# AFTER THE FALL

Nathan Bracher

# AFTER THE FALL

War and Occupation in Irène Némirovsky's

*Suite française*

The Catholic University of America Press
Washington, D.C.

The Catholic University of America Press
Washington, D.C.

Copyright © 2010
The Catholic University of America Press
All rights reserved

The paper used in this publication meets the minimum
requirements
of American National Standards for Information Science—
Permanence of
Paper for Printed Library Materials, ANSI Z39.48-1984.
∞

Library of Congress Cataloging-in-Publication Data
Bracher, Nathan, 1953–
After the fall : war and occupation in Irène Némirovsky's
Suite française / Nathan Bracher.
p. cm.
Includes bibliographical references and index.
ISBN 978-0-8132-1789-5 (cloth : alk. paper)
1. Némirovsky, Irène, 1903–1942. Suite française.
2. World War, 1939–1945—France—Literature and the war.
3. France—History—German occupation, 1940–1945.
4. War in literature.   I. Title.
PQ2627.E4S8534 2010
843'.912—dc22
                                        2010015209

# CONTENTS

## ACKNOWLEDGMENTS

I am grateful to Texas A & M University for the Faculty Development leave that allowed me to complete my research and draft the initial manuscript of this book, and for the generous grant awarded by the Program to Enhance Scholarly and Creative Activities through the Office of the Vice President for Research of Texas A & M University that allowed me to complete my project and prepare the manuscript for publication.

The discussion of historical ideology in chapter 1, "Timely Representations," incorporates several pages of my article "Timely Predications: The Use and Abuse of History in Contemporary France," *Soundings* 81, nos. 1–2 (1998): 234–56, reprinted by permission. Chapter 2, "Narrating the Fall," incorporates my article "Le Fin Mot de l'histoire: La *Tempête en juin* et les perspectives de Némirovsky," *Modern and Contemporary France* 16, no. 3 (August 2008): 265–77, reprinted by permission of the publisher, Taylor & Francis Ltd. (www.tandf .co.uk/journals). I thank both journals for allowing me to use this material in the present book.

The final version of this book has greatly benefited from the careful reading and helpful suggestions provided by Lynn Higgins, Israel Evans Professor of Oratory and Belles Lettres at Dartmouth College.

Most importantly, I want to thank my wife, Françoise, and my three boys, Christoph, Benjamin, and Andrew, without whom this project would never have come to fruition.

# INTRODUCTION

One would be hard-pressed to make a more compelling case for the enduring potency of World War II in contemporary French culture than that offered by Irène Némirovsky's *Suite française,* which was finally and dramatically discovered and published in 2004, over sixty years after the author's tragic death. A Russian Jewish émigré who had achieved literary stardom during the twenty years she had lived in France, Némirovsky wrote her novel during the first years of the Occupation from 1940 until 1942, when the persecutory measures imposed by both the Germans and the Vichy government had (among other things) forbidden Jews to publish or move from one place to another, thus taking away her livelihood and freedom of movement. In July 1942 she was arrested by French gendarmes and deported by the Nazis to her death at Auschwitz.[1]

Irène Némirovsky's daughters, however, managed to escape and preserve their mother's manuscript while in hiding. Mistakenly believing it to be a personal diary too painful to read, her oldest daughter did not realize that it was a novel until 2004, when she finally brought it to the attention of Olivier Rubinstein with the Denoël publishing house. When published shortly thereafter, the book produced an immediate sensation nationally and internationally: acclaimed

---

1  For a detailed, well-researched biography of Irène Némirovsky, see Olivier Philipponnat and Patrick Lienhardt, *La vie d'Irène Némirovsky* (Paris: Grasset-Denoël, 2007).

by the general public and critics alike, *Suite française* has recorded 600,000 sales of the French original and 1,300,000 of the English version, and has been translated into no less than twenty-six languages.[2] The author's own singular itinerary and tragic death doubtless gave renewed urgency to this long-lost voice from the Dark Years. In any case, success with critics and the general public was immediate and unanimous: Némirovsky's *Suite française* was acclaimed as a literary masterpiece providing a devastating portrayal of France's defeat and occupation.

The fact remains, however, that critics have issued confused and contradictory assessments of *Suite française*, particularly when attempting to formulate their various assessments in terms of memory or identity. Strictly speaking, neither *Suite française* nor the present study are about memory or identity as such. They rather propose a unique window on the French experience of World War II based on the knowledge and formulated in the terms available to laypersons, such as Némirovsky, who lived in those momentous times. As dramatic and decisive as these events appeared at the time, their ultimate outcome and true significance remained largely shrouded in uncertainty, particulary during the early phases of the war and the Occupation when Némirovsky penned her manuscript. Accordingly, the present book focuses primarily on exploring *Suite française* as a rare and particularly rich example of a literary text depicting with great nuance and in detail the attitudes of a large swath of French set against the unsettling backdrop of 1940–1942. My central thesis is that Némirovsky's novel not only offers valuable insights on a number of subjects (in particular, the civilian exodus of May–June 1940, the attitudes of French women vis-à-vis German soldiers, and class conflicts under the Occupation) that, up until now, have been too often neglected or misunderstood, but also displays striking originality when com-

---

2   According to Olivier Rubinstein, who on July 1, 2009, described various aspects of the book's discovery, publication, and reception for the Summer Seminar for Schoolteachers "Visions of the Dark Years: Legacies of World War II in France," sponsored by the National Endowment for the Humanities, directed by Richard J. Golsan and Nathan Bracher, from June 28 to July 30, 2009, in Paris, Lyon, Vichy, and Caen.

pared to other discourses and narratives dating from the same period, including Vercors's *Le Silence de la mer*. At the same time, a comparison with Jean Guéhenno's *Journal des années noires* will provide a clearer perception of *Suite française*'s lacunae and shortcomings.

Along the way, I hope to dispell a number of misconceptions that have arisen when critics and commentators have evaluated *Suite française* on the basis of rather hasty biographical assessments or on expectations of how writers should now represent World War II France. Some have heralded the work for offering unadorned testimony supposedly gleaned from the author's personal experience of events and their time and directly transposed onto the pages of her novel.[3] The book has thus been implicitly considered as a sort of documentary and valued for its presumed capacity to transmit intact to the contemporary reader the unmediated raw experience of history as tragically encountered by one of its victims. Such views lose sight of the crucial fact that *Suite française* constitutes an eminently literary text whose richly composed, multifaceted narrative must first and foremost be analyzed in relation to the literary and ideological contexts of its time.

Others have indeed seen *Suite française* as a literary masterpiece in the prestigious but highly traditional vein of Balzac, but have discounted the novel's representation of World War II France. Some have conceded that Némirovsky offers a rich and subtle depiction of fallen humanity, but complain that she ignores the sinister reality of Nazism.[4] Still others contend that Némirovsky's "cynical" outlook and lack of ideological commitment detract from her capacity to represent the World War II period for present-day readers. For their part, biographers Olivier Philipponnat and Patrick Lienhardt suggest that Némirovsky produced a literary narrative that remains largely and understandably amoral, apolitical, and disconnected from histo-

3   See, for example, Olivier Le Naire, "La Passion d'Irène," *L'Express*, September 27, 2004, and Clémence Boulouque, "Irène Némirovsky: échec à l'oubli," *Le Figaro Littéraire*, September 11, 2004.

4   Such is the case for Pascal Bruckner, "Elle s'appelait Irène," *Le Nouvel Observateur*, October 21, 2004, and René de Cecatty, "Le *Guerre et paix* d'Irène Némirovsky," *Le Monde des Livres*, September 30, 2004.

ry. Christopher Lloyd, on the other hand, is adamant in reading *Suite française* as an inherently and inescapably political representation of historical events. Touting Némirovsky as a "guardian of memory" who exposes the French state's betrayal of humane values, he claims that *Suite française* has occasioned "a sort of apologetic expression of French national guilt" and that the book has thus illustrated the Vichy syndrome of a past that will not go away.[5] Jonathan Weiss deplores on the contrary what he sees as just another example of Némirovsky's alleged indifference to politics and to the Jewish question, since her *Suite française* does not explicitly denounce Vichy's persecution of the Jews, issue clear condemnations of Pétain and Laval, or even endorse the armed Resistance.[6] Picking up on Weiss's allegations, Ruth Franklin has issued a scathing denunciation of a supposed "Scandale Française" (*sic*). Categorically condemning Némirovsky's early writings as rife with anti-Semitic stereotoypes and excoriating the novelist's contacts with right-wing publishing magnates, Franklin goes so far as to allege that Némirovsky was nothing but a second-rate novelist whose *Suite française* has fraudulently benefited from sympathy automatically accorded to its author as a Holocaust victim.[7]

These widely varying—and in several cases, highly erroneous —assessments nevertheless all have one important element in common. They tend to approach Irène Némirovsky's war narrative primarily either as a supposed source of biographical information (particularly concerning her attitudes and experiences as a Jew) or as a simple instrument of memory rather than as a specifically configured literary text whose voice can engage its readers in a critical dialogue with the dramatic era of the defeat and the Occupation. For anyone who has followed the seemingly unending series of widely publicized scandals and controversies concerning France's World War II past as well as the various representations of those traumat-

5   Christopher Lloyd, "Irène Némirovsky's *Suite française* and the Crisis of Rights and Identity," *Contemporary French Civilization* 31, no. 2 (2007): 161–69.

6   Jonathan Weiss, *Irène Némirovsky* (Paris: Éditions du Félin, 2005), 171–72.

7   Ruth Franklin, "Scandale Française: The Nasty Truth about a New Literary Heroine," *New Republic*, January 30, 2008, 38–43.

ic events, it comes as no surprise to see that both Irène Némirovsky and her literary works have occasioned a significant amount of criticism and praise based on the two most common pitfalls of our time: historical anachronism and ideological instrumentalization. Henry Rousso, the most eminent specialist on the memory of the Vichy years, has thoroughly documented and analyzed the propensity to perceive and judge events of yesterday through our deforming lenses of today. The much-heralded "duty to remember" invariably leads us to enroll the past, or at least our vision of the past, in the social and political struggles of the present. Although such telescoping of issues and contexts does often revive interest in long neglected and forgotten people and events and can spur long overdue research and even adjudication, it can also occasion a considerable amount of historical distortion and moral confusion.[8]

The polemics surrounding Némirovsky and her *Suite française* are just one more sign of the undeniably powerful impact that her work has had on readers on both sides of the Atlantic. Contemporary readers attempting to navigate the treacherous waters of time to revisit the dramatic context of the early 1940s in France must nevertheless steer clear of the Scylla of anachronism without falling into the Charybdis of instrumentalization. We must avoid assessing the work based simply on its usefulness in confirming what we already take for granted. The novel has its own unique contribution to make in conveying specific perceptions of the people and events of the early 1940s. In order to discern what is specific to Némirovsky's portrayal of the fall of France and the German occupation, we must accurately situate her discourse with respect to the multiple contexts of both World War II and the present. We must distinguish that which was prevalent in the conventional wisdom of one time or another from what is specifically conveyed by her historical narrative. We would do well to begin with the layer of assumptions that can often prove all the harder to discern in that they are closest to us. The fact of the matter is that our own age is so accustomed to conscripting the past

8   Henry Rousso, *La Hantise du passé* (Paris: Les Éditions Textuelles, 1998).

into the service of the present that we often have trouble interpreting all that does not fit into our preconceived categories. Eager to identify responsibilities and demand reparation for the iniquities of yesteryear, we summon history to our tribunals of memory without always remaining attentive to the complexities and ambiguities that may not conform to the binary logic (true or false, innocent or guilty) of judicial institutions.[9]

## The Lessons of History

We all too often expect writers to teach the lessons of history and even to formulate them in terms of our own present-day priorities. Readers of *Suite française* seem to demand that it set the record straight, that it repair past wrongs, and that it exhibit the author's cultural identity concretely, *hic et nunc*. Jonathan Weiss summons Némirovsky to his tribunal and indicts her on an interrelated battery of charges, including cultural apostasy (having allegedly attempted to escape her Jewish origins), social heresy (since she associated with right-wing magnates of French publishing), and political dereliction (having failed either to condemn Pétain or praise the Resistance while articulating an apolitical, moralistic worldview in her wartime writings).[10] Christopher Lloyd, on the other hand, touts Némirovsky's *Suite française* as a guardian of memory that finally broke the "taboo" that supposedly hung over the events of 1940 and forced the French to face up to their collective guilt.[11] In their otherwised nuanced and highly informative biography, even Philipponnat and Lienhardt delight in seeing the author immortalize acquaintances (Cécile Michaud, who served as a nanny for Irène's daughter, and Madeleine Avot, one of Irène's close friends), and visiting revenge on those who

9   See Rousso, *La Hantise du passé*, and Éric Conan and Henry Rousso, "Memory All Bent Out of Shape" and "The Future of an Obsession" in *Vichy, An Ever-Present Past*, trans. and annotated by Nathan Bracher (Hanover, N.H., and London: University Press of New England, 1998), 1–15 and 197–211.

10   Weiss, *Irène Némirovsky*, 7–9, 209–14.

11   Lloyd, "Irène Némirovsky's *Suite française* and the Crisis of Rights and Identity," 169.

allegedly lured her into religious conversion.[12] Whether we accept such narrow biographical interpretations as founded or not, they seriously limit the scope of investigation and ultimately lead to the twofold reductive fallacy of interpreting the author's work in function of her personal itinerary and judging her person based on a hasty, circumstantial reading of her novels.

However emotively evocative and historically significant the book may be—my underlying argument is that it must be taken seriously on all levels—*Suite française* is clearly a literary text, a fictional composition, and not an archival document or even an eyewitness testimony. The novel arranges the various fragmentary and chaotic elements of a historical trauma into a meaningful whole, without, however, subordinating them to some predetermined thesis, preconceived message, or overriding cause. The literary work has an integrity of its own whose precise contours we would do well to discern and delineate. In order to gauge Némirovsky's view of history, we shall first return to the text itself and engage in a close analysis of the various elements that contribute to a global perception of the defeat and Occupation. This attentive, detailed, and methodical reading of the primary text will avoid the common pitfall of fixating on one element while ignoring a host of others, and thus allow us to gauge Némirovsky's narrative representation of history.

The present book accordingly aims to clarify the nature and scope of her contribution to our understanding of the May–June 1940 debacle, the Vichy regime, and everyday life under German occupation. Instead of using biographical details to "explain" Némirovsky's war narrative, or, conversely, using her representation of the Fall of France and the Occupation to narrate the story of her own life, I argue that *Suite française* makes distinctive and important contributions to our intelligence of several often neglected facets of the war that were nevertheless dramatically crucial to those who lived through these events: namely, the May–June 1940 exodus of civilians who scattered themselves across French territory desperately seek-

---

12    Philipponnat and Liendhardt, *La Vie d'Irène Némirovsky*, 363, 382.

ing to escape calamity, the fierce rivalries of social class that intensified suffering and conflict throughout the Occupation, and the singular plight of the tens of thousands of French women who had to face the severe rigors of the German occupation on their own. Thus emphasizing Némirovsky's singular contributions to our present-day perception of the Dark Years in France, I also explain how she explores the ethical dilemmas arising from the clash of personal lives with collective destinies in the context of the war. Rather than use biographical details to assess her depiction of the people and events of the Occupation, I analyze her text by comparing it with the contemporaneous narratives on the war as well as with what the most recent historical research tells us about France's reaction to the catastrophic Fall of France and the ensuing Vichy years.

Just as Némirovsky's novel is composed of two narratives, *Tempête en juin,* which focuses on the May–June 1940 fall of France, and *Dolce,* which depicts provincial life in Bussy under the German occupation, the present study is divided into two major parts consisting of four chapters each. Part I analyzes the unique qualities of *Tempête en juin*'s representation of the defeat and the accompanying exodus of civilians. More than any other narrative of the debacle, *Tempête en juin* reveals the trauma experienced by the common people while at the same time mocking Vichy's official version of events.

Chapter 1, "Timely Representations," situates Némirovsky's narrative with respect to the multiple contexts of both World War II France and our present-day world. Close textual analysis reveals that, unlike the vast majority of observers of the early 1940s, Némirovsky refuses to put a spin on history, to teach "the morals of the story," or to rally behind ideology. *Tempête en juin* nevertheless dynamites the very foundations of Vichy's National Revolution which was so vigorously stigmatizing Jews, communists, the Popular Front, and Léon Blum. Instead of claiming to give a direct account of events, Némirovsky lets us see history through the highly charged reactions of those caught up in it, thus obliging us to view the debacle as mediated through multiple perspectives. By calling attention to the way in which different protagonists filter the Fall of France through their variously shaded lenses and interpret history according to their own purposes, Némirovsky subverts Vichy propaganda and implicitly delivers a stinging indictment of the conspiracy of lies that Vichy was disseminating in order to use war veterans and families with prisoners of war as pillars of power and authority.

Chapter 2, "Narrating the Fall," explains how Némirovsky not only subverts interpretations of events that were systematically favoring the privileged and the powerful, but also honors the plight of the common people. Némirovsky's narrative proceeds from one scene to the next, alternating the perspectives, juxtaposing mores, mind-sets, and specific behaviors with each other, then reversing the perspective to bring out not only socioeconomic dissonances but also everything that reveals the contradictions between words and acts, self-image and the judgment of others, and finally subjective perceptions and the violent reality of history. Némirovsky thus shows how France's collective ordeal is composed of a multitude of individual tragedies and betrayals. The result is a veritable cross section of the French populace. In portraying representatives of the aristocracy, the upper and lower echelons of the bourgeoisie, rural society, and even a bit of the working class, Némirovsky moreover gives epic dimensions to otherwise isolated episodes by depicting individual experiences as inextricably tied to the plight of the French nation as a whole. Contrary to certain accusations of political naivety or indifference, Némirovsky's *Suite française* links private lives and collective destiny in order to undermine the ideological foundations of Pétain's National Revolution by exposing the arrogance of the elite's extravagant lifestyle and the hypocrisy of their sententious patriotism.

Chapter 3, "Epic Suffering," shows that Némirovsky's representation of the debacle has in point of fact been confirmed by the most recent historical research on the May–June 1940 exodus of civilians seeking to flee the war.[13] Although herself tragically denied French citizenship, she narrates the cataclysmic defeat and occupation of

---

13   Hanna Diamond, *Fleeing Hitler* (Oxford and New York: Oxford University Press, 2007).

France from within the national community. It is precisely by portraying her desired compatriots' frequent failure to recognize and practice the solidarity that willy-nilly linked them all together as members of one common body politic that she identified with the French populace. Foregrounding the tidal wave of confused, panicked, and vulnerable civilians that has often been ignored in the traditional focus on military force, ideology, and political figures, Némirovsky has thus rekindled interest in an unjustly neglected event and underscored the aspects of the debacle that were not only foremost in the minds of those who endured the ordeal, but were also critical for determining public reaction to the creation of the Vichy regime and to its very first initiatives.

Chapter 4, "Accounting for Disaster: *Tempête en juin* and Its Contemporaries," compares Némirovsky's text with several other contemporaneous narratives of the Fall of France: René Benjamin's *Le Printemps tragique*, Antoine de Saint-Exupéry's *Pilote de guerre*, Marc Bloch's *L'Étrange défaite*, and Léon Werth's *33 jours*. Némirovsky's account takes on even greater significance when we observe just how uncommon it was at the time. René Benjamin's Pétainist novel excoriates the common people for abandoning traditional hierarchies and morality, while Saint-Exupéry's egocentric text filters everything through the mind of his first-person narrator who qualifies the refugees as "parasites" and "vermin," the very embodiment of France's disaster. The renowned Annales school historian and Resistance martyr Marc Bloch, on the other hand, emphasizes the shortcomings of the military and the government while considering the massive exodus of civilians fleeing the terror and mayhem of war as a secondary, if tragic, result. Bloch moreover castigates the very same egocentrism and social bigotry that are so implacably satirized by Némirovsky, and insists that the inextricable link between private lives and public destinies is crucial for democracy. In what is doubtless the most detailed and astute eyewitness account of the ordeal, Léon Werth parallels Némirovsky in linking the trauma of private lives with public destinies that suddenly appear to be inscrutable, confusing, and ambiguous. Werth's repeated and unavoidable contacts with the Germans force him to question his own conduct, sound the limits of national and personal integrity, and weigh humanitarian imperatives against moral and political compunction. Werth's analysis of interactions between French civilians and the German troops confirms the integrity of Némirovsky's depiction of the defeat and Occupation and leads us to the ethical quandaries studied in Part II.

Part II of *After the Fall* studies the incisive view of French provincial society during the early stages of the German occupation that is found in *Dolce,* the second part of *Suite française.* Chapters 4 through 8 explain how Némirovsky probes the dilemmas of ordinary citizens in order to reveal the unsettling ambiguities of daily contacts among the French and their German conquerors. Némirovsky's historical narrative can thus be read as one of the most uncompromising depictions of everyday life during the early phases of the Occupation.

Chapter 5, "Occupational Hazards," reveals how Némirovsky exposes the trenchant rivalries of social class and the highly ambivalent interactions of French people with German soldiers. Mocking Vichy's sententious moralism without espousing Gaullist idealism, *Dolce* underscores the economic inequities and class prejudices that clouded loyalties and ethical principles. Némirovsky's depiction of provincial life under the Occupation in fact proves to be much closer to the actual concerns of the vast majority of French population than was Vercors's *Le Silence de la mer:* without collaborating or resisting, people tended to lie low and ride out the storm, watching out first and foremost for what they considered to be their own vital interests. The reality is that most were driven by exactly the sorts of social and psychological factors that Némirovsky highlights: food shortages, prisoners of war, absence of men, social rancor, frequent contacts with omnipresent Germans, and the assertion of power and authority under Pétain and Vichy. By gauging the sharp divisions and deep-seated tensions in the rural provinces, we are much better equipped to understand the virtual civil war created by the German occupation. By exposing the fierce, unseemly rivalries of sex, cultural tradition, and social class at work in the fictional town of Bussy, *Dolce* moreover points to the gaping disparity between Vichy ideology and its schmalzy images, on the one hand, and the concrete reality of French society, on the other. As we will see in the following chapter, Némirovsky's narrative also delivers a brutally frank portrayal of French accommodation with the Occupation and of the relations between German soldiers and French women.

Chapter 6, "Portraits of the Nazis as Young Men," focuses on the political, social, and ethical implications in Némirovsky's depiction of the German soldiers. During the early phases of the Occupation, the image of the Wehrmacht in the eyes of the French proved to be highly charged and crucial not only for the Germans but also for the French populace, Vichy, and the early resistance movements. Like other writers of the time, such as Jean Guéhenno, François Mauriac, Jean Texcier, and Vercors, Némirovsky attests to a widely recognized, if often tacit, code of conduct requiring that the French population keep their distance from their unwanted visitors. Unlike Vercors's *Le Silence de mer,* however, Némirovsky dwells on the social divisions and resentments that led some French citizens to admire the Germans. Appearing in tandem, the Viscountess of Montmort and her tenant farmer Benoît Labarie provide a particularly dramatic case in point. Némirovsky has us view the Viscountess Mme de Montmort as clearly aligned not only with Pétain but also with the German occupying forces. As an aristocrat eager to bolster her own socioeconomic privilege, Mme de Montmort is attracted to the aura of order and discipline. Benoît's response to the German officer forcibly lodged in his modest rural home is diametrically opposed to the Viscountess's attitude. He shatters what had been a more or less peaceful coexistence between the residents of Bussy and their German occupiers, and therefore dissipates the illusion of neutrality by killing the German officer Bonnet, who was about to arrest him for possessing a gun. Benoît thus commits an act of radical disobedience to German power that ultimately forces Lucile to face the ethical implications of her seemingly idyllic friendship with the German officer lodged in her home.

In chapter 7, "Private Lives and Public Stories," we will see that Némirovsky's portraits of provincial women living through the Occupation carry serious historical implications for both her time and ours. By providing an early and unblinkered view of the direct association and frequent sexual encounters between French women and German soldiers, *Dolce* shows the young women of Bussy engaging in a whole range of behaviors, from furtive glances and casual conversation to stolen kisses, heart-to-heart discussions, and prolonged sexual adventures. Némirovsky's narrative constitutes a clear departure from both the dominant discourses of her own time and the common perspectives of our present era. Instead of representing one such relationship as paradigmatic of all women who consorted with enemy troops, her text offers an entire range of encounters between French women and soldiers of the Wehrmacht. The most dramatic case is the disturbing relationship between Lucile and the German officer Bruno von Falk. With his romantic notions of love, his Wagnerian musical exaltation, but also his amalgam of hatred, revenge, and pleasure all mixed together in the desire to personally kill Benoît, Bruno actually proves to be more sinister than the image projected by Vercors's von Ébrennac. While the latter finally resigns himself to a bitter fate of destruction, Bruno presents a much more flesh-and-blood human image of fears and desires. Némirovsky's narrative moreover squarely confronts the embarrassing reality of the many French women who without political motivation found Germans sexually attractive. Yet in the end Lucile suddenly and vigorously rejects Bruno's advances: this plot development constitutes a symbolic rejection of the New Order enticingly held out by German propaganda that is even more dramatic than the resolute silence immortalized by Vercors's *Le Silence de la mer.* Lucile's largely unexpected anti-German stance provides the central focus of our next chapter.

Chapter 8, "Reaching the Rendezvous with Destiny," analyzes what might be considered as the centerpiece of *Dolce:* Lucile's intimate conversations with Bruno von Falk, the Wehrmacht officer who appears to be as culturally refined and emotionally sensitive as Vercors's Werner von Ebrennac. Determined to pursue her own desire for personal fulfillment, Lucile defiantly flouts her mother-in-law's bourgeois strictures as well as Vichy's narrow definitions of women's roles in society. At the most critical juncture, however, Lucile suddenly rebuffs von Falk's sexual advances and resolves to protect a French fugitive at the risk of her own life. Far from anecdotal, Lucile's personal dilemma is in fact paralleled in several critical ways by those of a seamstress and of the farmwoman Madeleine Labarie. Indeed, *Dolce* depicts all three as women in love with German soldiers. Beyond obvious socioeconomic differences, all three are lonely women who find themselves neither respected nor appreciated, and who for this very reason yearn for a masculine presence that might offer both love and friendship beyond the crude desire for possession from which they have suffered in the company of their male compatriots. In depicting her protagonists's thought and actions as socially contingent, sexually anchored, and psychologically conflicted, Némirovsky elaborates a narrative that proves more plausible, and therefore more engaging, than Vercors's *Le Silence de la mer.* In the end, *Dolce* foregrounds a rejection of collaboration that is arguably more dramatic and more compelling than that featured in *Le Silence de la mer* precisely because the ambivalence of Lucile's feelings has made her decision infinitely more problematic.

Analyzed closely, Némirovsky's uncompromising representation of French women who are strongly attracted to German soldiers explores a widespread ethical dilemma with both honesty and sensitivity. All while holding up Vichy's moralism to ridicule by foregrounding highly sympathetic portraits of the seamstress and Lucile, who thoroughly flouted the National Revolution's exhortations for women to offer models of personal self-sacrifice and patriotic devotion, Némirovsky's narrative conveys a keen awareness of the urgent beckoning of ethics in the face of history. Without heavy-handed indications that such and such choices are reprehensible while others are laudable, Némirovsky's narrative nevertheless shatters the illusion of her protagonists' attempts to escape all that ties them to the social context and historical events of their time. The text accordingly presents their thoughts, speeches, and actions not as arising from the putatively unfathomable depths of "blood," as Philipponat and Lienhardt have suggested, but as inescapably frought with ethical implications.

*Suite française* thus presents a searing portrait of France and the French in the throes of what arguably constituted the most traumatic and decisive events in the history of the French Republic. In order to fully appreciate Némirovsky's literary achievement and judiciously assess what her *Suite française* can contribute to our present-day understanding of the war and its various protagonists, we must subject the work to thoroughgoing literary and historical scrutiny. Great care must be taken to situate the narrative and the author with respect to her time and ours without assimilating their many powerful features to our own ready-made categories. To do so, we must first realize that we ineluctably view this novel through our own multifaceted, kaleidoscopic lenses of history and memory.

# AFTER THE FALL

# CHAPTER 1

# TIMELY REPRESENTATIONS

## The Lessons of History

With respect to the traumatic events in 1940, Némirovsky presents an intriguing paradox that may explain a good deal of the present-day confusion surrounding her attitude toward the war. In the wake of Hegel, who, in surveying the succession of human events claimed to read the "prose of the world" written by the Absolute Spirit, and Marx, who saw the universal struggle of the exploited and oppressed as a progressive march toward the instauration of the classless society, History with a capital $H$ was deified by nineteenth- and twentieth-century ideologies. For her part, however, Némirovsky maintains a veritable agnosticism that refuses to recognize any preordained plan, overarching teleology, or immanent dialectic in historical events. Without espousing the perspectives of relativism, her narrative combines uncompromising socioeconomic and psychological analyses with a compassion for her characters, whose humanity transcends their specific historical determinations. It is precisely such ideological agnosticism and artistic depth that lend her historical novel its own specificity. *Suite française* provides us with one of the most painfully accurate depictions of France's debacle. What sets it apart from narratives of both her own time and ours, however, is her refusal to read into this tragedy "the signs of the times," to see in these momentous developments the presence of some judgment, sanction, or dialectical movement emanating from within, without, or beyond the realm of human affairs. Since this unwillingness to read the various elements of France's unmitigated military and political disaster as a coherent "prose of the world" conveying some interior or ulterior signification informs her entire narrative of France's defeat and of the Occupation, it requires close analysis.

It is crucial to observe that such a stance runs absolutely counter to the overwhelming tendency of her contemporaries to discern and disseminate the morals of the story, not only to draw lessons from the humiliating defeat but even more importantly to apply them to the domains of politics and culture. Such was the first priority of the most pivotal figure of the time, Marshal Philippe Pétain, who first officialized the defeat in his famous speech of June 17, 1940, and then quickly set about presenting it as the just desserts for France's political and moral transgressions. From the very moment he took power—and interestingly, it was another dubious "lesson" of history, namely, the fear of a repeat of the 1871 Parisian insurrection known as "La Commune," which encouraged the parliament of the Third Republic to hand all power to him[1]—Pétain repeatedly engaged in his own historical pedagogy, hammering on the notion that France's defeat constituted history's moral and political condemnation of the "decadent" France of the Third Republic.

This idea held heavy sway not only among the French public still traumatized by France's military collapse and the ensuing humanitarian catastrophe putting some eight to ten million civilians on the roads bombed and strafed by the *Luftwaffe,* the German air force, but also among the overwhelming majority of French political leaders, artists, and intellectuals. There was a virtual consensus that in the defeat, France was paying the heavy wages of the Third Republic's sins: those of an inept, tainted parliamentary regime, of morality undermined by intellectuals such as André Gide, and of the influence of foreigners and Jews, all of which had supposedly sapped the country's vi-

---

[1]    Philippe Burrin, *La France à l'heure allemande* (Paris: Éditions du Seuil, 1995), 23.

tality. Today, we know this pedagogy to be patently false: scholars are virtually unanimous in dismissing any notion of "weakness" or "decadence" in France's military forces, who engaged the enemy fiercely and with equal firepower. The loss can instead be attributed to such classic military factors as archaic strategy, errors by commanding officers, and deficient aviation. Ironically, one of these fundamental military errors is in turn attributable to the attempt to "learn the lessons" of World War I: the Maginot Line and the entire French military strategy built around it was based on the notion that what was needed to assure victory was heavy firepower along long, impenetrable lines.[2]

One of the precious few in France to perceive the fallacy of such historical pedagogy was a certain Charles de Gaulle: in his now famous call of June 18 that summoned the French to refuse the armistice and to rally around him, he notably abstained from drawing any moral conclusions from France's defeat, describing it instead in military terms, and explaining what military and geopolitical factors would lead America to join in a world war that would be the demise of Nazi Germany. But de Gaulle's prophetic exhortations hardly kept Pétain and Vichy from exploiting the seemingly unshakable idea that France's military failure constituted the sanction of history. Vichy ideologues and propagandists would never tire of reminding the French public just who was supposedly responsible for tarnishing France's proud legacy: the Jews, the intellectuals, the Freemasons, *bistrots, bordels,* the communists, and the Third Republic.

With twenty-twenty hindsight, and in the absence of the tremendous material and moral shock that France suffered in May and June 1940, we are obviously somewhat privileged observers. It is nevertheless stupefying to observe the large number of commentators (including, ironically enough, the *"immoraliste"* André Gide himself!) who concluded that the defeat contained a clear lesson from history illustrating France's political and moral inferiority to Nazi Germany. It was commonly assumed that military failure proved that a country was wrong, that its cause was not just, and that conversely, that if a country were right, it would be rewarded with victory. Even in this

2   Philippe Burrin, *La France à l'heure allemande,* 11.

simplistic form, such reasoning is symptomatic of the proverbial de-
ification of history, for it assumes that the march of human events
embodies a driving force or principle (be it survival of the fittest or
the struggle for the classless society) and that history is the Hegelian
"prose of the world" rendering its judgment on peoples and nations.
Perhaps the most vociferous literary exponent of this view is Henry de Montherlant, whose "Solstice de juin" claimed that the German conquest had not only marked the end of almost two millenia
of Christian civilization in Europe but that the leonine beauty of the
Nazi Panzer divisions had also ushered in a revitalized paganism.[3]

   To be sure, many of those who rushed in to spell out the morals
of history to their defeated compatriots were merely political oppor-
tunists who had no need of either Hegelian, Marxist, or Darwinist
metahistory to convince them that France's liberal democracy should
be scuttled in favor of an authoritarian, paternalist, and highly hierar-
chical "French State." Neither Marshal Pétain nor General Weygand,
both of whom played a key role in liquidating parliamentary rule in
favor of a Pétainist dictatorship, suddenly "saw the light" during the
course of France's military collapse. They and their fellow Vichy ideologues had been waiting for a chance to settle their social and political
scores for years. Their entire campaign of historical pedadogy was bo-
gus from the outset: far from ascertaining any "lesson" from the observation of historical events, they merely used the latter as a pretext
to apply a preconceived, preexisting, highly overdetermined ideology.
Historical events were not the origin of this ideology, but rather simply provided a convenient opportunity to give it popular support.

   Nothing is farther removed from such ideological exploitation of
history than Némirovsky's searing story of private lives caught up in
the maelstrom of events that totally outstrip their capacity to comprehend, much less control, their own destinies. We shall see, however,
that while her perspectives on the fall of France and on the overbearing presence of the German occupying forces differ radically from
those disseminated by Vichy propaganda, her *Suite française* has been

3    See Henry de Montherlant, *Essais* (Paris: Gallimard, 1963), 953–63.

composed in reference to those same historical developments, which ultimately provide the basic warp on which the narrative is woven.

## Doubting the Signs of the Times

For her part, and perhaps tragically, Irène Némirovsky remained impervious to the doctrines of history that defined French political orthodoxies of her time. She maintained a certain distance from open political stances, not so much because of ignorance or indifference, but rather because of a conscious artistic and personal choice made amid trying circumstances. While realizing that the conflicts of the day imperiled her own life and those of her loved ones, she nevertheless firmly resolved to situate her writing on another level. Besieged by restrictions and dangers, she resolved not to use her artistic talent to settle scores or advance a particular cause. In this sense, she was much like Lucile, the central character of *Dolce*. Seeking desperately to escape the solitude of a failed marriage that has left her wasting away in the clutches of the provincial bourgeoisie of the little town of Bussy, Lucile finds herself trapped between her irresistible attraction to the German officer and accomplished musician Bruno von Falk, on the one hand, and the inescapable realities of the war and the Occupation, on the other. She thus cries out for release:

Je veux être libre. Je demande moins la liberté extérieure, celle de voyager, de quitter cette maison (quoique ce serait un bonheur inimaginable!), que d'être libre intérieurement, choisir ma direction à moi, m'y tenir, ne pas suivre l'essaim. *Je hais cet esprit communautaire dont on nous rebat les oreilles. Les Allemands, les Français, les gaullistes s'entendent tous sur un point: il faut vivre, penser, aimer avec les autres, en fonction d'un État, d'un pays, d'un parti. Oh, mon Dieu! je ne veux pas!* Je suis une pauvre femme inutile; je ne sais rien mais je veux être libre! Des esclaves nous devenons, pensa-t-elle encore; la guerre nous envoie ici ou là, nous prive de notre bien-être, nous enlèvent le pain de la bouche; qu'on me laisse au moins le droit de juger de mon destin, de me moquer de lui, de le braver, de lui échapper si je peux.[4]

---

4  Irène Némirovsky, *Suite française* (Paris: Denoël, 2004), 457; emphasis mine. Here as throughout, the translations of Némirovsky's text are my own.

I want to be free. I'm not so much asking for outer liberty, such as the freedom to leave this house or to travel about (although that would be an unimaginable joy), as for inner liberty, the freedom to choose my own path, to stay on it instead of following the herd. *I hate this communitarian mind-set they keep on pounding into our heads. The Germans, the French, and the Gaullists all agree on one thing: you have to live, think, and love along with everybody else, on the basis of a State, a country, or a party. Oh God! I don't want to!* I'm just a woman who's of no use to anyone; I don't know anything but I want to be free! Slaves are what we are becoming, she moreover thought. The war throws us here or there, deprives us of our well-being, takes the bread out of our mouths; people should at least let me keep the right to assess my own plight, either to disregard it, to stand up to it, or to escape if I can.

Irène Némirovsky herself was certainly neither poor, nor useless, nor ignorant by any stretch of the imagination. However, just as the literary character Lucile stubbornly affirmed her own inalienable right to a life, a liberty, and a pursuit of happiness that transcended the imperatives of war, so the writer Irène persisted in creating a literary work undiminished by attempts to settle scores or advance specific causes. When scrutinized carefully, her determination to maintain her artistic endeavors outside of the ideological arena can be most fruitfully perceived not as some self-seeking compromise or compromission of her art, but on the contrary as an attempt to create a work that could withstand the passing of years and the expediencies of the moment.

We draw even closer to her innermost thoughts on the subject by considering the reflections consigned to her own personal notes in March 1942, at the very moment when ever-increasing restrictions, persecutions, and arrests had given her a sense of impending doom.[5]

Mon Dieu! que me fait ce pays? Puisqu'il me rejette, considérons-le froidement, regardons-le perdre son honneur et sa vie. Et les autres, que me sont-ils? Les Empires meurent. Rien n'a d'importance. Si on le regarde du point de vue mystique ou du point de vue personnel, c'est tout un. Conservons une tête froide. Durcissons-nous le coeur. Attendons.[6]

5   Philipponnat and Lienhardt, *La vie d'Irène Némirovsky*, 399.
6   Némirovsky, *Suite française*, 521.

My God! What does this country matter to me? Since it rejects me, let's contemplate it coolly, let's watch it lose its honor and its life. And the others, what are they to me? Empires die. Nothing has any importance. Whether you look at it from a mystical point of view or a personal point of view, it's all the same. Let's keep a cool head. Let's harden our heart. Let's wait.

These lines have erroneously been cited by Weiss and others as a long overdue awakening to the reality of injustice and anti-Semitism in the country that never accepted her request for citizenship in spite of her long residency, widely acclaimed novels, and love of things French.[7] The statements quoted above should in fact be understood not as some inchoate political revolt but on the contrary as a willful resolution to maintain intellectual composure. We must first clarify the meaning of Némirovsky's first sentence. Weiss interprets "que me fait ce pays?" as "What is this country doing to me?" In fact, however, Némirovsky is asking herself "What does this country matter to me?" or "What do I care about this country?" Just as in the expression "Ça ne me fait ni chaud ni froid" (It does not have any effect on me, I don't care one way or another) and "Ça me fait quelque chose" (It does not leave me indifferent, it moves me), the words "Que me fait" point to the affective impact of some occurrence. The immediate context as well as the other passages that we are examining moreover make it abundantly clear that Némirovsky is pondering first and foremost what attitude to adopt in the face of tragedy, since she continues by asking what other countries matter to her ("Et les autres, que me sont-ils?"), and then admonishes herself to keep a cool head and to focus on the essential, which can only be discerned from a viewpoint that she terms "mystique" or "personnel."

Three months later, only a few weeks before her arrest and deportation, Némirovsky reaffirms her determination to compose a novel with material that would resist the passing of time better than political commitments and inclinations of the moment:

---

7   Jonathan Weiss, *Irène Némirovsky* (Paris: Éditions du Félin, 2005), 188.

*2 juin 1942:* ne jamais oublier que la guerre passera et que toute la partie historique pâlira. Tâcher de faire le plus possible de choses, de débats ... qui peuvent intéresser les gens en 1952 ou 2052. Relire Tolstoï. Inimitables les peintures mais non historiques. Insister sur cela.[8]

2 June 1942: never forget that the war will pass and that the whole historical part will fade. Strive to do as many things as possible, debates ... that can interest people in 1952 or 2052. Reread Tolstoy. The depictions are inimitable but not historical. Emphasize that.

It is not possible to be more explicit—nor more tragically justified — in the desire to write "for posterity," which she again expressed in one of her very last letters. On July 11, 1942, only two days before French gendarmes would come to arrest her at her residence, she confided to Robert Esménard, director of the Albin Michel publishing house in Paris, that "J'ai beaucoup écrit, ces derniers temps. ... Je suppose que ce seront des oeuvres posthumes mais cela fait toujours passer le temps" (I have written a lot of late. ... I suppose that these will be posthumous works, but it nevertheless makes the time go by).[9]

Yet another series of maxims expresses even more clearly Némirovsky's repeated efforts to avoid skewing her artistic project by seeking to prove preconceived ideas or achieve predetermined political ends:

Ne rien prouver surtout. Ici moins que partout ailleurs. Ni que les uns sont bons et les autres mauvais, ni que celui-ci a tort et un autre raison. Même si c'est vrai, surtout si c'est vrai. Dépeindre, décrire.[10]

Above all, do not try to prove anything. Here less than everywhere else. Not that some are good and others bad, nor that this one is wrong and another right. Even if it is true, especially if it is true. Depict, describe.

These lines give evidence of a certain artistic, intellectual, and personal tension. Némirovsky is clearly far from indifferent to the restrictions that were slowly tightening their stranglehold on her life and career amid the oppression of the German occupation and Vi-

---

8   Némirovsky, *Suite française,* 531.

9   Cited by Philipponnat and Lienhardt, *La vie d'Irène Némirovsky,* 415.

10  Cited by Philipponnat and Lienhardt, *La vie d'Irène Némirovsky,* 401.

chy's reactionary dictatorship. She has, as we shall see, her own ideas on who and what are right and wrong. However ambivalent her characters and their actions may be, she recognizes a distinction between just and unjust, truth and falsehood. Her intention is not to turn her back on these realities nor to escape their disturbing implications. Rather than using her fictional narrative to systematically inculcate those distinctions in ideological terms, however, she sets about giving close, careful descriptions of how persons from various socioeconomic origins experience their individual and collective plights. Instead of loading the proverbial dice or skewing her portrayals, she aims to craft a work that will make events and personnages appear sub specie aeternitatis.

In short, Némirovsky was intent on observing a certain authorial detachment. Maintaining a critical distance between her own preferences and inclinations does not, however, prevent her from pitting a diverse and complex set of characters against the chaos, terror, and proteiform upheavals of the May–June debacle and its aftermath in France. We readers should therefore be wary of hasty judgments based on the twists and turns of fate—that is, of history—as presented by her narrative. We could take a cue from the singular perspective developed by her character Maurice Michaud, the modest bank employee: along with his wife Jeanne, he constitutes one of the very few who manage to act and speak with honesty and courage throughout all of the various phases of the ordeal. That is why Némirovsky reminds herself to keep him in the foreground of her narrative: "Insister sur les figures de Michaud. Ceux qui trinquent toujours et les seuls qui soient nobles vraiment"[11] (Stress the Michaud figures. Those who always take it on the chin and the only ones who are really noble).

In order to trace the contours of Némirovsky's general perspective on the ebb and flow of history, we can therefore analyze the debacle as seen by the Michauds. Némirovsky first articulates Maurice Michaud's distinctive manner of viewing the catastrophe when she

11 Némirovsky, *Suite française,* 525.

depicts him and his wife Jeanne caught up in the very middle of it along with the thousands of others fleeing Paris on foot out on the open road. The passage clearly foregrounds the Michauds as figures conveying Némirovsky's own perception of events, since her text situates them at a strategic point, "sur une de ces hauteurs légères qui coupaient les routes de place en place"[12] (on one of these little high spots that the road led over in a few places). Reaching the top of a hill, the Michauds survey the panorama of the vast exodus as the disaster unfolds: "ils voyaient jusqu'à l'horizon, aussi loin que pouvait porter leur regard"[13] (they saw as far as the horizon, as far as the eye could see). At the same time, the Michauds share the plight of the common people, who find themselves the most exposed to the bombings, strafings, and chaos. These commoners are clearly the most vulnerable to the dire lack of food, water, shelter, and medical care that jeopardize the well-being of the eight to ten million civilians seeking to flee the horrors of war.

Since he articulates a general perception that goes beyond his immediate individual situation and places the traumatic upheaval of the civilian population in the larger historical perspective, Maurice seems to have a particularly privileged vantage point:

Malgré la fatigue, la faim, l'inquiétude, Maurice Michaud ne se sentait pas trop malheureux. Il avait une tournure d'esprit singulière, il n'attachait pas beaucoup d'importance à lui-même; il n'était pas à ses propres yeux cette créature rare et irremplaçable que chaque homme voit lorsqu'il pense à lui-même. Envers ses compagnons de souffrance, il éprouvait de la pitié, mais elle était lucide et froide. Après tout, ces grandes migrations humaines semblaient commandées par des lois naturelles, songeait-il. Sans doute des déplacements périodiques considérables de masse étaient nécessaires aux peuples comme la transhumance l'est aux troupeaux. Il y trouvait un curieux réconfort. *Ces gens autour de lui croyaient que le sort s'acharnait particulièrement sur eux, sur leur misérable génération; mais lui, il se souvenait que les exodes avaient eu lieu de tout temps.*[14]

---

12   Némirovsky, *Suite française*, 100.     13   Némirovsky, *Suite française*, 100.

14   Némirovsky, *Suite française*, 101; emphasis mine.

In spite of fatigue, hunger, and anxiety, Maurice Michaud did not find himself too poorly off. He had an unusual way of thinking; he did not attach a lot of importance to himself; he was not in his own eyes that rare and irreplaceable creature that every man sees when he thinks of himself. Toward his companions in suffering, he felt pity, but it was lucid and restrained. After all, these great migrations of humans seemed to be commanded by natural laws, he thought. Doubtless such considerably massive periodic movements were necessary for people, as for herds of animals moving from one grazing area to another. He found a strange comfort in this thought. *These people around him believed that fate was being particularly harsh with them and their miserable generation; as for Maurice, however, he remembered that exoduses had always taken place.*

Instead of yielding to the panic gripping an ever-increasing number of these refugees, Maurice manages to transcend his own suffering with philosophical considerations. It is this rare capacity to carry his thought beyond his own fear and trembling to contemplate the event in a universal context that enables him to avoid an egocentric, teleological, and anthropomorphic interpretation of history. Némirovsky's text explicitly underscores the attitude that so strikingly sets Maurice apart from his contemporaries: even under duress, he refuses to put a self-interested spin on dramatic events. He persists in lucid analysis to the detriment of tendentious moralization. In short, he resists the temptation to read into the traumatic events of France's debacle some "prose of the world" offering a lesson to be learned, inculcated, or politically exploited to the benefit of some and the detriment of others.

To decry the supposed failure by Némirovsky to take sides, to allege an unwillingness to delineate political responsibility, or to contend that Némirovsky advances an amoral vision of events is anachronistic in that such charges implicitly carry the expectation that the novelist writing in the early stages of the Occupation in 1940 and 1941 should advance the perspectives elaborated in the final decades of the twentieth century only after an unshackled historiography had dispelled myriad myths and misperceptions, and after the "duty to remember" had demanded that perpetrators of historical crimes be clearly designated. Expecting Némirovsky's *Suite française* to correspond to current priorities, moreover, prevents us from appreciating the novel's significance as a narrative penned at the heat of the moment. Viewed in the context of its own times, her representation of France's collapse under the brunt of the German invasion distinguishes itself from other narratives by its capacity to step back from the shock of the moment and view events from a perspective that transcends the immediate time and place.

As we will see in detail in the last two chapters of the present book, viewing war through metaphors of natural disasters proves problematical on several levels. Seen as a recurring pattern in a universal context, however, events no longer lend themselves to the self-serving moralistic and ideological interpretations of the defeat that were very deliberately being used by Pétain in particular and Vichy in general to fuel the exercises of public self-flagellation and scapegoating. Rejecting any notion that the disaster represented some sort of divine sanction or Hegelian verdict, Maurice Michaud instead views the surrounding chaos, death, and destruction as another periodic eruption of the senseless violence of history.

Que d'hommes tombés sur cette terre (comme sur toutes les terres du monde) en larmes de sang, fuyant l'ennemi, laissant des villes en flammes, serrant leurs enfants sur leur coeur: personne n'avait jamais pensé avec sympathie à ces morts innombrables. Pour leurs descendants, ils n'avaient pas plus d'importance que des poulets égorgés. Il imagina leurs ombres plaintives se levant sur le chemin, se penchant vers lui, murmurant à son oreille:
—Nous avons connu tout cela avant toi. Pourquoi serais-tu plus heureux que nous?
Une grosse commère, à côté de lui, gémissait:
—On n'a jamais vu des horreurs pareilles!
—Mais si, madame, mais si, répondit-il doucement.[15]

So many people had fallen on this land (as on every land in the world) amid tears of blood, fleeing the enemy, leaving behind cities in flames,

15  Némirovsky, *Suite française*, 101–2.

clutching their children to their breast: nobody had ever given a sympathetic thought to these countless dead. For their descendents, they had no more importance than slaughtered chickens. He imagined their plaintive shadows rising above the road, leaning over him, murmuring in his ear:

"We experienced all this before you. Why should you be more fortunate than us?"

A big garrulous woman beside him was groaning:

"People have never seen anything so horrible!"

"Oh yes they have, ma'am, oh yes they have," he replied softly.

This unequivocal refusal to see "des horreurs pareilles" (such horrors) as exceptional, that is, specific to the France of May–June 1940, makes it impossible to blame the civilian and military debacle on any particular group, party, regime, person, or moral behavior. Without specifically mentioning Pétain or Vichy, Némirovsky has implicitly dynamited the very foundations of the National Revolution which was so vigorously stigmatizing Jews, communists, the Popular Front, Léon Blum, and the frequentation of bars, *bistrots,* and *bordels.*

We can confirm Nemirovsky's refusal to skew her representation of the debacle in view of seeking revenge or delivering an indictment by noting the image of the retreating French army that she presents through the eyes of Maurice and Jeanne Michaud crossing paths with "les premiers régiments en déroute"[16] (the first routed regiments). Her depiction of these troops contrasts sharply with the portrayals that we get from the most prominent discourses of the time. In his speech of June 17, 1940, announcing both his accession to power as France's premier and the necessity of coming to terms with the Germans, Pétain drew on his legacy as the "Vainqueur de Verdun" (Victor of Verdun) and the "médecin des soldats" (the soldiers' doctor).[17] Pétain thus sought to bolster his authority as a leader and heighten his popularity among war veterans by touting the ar-

16   Némirovsky, *Suite française,* 102.

17   See Ian Ousby, *Occupation: The Ordeal of France, 1940–1944* (New York: St. Martin's Press, 1998), 6–12, and Julian Jackson, *France: The Dark Years, 1940–1944* (New York and London: Oxford University Press, 2003), 28–30.

my's "héroïsme digne de ses longues traditions militaires" (heroism worthy of its long military traditions) and "sa magnifique résistance" (its magnificent resistance). As would many other collaborationists, Henry de Montherlant similarly claimed in his "Le Solstice de juin" dating from the immediate aftermath of the defeat in July 1940 that the French military's lack of discipline and virility was emblematic of France's decadent morals and effeminate culture, and thus that the defeat was largely deserved.

Némirovsky's text offers no trace of either any chauvinist fanfares or such snide denigration. *Tempête en juin* foregrounds instead the hagard, forlorn, and exhausted faces visible to the fleeing refugees.

Les soldats ne se montraient pas loquaces. Presque tous étaient sombres et pensifs. Quelques-uns dormaient au fond des camions. Les chars avançaient lourdement dans la poussière, camouflés de branchages légers. Entre les feuilles fanées par le soleil ardent paraissaient des visages pâles, fatigués, avec une expression de colère et de fatigue.[18]

The soldiers did not prove to be talkative. Almost all were somber and lost in thought. A few were sleeping in the back of the trucks. The tanks lumbered through the dust, camouflaged with small branches. Among the leaves faded by the hot sun there appeared pale, tired faces that expressed anger and fatigue.

Némirovsky prefaces this grim picture of "les premiers régiments en déroute"[19] (the first routed regiments) by pointing out the discrepancy between the refugees' belief that these troops were about to confront the German army when in fact they were retreating in disarray. Even in the midst of defeat, fleeing civilians point to France's overconfidence. Instead of using either the rout of French troops or the failure of the populace to perceive the defeat as a pretext for moral resentment or political indictment, however, Némirovsky focuses on the pathos of such widespread human distress.

Just as Maurice Michaud exemplifies lucid analysis of history in

18   Némirovsky, *Suite française*, 102.
19   Némirovsky, *Suite française*, 102.

its *longue durée,* that is, its long-term, virtually imperceptible evolution, so Jeanne Michaud embodies empathy with the acute suffering in the *hic et nunc.* Noting that Jeanne had learned as a child to be sensitive to what was both funny and moving in other people, Némirovsky uses Jeanne's voice in the recurrent indirect free style, the narrative device that gives the reader direct access to characters' thoughts and perceptions without having those characters speak in the first person. *Tempête en juin* thus gives us a more concrete, close-up view of people caught up in the drama of the civilian exodus. Preoccupied by the unknown fate of her own son, Jean-Marie, who is a French soldier, Jeanne can only presume him to be caught up somewhere in the maelstrom. Jeanne understandably "croyait sans cesse reconnaître"[20] (constantly thought she recognized) her son among the retreating troops. She nevertheless proves equally capable of going beyond the stress and emotion of the moment and putting the event into an analytical perspective.

Elle souffrait donc moins de la fatigue que ses compagnons, mais cet incessant kaléidoscope, ces visages inconnus passant devant elle, apparaissant, s'éloignant, disparaissant, lui causaient une sensation douloureuse pire que la lassitude physique. "Un carrousel, dans un piège," songeait-elle. Dans la foule, les autos étaient prises comme ces herbes qu'on voit flottant sur l'eau, retenues par des liens invisibles tandis que le torrent coule tout autour. Jeanne se détournait pour ne plus voir.[21]

She was therefore suffering less from fatigue than were her companions, but this incessant kaleidoscope, these unknown faces passing in front of her, appearing, going off, disappearing, was producing a painful sensation worse than physical fatigue. "A merry-go-round, in a trap," she thought. In the crowd, cars were caught like these weeds one sees floating on the water, held by invisible ties while the torrent flows all around. Jeanne turned away so as not to see them anymore.

---

20  Némirovsky, *Suite française,* 102.
21  Némirovsky, *Suite française,* 104.

In her own more proximate and concrete formulation, Jeanne sees the event much as does Maurice: the mayhem of history appears neither as a divine scourge nor as a dialectical verdict, but rather as an impersonal mechanism, figured in the above passage by the images of the merry-go-round and the plants floating in the stream of water. Némirovsky thus depicts individual human beings swept up in historical movements that far surpass their ability to control or even understand their own destiny. At the same time, however, Némirovsky's indirect free style gives us a multiplicity of fragmentary views from within and without the specific perspectives of a number of protagonists that appear within the debacle unfolding over wide expanses of French territory. We readers are consequently able to view the catastrophe sub specie aeternitatis as part of a pattern of the ebb and flow of human affairs.

That the various protagonists of her narrative are simply overwhelmed by the violence of history is dramatically conveyed by Némirovsky's narration of the refugees being strafed for the first time.

Ils n'avaient pas été mitraillés encore. Lorsque cela arriva ils ne comprirent rien, tout d'abord. Ils entendirent le bruit d'une explosion, d'une autre, puis des cris: "Sauve qui peut! A terre! Couchez-vous!" Ils se jetèrent instantanément face contre le sol, et Jeanne songeait confusément: "Ce que nous devons être grotesques!"[22]

They had not yet come under machine gun fire. When they did, they were confused at first. They heard the sound of an explosion, then another, and then people shouting: "Run for your life! Hit the ground! Flatten out!" They immediately threw themselves face down against the ground, as Jeanne thought to herself distractedly: "We must really look ridiculous!"

Thanks to the figure of Jeanne Michaud, who in spite of the absolute terror that grips her manages to think about how she must appear to outside observers, Nemirovsky once again has us view one of the most hellish moments of the ongoing exodus from perspectives both

22  Némirovsky, *Suite française*, 105.

interior and exterior to the event. We should not confuse this singular ability to step back from immediate experience with either a simple refusal to face reality or callous indifference, for through the eyes of the Michauds, Nemirovsky proceeds to have us take a close, careful look at some of those who fell victim to the machine gun fire.

Calming her pounding heart as best she can, Jeanne picks herself up off the ground and tries to continue her flight with her husband. It is at this juncture that she is forced to look death in the face:

Mais après quelques instants de marche, ils virent les premiers morts, deux hommes et une femme. Leurs corps étaient déchiquetés et par hasard leurs trois visages demeuraient intacts, de si mornes, de si ordinaires visages, avec une expression étonnée, appliquée et stupide comme s'ils essayaient en vain de comprendre ce qui leur arrivait, si peu faits, mon Dieu, pour une mort guerrière, si peu faits pour la mort.[23]

But after walking for a few minutes, they saw the first to have died, two men and a woman. Their bodies were torn apart, but their three faces just happened to remain intact: they were such dreary, ordinary faces with a studied, silly expression of surprise, as if they had been trying in vain to understand what was happening to them. They seemed so ill-suited, my God, for a warrior's death, so ill-suited for death.

The key word here is "ordinaires": even though her text has previously indicated that the mass of people fleeing on foot are common folk who could not afford the luxury of a car, Némirovsky presents these faces as mere humanity with no allusion whatsoever to any particular social, religious, political, or national (a good number of foreign nationals were in fact caught up in the exodus) identity. The emphasis remains clearly on the absurdity of these deaths, in which neither Jeanne nor the reader can find any ulterior or exterior signification. In terms of History, such as invoked by Hegel, Marx, or Pétain, they are meaningless, that is, not attributable to any divine scheme or earthly teleology.

The passage moreover underscores the intrinsic dignity and worth

23  Némirovsky, *Suite française*, 105–6.

of these unremarkable people whose lives have been claimed by the violence and chaos of events. These were modest folk, doubtless preoccupied with rather mundane cares, presumes Jeanne: "La femme, de toute sa vie, n'avait pas dû prononcer autre chose que 'les poireaux ont encore augmenté' ou bien 'qui c'est le cochon qui a sali mes carreaux'?"²⁴ (All her life, this woman had most likely not said much of anything other than "leeks have gotten more expensive again" or "who was the pig who made this mess on my tile floor"?) Yet through the keen human sensitivity that she has lent to Jeanne Michaud, Némirovsky remains epistemologically modest. Just as she respects the opacity of history in eschewing simplistic causal "explanations," so she respects human alterity by refusing to assimilate people to ready-made stereotypes and clichés (which, as we will see, however, in no way prevents her from delivering an implacable portrait of social pretension, privilege, and exploitation). Jeanne therefore warns herself against devaluing the lives of these simple persons by reducing them to their social categories.

Mais qu'est-ce que j'en sais? se dit Jeanne. Il y avait peut-être des trésors d'intelligence et de tendresse derrière ce front bas, sous ces cheveux ternes et défaits. Que sommes-nous d'autre aux yeux des gens, Maurice et moi, qu'un couple de pauvres petits employés? C'est vrai en un sens, et dans un autre nous sommes précieux et rares. Je le sais aussi. "Quel gaspillage immonde," songea-t-elle encore.²⁵

But what do I know? wondered Jeanne. There may have been treasures of intelligence and affection underneath those heavy brows, and that dull, disheveled hair. What else do people see in Maurice and me, other than a couple of poor little employees? That's true in a sense, but in another sense we are precious and rare. I know that also. "What an ungodly waste," she thought to herself again.

Jeanne thus refrains from issuing judgments on the value of persons as well as from interpretating the "meaning" of the catastrophic

24   Némirovsky, *Suite française*, 106.
25   Némirovsky, *Suite française*, 106.

event that occasioned their destruction. She instead ponders the partial, contingent nature of her own perception and decries the senseless nature of the devastation.

Viewed from within, through the eyes of Maurice and Jeanne Michaud caught up in the heat of the event, the mass exodus of civilians fleeing the Nazi onslaught appears as a tragedy of history akin to the natural disasters occasioned by earthquakes, floods, or volcanoes wreaking havoc among a vulnerable human population. The scandal seems more metaphysical than political. As if to drive the point home, Némirovsky provides a second iteration of this perspective after the historical disaster of France's defeat has been thoroughly consummated by the signing of an armistice, leaving the country deprived of two million prisoners of war. Having survived the harrowing ordeal and returned to Paris on foot, the Michauds learn not only of the collective humiliation but also of the severe blow dealt to their private lives: still without news from their son, they are informed by letter that they have lost their livelihood as bank employees.

Unable to retain her despair and indignation any longer, Jeanne lashes out against the injustice of their plight, asking why the little people always wind up bearing the brunt of the suffering: "Mais pourquoi la souffrance est-elle toujours pour nous? et pour des gens comme nous? Pour les gens ordinaires?"[26] (But why are we, and people like us, ordinary people always the ones who suffer?). Maurice once again likens the cataclysmic events that they have experienced to natural disasters that crop up without warning or explanation: "Il n'y a rien à comprendre. . . . Il y a des lois qui régissent le monde et qui ne sont faites ni pour ni contre nous"[27] (There's nothing to understand. . . . There are laws that govern the world and that are not made either for or against us). Even when Jeanne objects that humans are behind the war, Maurice persists in attributing such outbreaks of war to natural cycles of alternately calm and stormy weather: "Pour notre malheur nous sommes nés dans un siècle d'orages,

26  Némirovsky, *Suite française*, 267.
27  Némirovsky, *Suite française*, 267.

voilà tout"[28] (It has been our misery and misfortune to have been born into a century full of storms, that's all).

## The Contingencies of Mediation

The perspectives on history provided by these two central characters nevertheless have their limits. However endearing the Michauds may prove to be, it is not possible to accept Maurice's detached naturalistic skepticism at face value. Némirovsky clearly (and as we have seen, explicitly) privileges the Michauds' perspective by presenting them as eyewitnesses with firsthand experience who at the same time provide us an overview of the exodus. She moreover situates their historical discourse prominently at all three phases of the disaster at the outset, the crux, and the aftermath. However, theirs is not the unique point of view that her narrative affords to the reader, nor is it the only credible take on the events. Ultimately their commentary and observations reflect as much the mettle of their own character as the reality of events. Their discourse is perhaps more emblematic of the courage and quiet strength that enable them to carry on with dignity in the face of terror and suffering than a basis for definitive pronouncements on France's debacle. Indeed, Némirovsky's text provides a measure of critical distance within the Michauds' own dialogue, for while marveling at her husband's equanimity, Jeanne reminds him of his own stated desire to spit in the face of the rich and arrogant banking magnate who has just fired them both.[29]

There, as in the various panoramas of disaster, Nemirovsky makes us view the historical event as filtered by the multiple perspectives of her characters. Her narrative thereby foregrounds the fact that, instead of having a clear, straightforward, or direct perception, we are seeing history through the often highly charged reactions of those caught up in it. One of the most interesting cases to study in this regard is that of Hubert Péricand, whose decision to throw himself into the battle

---

28   Némirovsky, *Suite française*, 268.
29   Némirovsky, *Suite française*, 268.

in hopes of preventing defeat brusquely transports him from the confines of his smugly self-righteous Catholic upper-class family into the thick of the defeat. Hubert is finally reunited with his family in Nîmes after having a brush with combat on the rapidly disintegrating front lines and after having lost not his life, but only his virginity, to the irresistible legs of Arlette Corail, the professional dancer and banker's mistress who had invited him to the shelter of her hotel room upstairs while German soldiers heartily celebrated their victory in the ground-floor tavern. Upon arriving, Hubert finds his family all decked out in their Sunday best just about to attend a grandiose memorial service in honor of the members of the immediate family whose lives have been claimed by upheaval: grandfather Louis-Auguste Péricand, whose frail health could not withstand the stress, brother Philippe Péricand, a priest brutally murdered by the delinquent youth that he was leading to safety, and Hubert Péricand himself, presumed to have been killed in battle.

While the situation in which Némirovsky places Hubert's ensuing assessment of the fall of France is clearly not without a humor reminiscent of a famous episode in Mark Twain's *Tom Sawyer,* the serendipitous irony of his itinerary serves an important purpose. Having escaped the blinkered perspectives imposed by his family, Hubert has had a sobering taste of reality and has witnessed firsthand how his compatriots comported themselves amid the indescribable chaos and terror of the military rout and civilian exodus. The experience has stripped him of illusions and left him with little patience for the ostentatious displays of piety and patriotism that he now finds disguising the brutal reality of what has taken place on French soil. Madame Péricand, for example, has been exhorting her remaining children not to cry but to thank God for rewarding Philippe and Hubert with the crown of martyrdom.[30] Némirovsky moreover tells us that the throng assembled for the memorial service is intent on seeing the hand of Providence in this singular turn of events:

---

30  Némirovsky, *Suite française,* 231.

toute la ville était là. Tous purent voir le rescapé qui venait rendre grâces
à Dieu pour sa délivrance le jour même où l'on priait pour les défunts de
sa famille. En général, les gens étaient contents: un bon petit garçon
comme Hubert échappé aux balles allemandes, cela flattait leur sens de
la justice et leur appétit de miracles. Chaque mère privée de nouvelles
depuis le mois de mai (et elles étaient nombreuses!) sentait son coeur
battre d'espoir![31]

the whole town was there. Everyone could see the survivor who had come
to give thanks to God for his deliverance on the very day when everyone
was praying for the members of his family who had died. All in all,
people were happy: a nice young boy like Hubert who had escaped
German bullets appealed to their sense of justice and their appetite for
miracles. Every mother (and there were many of them!) who had not
heard from her own son since May felt her heart beating with hope!

With these lines, Némirovsky underscores the human-all-too-human
inclination to perceive events through the proverbially rose-colored
glasses, which in this case take on the form of a collective yearning
for a happy ending to France's misery and individual desires for the
safety of loved ones sent to battle.

The text of *Tempête en juin* exposes the illusory nature of such
yearnings by juxtaposing them with the sharply contrasting perspective of Hubert. Stung by the death of his brother and disillusioned
by the panic and cowardice that he has witnessed, Hubert will have
none of the sugarcoated rationalization that prevails at the ceremony.
He pointedly ignores the benevolent smiles of those in attendance
and freely vents his anger, raging first against the singular injustice
of his brother Philippe's death:

Si nous étions tous pareils, cochons et chiennes ensemble! pensait-il en
contemplant l'assistance, ce serait encore compréhensible, mais des
saints comme Philippe, qu'est-ce qu'on les envoie faire ici? Si c'est pour
nous, pour racheter nos péchés, c'est comme si on offrait une perle en
échange d'un sac de cailloux.[32]

31   Némirovsky, *Suite française*, 235.
32   Némirovsky, *Suite française*, 236.

"If we were all just the same, pigs and dogs all together," he thought while surveying those in attendance, "it would still be understandable, but what on earth are saints like Philippe doing here on this earth? If it is for us, in order to redeem our sins, then it is as if they were offering a pearl in exchange for a sack of pebbles."

Hubert's protest echoes the cries of injustice voiced by Jeanne Michaud. Outraged at seeing scoundrels fare so well while noble souls are crushed, he proceeds to turn his anger against hollow pretensions and lies emanating from his own upper-class milieu who, he knows, will seek to cover up their own scandalous behavior with a pious official version of these traumatic events. Through the voice of the eighteen-year-old Hubert so recently catapulted to manhood, Némirovsky thus provides one of her most stinging indictments both of the human failings so evident in France's debacle and of the self-serving spin put on these traumatic events by Pétain and his attendant ideologues. The passage deserves to be cited at length:

Ceux qui l'entouraient, sa famille, ses amis, éveillaient en lui un sentiment de honte et de fureur. Ils les avait vus sur la route ceux-là et leurs pareils, il se rappelait les voitures pleines d'officiers qui fuyaient avec leurs belles malles jaunes et leurs femmes peintes, les fonctionnaires qui abandonnaient leurs postes, les politiciens qui dans la panique semaient sur la route les pièces secrètes, les dossiers, les jeunes filles qui après avoir pleuré comme il convenait le jour de l'Armistice se consolaient à présent avec les Allemands. *"Et dire que personne ne le saura, qu'il y aura autour de ça une telle conspiration de mensonges que l'on en fera encore une page glorieuse de l'Histoire de France. On se battra les flancs pour trouver des actes de dévouement, d'héroïsme. Bon Dieu! ce que j'ai vu, moi!* Les portes closes où l'on frappait en vain pour obtenir un verre d'eau, et ces réfugiés qui pillaient les maisons; partout, de haut en bas, le désordre, la lâcheté, la vanité, l'ignorance! Ah! nous sommes beaux!"[33]

Those who were standing all around him, his family, his friends, all stirred up a feeling of shame and anger in him. He had seen them and their like on the road, he recalled the cars full of officers who were

---

33  Némirovsky, *Suite française*, 236; emphasis mine.

fleeing with their fine yellow trunks and their women covered with makeup, the civil servants who had abandoned their posts, the politicians who in their panic had strewn the road with secret files and dossiers, the girls who after having wept as properly expected on the day of the Armistice were now seeking consolation with the Germans. *"And to think that nobody will know about it, that there will be such a conspiracy of lies around all it that they will once again make it into a glorious page of French history.* They will make a big deal out of anything they can find to present as acts of devotion and heroism. Good God! The things I've seen! The closed doors where people would knock in vain in order to get a glass of water, and those refugees who were looting houses; everywhere, from top to bottom, disorder, cowardice, vanity, ignorance! Ah, what a fine lot of people we are!"

In order to fully appreciate the significance of this devastating assessment, we must once again situate it precisely. If, on the one hand, Némirovsky uses Hubert's caustic remarks to expose some of the unseemly behavior occasioned by France's fall, we must not lose sight of the prime targets of his outrage. Instead of targeting communists, Freemasons, intellectuals, and Jews as did Vichy propaganda in seeking to use them as scapegoats for the defeat, Hubert castigates on the contrary "le désordre, la lâcheté, la vanité, l'ignorance" (disorder, cowardice, vanity, ignorance) that he has observed at all levels, "de haut en bas" (from top to bottom) of French society, and in particular among the most privileged upper-class people that we now know to have been largely favorable to the Vichy regime for a long time: army officers and high-level civil servants. He furthermore reserves his most implacable attack for the "conspiracy of lies" that Vichy was disseminating in order to use war veterans and families with prisoners of war as pillars of power and authority. Written at the height of the National Revolution in 1941 and 1942, these words blast away the bedrock foundations of Vichy ideology.

More significantly for us today, the passage calls attention to the way in which different protagonists filter events through their variously shaded lenses and interpret history according to their own purposes. Even the commentary that Némirovsky shows Hubert formulating in his mind is no exception. While sharply undercutting the National Revolution's unctuous devotion to military, social, and religious authority, his own interpretation is explicitly linked to the particular experience that he has recently acquired from his direct involvement in the drama of France's debacle:

Il avait acquis une riche expérience; il savait, et non plus d'une manière abstraite, livresque, mais avec son coeur qui avait battu si follement, avec ses mains qui s'étaient écorchées en aidant à la défense du pont de Moulins, avec ses lèvres qui avaient caressé une femme tandis que les Allemands fêtaient leur victoire. . . . Il ne verrait plus jamais par les yeux d'autrui, mais aussi ce qu'il aimerait et croirait désormais, ce serait bien à lui et non inspiré par d'autres.[34]

He had acquired a rich experience; he now knew, not in abstract, bookish terms but with his heart that had beat so wildly, with his hands that he had skinned when helping defend the bridge at Moulins, with his lips that had caressed a woman while the Germans were celebrating their victory. . . . Not only would he no longer see through the eyes of others, but what he would henceforth love and believe would come from his own heart instead of being inspired by others.

However perspicacious we find them today, Hubert's acid criticisms of the official public versions of the defeat remain inseparable from his newly acquired moral and intellectual autonomy. While largely validated by the evidence that Némirovsky provides in the rest of her narrative, as well as by historical research, Hubert's perception nevertheless appears in all its contingent and partial subjectivity. Even his vehement denunciation of the upper-class hypocrisy that seeks to veil the sordid reality of the disaster is tempered by an inner voice enjoining him to respect a certain epistemological modesty and refrain from categorical, unqualified condemnations: "Tu es bien sévère, tu n'as vu que les événements extérieurs, tu ne connais pas les âmes"[35] (You are quite harsh; you have only seen what has happened on the outside,

34    Némirovsky, *Suite française*, 238.
35    Némirovsky, *Suite française*, 237.

you do not know their souls). Even though *Tempête en juin* clearly presents Hubert's narrative in a favorable light, the text calls attention to the limits of Hubert's perspective. In approaching varying versions of the historical catastrophe that has thrown France into upheaval, both Hubert and the reader must accordingly remain critical and skeptical. Far from being an anomaly, this conspicuous mediation of historical events constitutes an essential aspect of her entire *Suite française*. Némirovsky's own notes explicitly describe this technique:

Si je montre des gens qui "agissent" sur ces événements c'est la gaffe. Si je montre des gens agir, cela se rapproche certes de la réalité, mais aux dépens de l'intérêt. Cependant il faut s'arrêter à ça.

C'est assez juste (et d'ailleurs banal, mais admirons et aimons la banalité), ce que dit Percy—que les scènes historiques les meilleures (voir *Guerre et Paix*), sont celles qui sont vues à travers les personnages. J'ai tâché de faire la même chose dans *Tempête*. . . .[36]

If I show people who "act" on events, it's a gaff. If I show people acting, that indeed does approximate reality, but at the expense of interest. Nevertheless, one has to leave it at that.

What Percy says is pretty accurate (and furthermore commonplace, but let us admire and love the commonplace), that the best historical scenes (see *War and Peace*) are those seen through the characters. I have strived to do the same thing in *Tempête*. . . .

While at times providing a direct narration of events, Némirovsky most often obliges the reader to approach history through the mediation of multiple protagonists with varying several socioeconomic origins who must confront different aspects of the fall of France. Her narrative thus focuses first and foremost not on the defeat and the Occupation themselves, but on the mediation of those events through the contrasting and at times conflicting discourses of Hubert, Madame Péricand, Gabriel Corte, the Michauds, and others who interpret the historical drama according to their own desires and experience. In other words, Némirovsky continuously filters history

36  Némirovksy, *Suite française*, 534.

through the deforming lenses of her characters who approach the specific episodes of their own involvement. *Tempête en juin* as well as *Dolce* thus foreground her various protagonists' reaction to the maelstrom of history.

It is precisely because Némirovsky obliges us to approach the fall of France from a multiplicity of perspectives and interpretations that her *Suite française* prevents us from taking any single one account or commentary too literally as a formulation of some supposed absolute, definitive truth, even if, as we have seen, Vichy's lies and upper-class pretensions are clearly exposed, mocked, and discredited. Such is the nature of Némirovsky's historical agnosticism: we never get any full, unadorned rendering of events, only a number of constrasting and at times contradictory perspectives. Instead of seeking to camouflage or minimize the contingent and partial character of the discourses narrating the historical event, Némirovsky's text underscores this mediation by using her indirect free style to reveal the dramatic variation of perspectives. In other words, her narrative strategy proves to be the opposite of texts seeking to create the "documentary effect" by encouraging the reader to ignore the act of narration and accept the narrative as direct, spontaneous testimony.[37] We should not, however, confuse her pointed aloofness from ideology with political neutrality or ethical relativism. While she firmly refuses to arrange her narrative to confirm some predetermined doctrine, this emphatic and conspicuous historical skepticism clearly situates *Suite française* in opposition to Vichy's relentless exploitation of the shock and humiliation of defeat to scapegoat the Popular Front, communists, and Jews while lionizing the traditional hierarchies of the French army, the Catholic Church, and agrarian provinces. In the following chapter, we shall see how Némirovsky subverts accounts that were systematically favoring the privileged and the powerful, and instead honors the plight of the common people in representing their reaction to the upheavals of that fateful summer of 1940 in France.

37  See Andrew Sobanet, *Jail Sentences: Representing Prison in Twentieth-Century French Fiction* (Lincoln: University of Nebraska Press, 2008), 32, 71–77.

CHAPTER 2

# NARRATING THE FALL

Irène Némirovsky, as we have seen, refused to rally her *Suite fran-çaise* under any particular banner and resolved to maintain her composure in the face of the increasingly sinister events of the early war years. In her fictional narrative as well as in her personal life, she displayed neither cynical detachment nor wounded isolationism. By all accounts, her situation was indeed highly precarious and warranted a great deal of reserve. She was after all the sole breadwinner for her household, and her husband had been fired from la Banque des Pays du Nord after the May–June 1940 debacle in circumstances not unlike those depicted for the Michauds in chapter 28 of *Tempête en juin*.[1] She moreover remained unsuccessful in seeking French citizenship for herself and her family. As a Russian Jewish émigrée, she appeared doubly suspicious in the eyes of the Nazis as well as the French State, which in spite of her brilliant literary career in Paris and long residency in France had denied her persistent applications for naturalization. Given such increasingly difficult circumstances, it would indeed not be surprising to find that she, like the overwhelm-

---

1  See Philipponnat and Lienhardt, *La vie d'Irène Némirovsky*, 345, and Némirovsky, *Suite française*, 263–65.

ing majority of French people, had been deeply unsettled by France's defeat and the ensuing hardships. Traumatized by the collapse of institutional infrastructure and terrified by the violence of the war unfolding on their territory, the masses that Henri Amouroux famously if abusively labeled "40 millions de Pétainistes"[2] flocked into the waiting arms of the paternalistic savior figure skillfully projected by "le Vainqueur de Verdun." As notes Philippe Burrin, their weariness of the war and their yearning for consolation and respite from the storms of history made it all the harder for them to face the sinister nature of the Third Reich.[3]

### Personal Destinies

As a stateless Jew specifically targeted early in the Occupation by the persecutory measures imposed by the Germans and legislated by Vichy, Irène Némirovsky found herself hemmed in on all sides. She was in fact keenly aware of the autobiographical factors preventing her from more clearly favoring the Resistance in *Suite française*. Her own assessment of the political posture of Jean-Marie Michaud, the wounded soldier destined to appear as a Resistance hero in a subsequent section of *Suite française*, thus takes on a particulary poignancy:

Pour que Jean-Marie ait une attitude politique juste il faudrait 1) que je connaisse l'avenir 2) que j'aie moi une attitude politique juste, autre que celle qui consiste à grincer des dents et à mordre mes barreaux ou à faire des trous dans la terre pour m'échapper.[4]

In order for Jean-Marie to have the right political stance, it would be necessary 1) for me to know the future 2) for me to have the right political stance, other than that which consists of gritting my teeth and biting at the bars of my cell or digging holes in the ground to escape.

---

2  Henri Amouroux, *Quarante millions de Pétainistes* (Paris: Robert Laffont, 1977).

3  Philippe Burrin, *La France à l'heure allemande* (Paris: Éditions du Seuil, 1995), 39.

4  Philipponnat et Liendhardt, *La vie d'Irène Némirovsky*, 401.

When analyzed carefully, *Suite française* reveals some of the scars inscribed onto those figurative prison bars by an author otherwise unable to lash out against her oppressors. We have amply demonstrated that her refusal to adhere to any specific didactic purpose sets her depictions of the May–June 1940 debacle apart from those of her contemporaries. We have similarly noted that she consciously resisted the urge to denounce villains while praising heroes with her fictional narrative of the historical event. Ultimately, however, novelists and historians alike choose their material, configure their "facts," and sequence their discourse into coherent narratives. Whether they be true to life or imaginary, some words and actions are selected, highlighted, and developed while countless others are consigned to oblivion.[5] To borrow from Sartre's famous dictum, authors cannot but situate themselves historically by situating the specific elements of their narrative—in Némirovsky's case, her characters, their discourse, and her own indirect free-style commentary—with respect to their own time and ours. One could of course argue that any and every representation of these events is inherently and inescapably political. To be sure, it is virtually inevitable that historical narratives in particular take on political dimensions. But that does not mean that political agendas always dictate the content of such narratives, or that such narratives consciously or unconsciously advance specific political imperatives, nor even that all narration is necessarily skewed in favor of one specific cause or aligned with a particular social group.

Such is eminently the case for Némirovsky's representation of the fall of France and the concomitant civilian exodus in *Tempête en juin*. For her time as well as ours, it would be virtually impossible for either a novelist or a historian to produce a strictly "neutral" account of an event that was so intensely experienced and subsequently so susceptible to the most tendentious and vindictive of interpretations. In order to narrate that historical tidal wave, it is first of all necessary to make the traumatic event intelligible for those who were too over-

5   See Tzvetan Todorov, *Mémoire du mal, tentation du bien* (Paris: Robert Laffont, 2000), 133ff.

whelmed to grasp it clearly as it was unfolding as well as for those who never experienced it directly. It is moreover indispensable to account for the military defeat and the exodus of civilians in order to assess political and social responsibilities. Finally, the May–June 1940 disaster proves to be not only pivotal for understanding the subsequent evolution of the war but also emblematic of the ideological divisions and sociocultural malaise playing themselves out before and after the war years. For Némirovsky writing in the immediate aftermath of the upheaval as well as for historians revisiting the catastrophe over half a century later, the stakes are critical.[6]

As we shall clearly see when studying other depictions of the debacle, Némirovsky's subject matter is in and of itself neither original nor unique. Her narrative nevertheless offers an invaluable perspective on the tragic events of 1940 for several reasons. Instead of seeking to provide an overarching explanation of how and why France's military forces and political leadership collapsed under the strain of invasion, Némirovsky presents an entire range of discourses on the defeat and debacle. These multiple perspectives enable her to scrutinize her protagonists' various attempts to make sense of the defeat in their own minds while at the same time situating themselves in the suspicious yet gullible eyes of their compatriots. *Tempête en juin* thus reveals how these people experienced the sheer terror and anxiety created by strafing, bombing, separation from loved ones, and the loss of dependable food and shelter. More importantly, by foregrounding the impact on their private lives, the text shows us how they tried to interpret these traumatic events for themselves and for others.

*Suite française* focuses intensely on the private. Yet we would be mistaken to conclude that Némirovsky simply turned her back on the public arena and national destiny. Several critics have called attention to the dramatic tension between the public and the private realms in

6   Henry Rousso (*Le régime de Vichy* [Paris: Presses Universitaires de France, 2007]), Philippe Burrin (*La France à l'heure allemande*), Ian Ousby (*Occupation: The Ordeal of France, 1940–1944*), Julian Jackson (*France: The Dark Years, 1940–1944*), and Hanna Diamond (*Fleeing Hitler*) all emphasize that it is impossible to understand Pétain, Vichy, and the Occupation without analyzing the defeat, the debacle, and the ensuing aftershocks.

*Suite française.* They have not, however, analyzed how that conflict between individual existence and historical events plays out on several interrelated levels, nor have they explained exactly how Némirovsky has placed this conflict at the heart of her artistic enterprise. In pursuing such inquiries, we should first recall her own rhetorical question that we have already cited in the previous chapter: "Mon Dieu! que me fait ce pays! Puisqu'il me rejette, considérons-le froidement, regardons-le perdre son honneur et sa vie"7 (My God! What does this country matter to me? Since it rejects me, let's contemplate it coolly, let's watch it lose its honor and its life). The tension between the author's personal destiny and the plight of the nation that she had adopted is evident in the irony of these words, which in fact convey the very opposite of what they ostensibly affirm: bitterly observing that France has rejected her, she scoffs that she does not care about the country whose language and culture she had passionately appropriated as her own from early childhood.

## The Fate of a Nation

Although *Tempête en juin* only marginally represents the institutional apparatus of state and the armed forces that are so often considered to embody a country, a number of textual elements testify to a literary project consonant not only with other prominent representations of the French nation and of the "volonté de vivre ensemble" (will to live together) that since the French Revolution has in fact defined the "nation" as such. Under the Republic, citizenship was (and is still) to be based neither on bloodlines nor ethnicity, as is the case in many other countries, but rather on the affirmation of a common destiny. To participate in "la nation" is thus to be a part of the French people constituted not as subjects but as body politic. To adhere to "la nation" has thus meant affirming one's desire to embrace a common (if selective) historical heritage and to join in a cohesive political project for the future, namely, the political ideals and institutions of the

7   Irène Némirovsky, *Suite française*, 521.

French Republic.[8] So it is for Némirovsky's *Tempête en juin*. The text situates the people and events in her narrative with respect to a universal history of humanity as conceived by Maurice Michaud's philosophical contemplations. More concretely, Némirovsky also presents her protagonists as members of a national community collectively confronting the ordeal of the fall of France, even though with precious little equity, justice, or solidarity.

The very title *Suite française* clearly links the narrative to the nation. Némirovsky moreover stated her desire to portray the French nation as such by comparing her project to that of Louis Bromfield, who had elaborated a monumental fresco of India in *La Mousson:* "Bromf. a voulu faire aussi un tableau de l'Inde éternelle au début et à la fin, *comme je veux faire le tableau de la France*"[9] (Bromfield also tried to paint a timeless picture of India from start to finish, *as I want to paint the picture of France*). Instead of depicting the "great men" carrying out their political and military actions as had so many historical narratives before the historiographical innovations introduced by Marc Bloch, Lucien Fèvre, and the *Annales* school, Némirovsky was intent on devoting her attention to the fabric of the nation, the French people who experience the brunt of the historical catastrophe: "Il faut surtout montrer la foule. Cela doit être le véritable héros, la foule de ceux qui souffrent sans comprendre, et ses sentiments élémentaires de faim, de colère, de peur. Ceux qui meurent sans savoir pourquoi. L'horrible gâchage des hommes, le gaspillage de toutes ces forces"[10] (Above all, it is necessary to show the crowd. That must

---

8    See Alain Finkielkraut, "Qu'est-ce qu'une nation?" in *La défaite de la pensée* (Paris: Gallimard, 1987), p. 43–52, and Pierre Nora, "Le nationalisme nous a caché la nation," *Le Monde*, 17 March 2007.

9    Cited by Philipponat and Liendhardt, *La vie d'Irène Némirovsky*, 358; emphasis mine.

10    Cited by Philipponnat and Lienhardt, *La vie d'Irène Némirovsky*, 359. As further evidence for her deliberate emphasis on people in their everyday lives, we can cite from the notes published in annex to *Suite française:*

> D'un côté je voudrais une sorte d'idée générale. De l'autre . . . Tolstoï par exemple avec une idée générale gâte tout. Il faut des hommes, des réactions humaines, et voilà tout . . . . (531)
> Le plus important ici et le plus intéressant est la chose suivante: les faits histo-

be the real hero, the crowd of those who suffer without understanding, and all their basic feelings of hunger, anger, fear. Those who die without knowing why. The horrible waste of human lives, the waste of all these resources).

While certain passages of *Tempête en juin* give us an epic panorama of frightened crowds in Paris and out on the open road, Némirovsky by no means conceives of them as faceless masses serving only to represent some impersonal historical process. Her text rather gives us an acute sense of chaos and suffering while at the same time delineating the protagonists' particular socioeconomic position in relation to others. The result is a veritable cross section of the French populace, as evident from her own enumeration of the novel's cast:

Paysans, grands bourgeois, officiers, réfugiés juifs intellectuels, hommes politiques, vieillards que l'on oublie, de ceux qu'on faisait profession de respecter, et que l'on abandonne comme les chiens, les mères qui montrent des prodiges d'endurance et d'égoïsme pour sauver leurs gosses. Ceux qui plastronnent et se dégonflent tour à tour, la jeunesse meurtrie, mais non abattue.[11]

Farmers, wealthy bourgeois, officers, Jewish intellectual refugees, politicians, elderly people that are forgotten, some of those that people ostensibly respected and who were abandoned like dogs, mothers who display incredible wonders of endurance and selfishness in order to save their kids. Those who boast and then pipe down, the young people who are beaten down, but not crushed.

---

riques, révolutionnaires, etc. doivent être effleurés, tandis que ce qui est approfondi, c'est la vie quotidienne, affective et surtout la comédie que cela présente. (537)

On the one hand, I would like a sort of general idea. On the other . . . Tolstoy for example spoils everything with a general idea. You have to have human beings, human reactions, and that's all.

The most important thing and the most interesting is the following: historical, revolutionary facts must be touched on, but what is explored in depth is everyday, emotional life and especially the spectacle that it presents.

11   Cited by Philipponnat and Lienhardt, *La vie d'Irène Némirovsky*, 358–59.

In portraying the aristocracy, the upper and lower echelons of the bourgeoisie, rural society, and even a bit of the working class, Némirovsky's narrative offers a mosaic of French society as a whole, even if her cast of characters is not exhaustive.[12]

For Némirovsky, the nexus of social and intersubjective relations constituted the crux of her narrative, as we can infer from the comments found in her biography of Chekhov dating from precisely the same period as *Tempête en juin:* "lorsque, dans une nouvelle ou un roman, on met en relief un héros ou un fait, on appauvrit l'histoire; la complexité, la beauté, la profondeur de la réalité dépendent de ces liens nombreux qui vont 'd'un homme à un autre, d'une existence à une autre existence, d'une joie à une douleur'"[13] (when you make one hero or one fact stand out in a novella or a novel, you impoverish the story; the complexity, beauty, and depth of reality depend on the numerous ties that go "from one human being to another, from one existence to another existence, from joy to pain and suffering"). Although Lucile's impassioned protest against "l'esprit communautaire" (community mind-set) closely echoes the author's own inclination, it ultimately proves impossible, as we shall see in chapters 7 and 8, for her protagonists to conduct their private lives in isolation from the cataclysmic events unfolding all around them. *Suite française* not only presents each individual character as linked to others, but also depicts individual experiences as inextricably tied to the plight of the French nation as a whole. Hence the title *Suite française:* each individual calamity provides a contrapuntal development of the overall depiction of the fall of France. At the end of the day, what happens to France matters profoundly to each individual protagonist and vice versa.

We can confirm the eminently national character of Némirovsky's

---

12    In spite of the stated intentions, there are, as many commentators have noted, no Jews and almost no foreigners (except for a glimpse of a few Spanish refugees in chapter 27 of *Tempête en juin* and of course the Germans) in *Suite française*. We shall have more to say about this lacuna, the text's epic dimensions, and about the general portrait of the French people at a later juncture in chapters 3 and 4.

13    Cited by Philipponnat and Lienhardt, *La vie d'Irène Némirovsky*, 360.

narrative of the fall of France when we observe that all of its salient features, including the intertwining of the public fate of the nation and the private lives of individual persons, the panoramic sweeps, the explicit intent to compose a "tableau de la France," and, above all, the keen interest in portraying the plight of the common people who, both in actual events as well as in textual accounts, have all too often remained the faceless pawns of history, are precisely those of the nineteenth-century historian whose writings galvanized the ideal of "the nation" for countless writers and citizens of the Third Republic: Jules Michelet. Nothing is more central to Michelet's project of telling the saga of France's history than his passion for the common people whose lives constitute the story of the nation. As Paule Petitier points out, Michelet considers the essence of the nation to be the French people: "la réalité fondamentale de la nation réside dans le peuple qui la constitue"[14] (the fundamental reality of the nation resides in the people that constitute it).

Petitier moreover observes that Michelet places the biographical narrative at the center of his project, which he presents as a "Méthode intime: simplifier, biographer l'histoire comme d'un homme, comme de moi" (Intimate method: simplifying history, making it into the biography of one person like me). It is accordingly from Michelet that we get an oft-cited metaphor of France's singular identity: "La France est une personne" affirme-t-il dans le "Tableau de la France"[15] ("France is a person," he states in his "Panorama of France"). Adopting Michelet's terms to her own approach, Némirovsky could simply pluralize his "méthode intime," since she clearly presents her own "Tableau de la France" at war as a multiplicity of persons whose fragmentary biographical sketches compose a tableau of the events of her own period in history. Hence the motif of the panorama in both spatial and temporal terms. Just as the idea of the nation circumscribes the space of French territory, so the project of constituting the people

---

14  Paule Petitier, "Introduction," in Jules Michelet, *Histoire de France: Choix de textes présentés par Paule Petitier* (Paris: Flammarion, 2008), 16.

15  Petitier, "Introduction," 10.

into the body politic defines the focus of the narrative of the French nation: "L'historien moderne substitue la nation au roi comme sujet de l'histoire"[16] (The modern historian substitutes the nation for the king as the subject of history). Michelet therefore is intent on writing the history of how, from the arrival of Caesar's conquering army to the rising up of the downtrodden masses in the French Revolution to overthrow the monarchy and protect the fledgling Republic against Prussian and Austrian invaders, the French nation came to be. Michelet's narrative composition is crucial to his project. Instead of a mere succession of dates, princes, wars, and royalty, Michelet concentrates his subject by presenting history as a dramatic narrative, a constant struggle of opposing forces: each drama is moreover linked to another, or gets transformed into another problem: "L'histoire de France avance par l'enchaînement des drames les uns aux autres" (French history advances with the unbroken succession of ordeals leading from one crisis to the next) notes Petitier.[17] Némirovsky offers a lyrical formulation of just such interconnections in the story aptly title "Destinées," published on December 5, 1940. This narrative displays important implications for her depiction of historical events on at least two counts. First, Némirovsky precisely identifies the time and place at the outset as being the day of the fateful Nazi invasion of France: "Le 10 mai 1940, nuit d'alerte à Paris"[18] (May 10, 1940, a night when Paris was under a bombing alert). Second, as her protagonists apprehensively wait for the end of the alert amid the sound of distant planes and cannon fire, they speak of the link between personal lives and public destinies:

Nous parlions de guerres et de révolutions et des incalculables conséquences qu'un mot, un geste, une pensée peuvent faire naître dans ces moments qui sont en dehors de la vie commune. . . .

. . . cela donne, disions-nous, une extraordinaire responsabilité à

---

16  Petitier, "Introduction," 16.

17  Petitier, "Introduction," 15.

18  Irène Némirovsky, *Destinées et autres nouvelles* (Pin-Balma: Sables, 2004), 245.

chaque être humain. Chaque mouvement de mauvaise humeur, chaque parole impatiente et dédaigneuse seraient ainsi redoutables.[19]

We were talking about wars and revolutions and the incalculable consequences that one word, one gesture, one thought can create in these moments that are outside of our common life experiences. . . .

. . . that gives an extraordinary responsibility, we were saying, to each human being. Every ill-tempered gesture, every word of impatience and disdain would thus be dreadful.

The narrator of "Destinées" later reiterates these unsuspected links between the public and the private realms, emphasizing that all ultimately find themselves linked to historical tragedy:

—Si vraiment, dis-je, des sources de haine peuvent surgir ainsi d'un mot, d'un geste de chacun de nous, alors nous avons tous quelque chose de lourd sur la conscience; en ce sens on peut dire que, dans les calamités publiques, personne n'est innocent.[20]

"If, I said, sources of hatred can truly spring from one word or gesture from any one of us, then we all have a bit of a heavy conscience; in this sense, we can say that, concerning public calamities, no one is innocent."

We find a remarkable echo of such unsuspected links between past and present, public and private life in what Petitier sees as the biographical archeology central to the enterprise of Michelet, who described these invisible connections in the following terms:

Ces traces du vieux temps, elles sont dans nos âmes, confuses, indistinctes, souvent importunes. Nous nous trouvons savoir ce que nous n'avons pas appris, nous avons mémoire de ce que nous n'avons pas vu; nous ressentons le sourd prolongement des émotions de ceux que nous ne connûmes pas.[21]

These traces of the distant past, blurred, murky, often nagging and untimely, are in our souls. We find ourselves knowing what we never

19  Némirovsky, *Destinées et autres nouvelles*, 246.
20  Némirovsky, *Destinées et autres nouvelles*, 253.
21  Michelet's words are cited by Petitier in her "Introduction," 10.

learned; we have a memory of what we never saw; we sense the silent aftermath of emotions that we never experienced.

Only by delving into these unseen realms of the past hidden in personal lives can Michelet reveal the sources and intimate nature of national identity. While *Tempête en juin* provides an infinitely more detailed and complex portrayal of the events that are merely adumbrated in "Destinées," the two texts share Michelet's perspective. Némirovsky's own notes furthermore identify the intertwining of past and present, public and private lives as one of the key components of her never completed third part of *Suite française:* "Dans le 3e, *Captivité,* le destin communautaire et le destin individuel sont fortement liés"[22] (In the third part, *Captivity,* community destiny and individual destiny are strongly tied). Although tempered by a good measure of cowardice and a few isolated acts of courage, the image of the French people that ultimately emerges in *Tempête en juin* is that of a community of suffering. The characters who appear the most unsavory are precisely those who either think that they are too good to suffer the same plight as the common folk (Corte, Langelet, Corbin) or those who thanks to their material and social privileges manage to avoid many of the frustrations and sufferings of the plebe (Mme Péricand, Corbin, and even Arlette). However, Némirovsky herself as narrator never explicitly denounces these scoundrels and hypocrites for what they are: she rather holds them up for contempt (but also, as we shall see, compassion) by juxtaposing their various responses to the mayhem. The text articulates her stinging (though contrasting and at times conflicting) indictments through the voices of those who are subjected to the cowardice and selfishness of their compatriots.

Throughout the novel, Némirovsky artfully sequences her changing narrative voices to create a symphony of personal and collective stories. The resultingly frequent and dramatic reversals of perspective constitute one of the linchpins not only of her novelistic technique but also of her distinctive representation of the May–June ex-

---

22  Némirovsky, *Suite française,* 532.

odus. We must therefore engage in a close, detailed analysis of this changing narrative voice. Shortly before the war in 1938, when a certain young philosophy teacher destined to gain renown as the quintessential French intellectual and master thinker for an entire generation decided to take on an established novelist and member of the French Academy at the pinnacle of his career, he created quite a stir in the most prestigious Parisian literary circles. We are of course referring to Jean-Paul Sartre's often cited article "M. François Mauriac et la liberté." With his razor-sharp wit, the young philosopher deftly skewered Mauriac for the latter's alleged philosophical and literary transgressions. Sartre delivered a particularly harsh indictment against the novelist's narrative voice, which failed to maintain a single, consistent perspective to describe action either from the outside or the inside of such and such a character. Mauriac, objected Sartre, kept acting like an all-powerful narrator, intervening everywhere, reporting plot developments from an omniscient perspective at one point while at other junctures making the reader privy to the innermost thoughts of his characters. Moreover, the stridently atheistic Sartre did not fail to savor the irony of his most stinging criticism, which roundly castigated the Catholic novelist for sacrilege: by acting in such an omniscient and ubiquitous manner, charged the philosopher, Mauriac was consciously or unconsciously trying to play God.[23]

It is of course no secret that divine perspectives have long had bad press in literary domains. Who could forget the verdict so implacably slammed down on Mauriac by the young iconoclast: "Dehors ou dedans. Dieu n'est pas artiste. M. François Mauriac non plus"[24] (In or out. God isn't an artist. Neither is Mr. François Mauriac). It has even been suggested that this deft barb announced the execution of Mauriac the novelist and delivered a veritable coup de grace announcing the definitive demise of the psychological novel in general.[25] It has in any case long been the conventional wisdom to cite Sartre's famous

23   Jean-Paul Sartre, "M. François Mauriac et la liberté," *Situations I* (Paris: Gallimard, 1947), 36–57.

24   Sartre, "M. François Mauriac et la liberté," 57.

25   Welch, *François Mauriac: The Making of an Intellectual* (Amsterdam and New York: Rodopi, 2006), 80–82.

line as a verdict, maxim, and watchword while echoing his epistemological sneers. It would indeed be tempting to consider Mauriac's
narrative technique to have been irreversibly relegated to the dust-
bins of literary history.

We would nevertheless do well not to follow Sartre's arresting formulation too literally. For it turns out that Némirovsky's most crucial
technique consists precisely of such a variable narrative point of view
that makes it possible to lead her narrative voice everywhere while nowhere allowing it become permanently fixed in any particular perspective. She accordingly directs the eyes and ears of her narrator
and her readers from character to character, scene to scene, individual consciousness to individual consciousness, and even from human
consciousness to imagined animal experience. When all is said and
done, it is actually Mauriac who provides the key to Némirovsky's narrative enterprise: "Mais par habitude professionnelle, je me mets à la
place des gens"[26] (But out of professional habit, I put myself in other
people's shoes). In its candid simplicity, which so strikingly contrasts
with the convoluted paradigms of theoretical purists, Mauriac's state-
ment aptly describes Némirovsky's literary practice in *Tempête en juin*.

We have only to cite Petitier's description of Michelet's writing of
his *Histoire de France* to see that here again Némirovsky's project inter-
sects with that of the nineteenth-century historian: "Écrire l'histoire,
c'est la faire: cela signifie aussi qu'en écrivant l'histoire on s'efforce de
se mettre à la place de ceux qui la vivent. On n'écrit pas depuis le point
de vue surplombant du présent, mais on participe à une expérience
de l'histoire"[27] (To write history is to make it [history]: that also means
that in writing history we strive to put ourselves in the shoes of those
who live it. We do not write from the perspective that looks down from
above, we rather take part in an experience of history). In having us
share the anxieties, cowardice, fear, pain, humiliations, irrationality,
pettiness, and on a few rare occasions, even the generosity and courage, of all sorts of people, ranging from Parisian banking magnates

26    François Mauriac, "Mussolini envahit l'Abyssinie—Un Dessin de Sennep," *Journal
Mémoires politiques* (Paris: Robert Laffont, 2008), 704.

27    Petitier, "Introduction," 29.

to small farmers without forgetting uppercrust Catholic families and hardworking middle-class employees, Némirovsky proves herself capable of putting herself and her readers in their place.

Sartre and his disciples would doubtless look askance on such a quasi-divine narrator capable of peering into the intimate depths of individual persons while at the same time enjoying the global vision of a privileged observer far above looking down from Sirius to survey the expanses of French territory dotted with civilians desperately fleeing the German onslaught. Yet it is precisely such a dramatic alternation—or perhaps felicitous alliance—of perspectives that we find from the outset of *Tempête en juin:* "Chaude, pensaient les Parisiens"[28] (Hot, the Parisians were thinking). These words immediately enable us to assess the tacit inner apprehensions not just of one character in particular but of the entire city's population, "les Parisiens." Némirovsky's narrative voice seems capable of going beyond spatial and psychic barriers. To the extent that she observes "les gens," "les enfants," "les dormeurs," "les mères," "les femmes," "les habitants du sixième," "les pauvres," and "les riches"[29] (the people, the children, those who were sleeping, the mothers, the women, the inhabitants of the sixth arrondissement, the poor, the rich), Némirovsky situates her narrative within and without, relating the thoughts and words of all the various groups mentioned. Her use of the impersonal subject pronoun "on" is in this respect particularly revealing: "On n'y croyait pas," "on ne savait pourquoi," "on devait la voir [la Seine] couler blanche," "on voyait descendre," "On baissait instinctivement la voix," "On entendait battre les unes après les autres les portes refermées," "on avait calfeutré les fenêtres"[30] (They didn't believe it, they didn't know why, one had to see it flowing white, one saw descending, people instinctively lowered their voices, one heard doors closing one after another, people had sealed the windows). The ambiguity of this pronoun "on," which can serve either as the equivalent of the subject pronoun "nous" or as a substitute for the imper-

---

28   Némirovsky, *Suite française*, 33.      29   Némirovsky, *Suite française*, 33–35.

30   Némirovsky, *Suite française*, 34–35.

sonal third-person plural subject pronoun "ils," corresponds precisely with the alternating narrative perspectives that we have pointed out here. While giving a sweeping panorama of the Parisian population and landscape at the outset of the disaster, the narrative voice also takes the liberty of slipping in the most intimate of insights by conveying the thoughts of those on the verge of death: "Aux oreilles des mourants, les coups de canon semblaient faibles et sans signification aucune, un bruit de plus dans cette rumeur sinistre et vague qui accueille l'agonisant comme un flot"[31] (In the ears of those who were lying on their deathbed, the cannon fire seemed weak and meaningless, just one more sound amid the vague, sinister drone that washes over a dying person like a wave). With this one single sentence, Némirovsky situates her narrative perspective both within, since she gives us access to the sensory perceptions and even the affectivity of those about to die, and without, since she comments on the state of such dying persons in general.

Even when occurring within the space of a few words, this multiplicity of viewpoints represents neither epistemological naivete nor technical oversight. It rather constitutes one of the main components of Némirovsky's narration of the civilian exodus, a large-scale event unfolding over a broad expanse of French territory and overwhelming millions of what Jean-Louis Crémieux-Brilhac has termed "Les Français de l'An 40"[32] (The French of the Year 40). Némirovsky proceeds from one scene to the next and from one narrative voice to another, juxtaposing mores, mind-sets, and specific behaviors, then reversing the perspective to bring out not only socioeconomic dissonances but also all that reveals the contradictions between words and acts, self-image and the judgment of others, and, finally, subjective perceptions and the violent reality of history. On a psychological level, Némirovsky accurately depicts a Parisian population oscillating between the anxiety of bombardment and the reassuring words of public officials. On a social level, these repeated, radical shifts of per-

---

31  Némirovsky, *Suite française*, 35.
32  Jean-Louis Crémieux-Brilhac, *Les Français de l'An 40*, 2 vols. (Paris: Gallimard, 1990).

spective lay bare the schisms, inequities, perversities, prejudices, and grudges that were severely fraying the fabric of French society in the early 1940s. Yet on a more general level, these variations of narrative voice paradoxically testify to the common humanity of the numerous groups and individuals caught up in historical disaster.

## Portrait of the Novelist as Aesthete and *Grand Bourgeois*

We can see just how central this narrative technique proves to *Tempête en juin*'s very particular representation of the May–June 1940 historical trauma by a close-up, detailed examination of a few prime examples. Particularly telling is the case of Gabriel Corte, the character whom we follow over the course of several chapters as he proceeds from his posh Parisian residence overlooking the Seine river at Saint-Cloud onto the chaotic highways and byways of the central provinces before ending up in the most lavish hotel in Vichy. In order to situate this highly egotistical bourgeois novelist with respect to other characters, Némirovsky composes a tableau worthy of the seventeenth-century moralists La Bruyère and La Rochefoucauld. By painting a detailed portrait of one personage in particular, she paradigmatically sketches the psychological and social behavior of an entire category of persons, which in this case are the sort of Parisian writers such as André Gide, Jean Giraudoux, and Paul Valéry, who at the time were virtually worshipped by a country that made literature into a sort of secular religion.

The satirical element becomes even more interesting when one realizes that Corte reflects certain aspects of Némirovsky's own status and outlook as a writer of fiction. We find, for example, that the upper-class Parisian novelist conspicuously displays on his desk the first part of the very same verses invoking Sisyphus that, according to Myriam Anissimov, Némirovsky herself had inscribed at the very beginning of her own working notes for *Suite française:* "Pour soulever un poids si lourd, Sisyphe, il faudrait ton courage"[33] (In order to

---

33  Némirovsky, *Suite française*, 50. See also Anissimov's "Préface" in *Suite française*, 25.

lift such a heavy weight, Sisyphus, it would take your courage). Corte moreover shares Némirovsky's admiration for the art of the novel that Tolstoy had implemented in writing *War and Peace*.[34] While it is not impossible that Némirovsky may be chastising her own artistic vanity and supposed political nonchalance, as Weiss has suggested,[35] Philipponnat and Lienhardt offer a more plausible hypothesis: Corte is modeled after André Chaumeix, the director of the *Revue des Deux Mondes*, a prestigious bulwark of literary conservatism. During the Occupation, Chaumeix became a notable voice of Pétainism who moreover often visited Pétain's residence in the Hôtel du Parc in Vichy.[36] The connection is all the more interesting in that Némirovsky's notes reveal her intention to present Corte as a collaborator in subsequent parts of *Suite française*.[37]

We shall have occasion to see that Némirovsky has Corte check in to the most prestigious hotel in Vichy as well. At the outset, however, she sketches a portrait of the famous Parisian novelist Gabriel Corte as an overbearing, pompous aesthete displaying distinct strains of narcissism and megalomania:

L'écrivain Gabriel Corte travaillait sur sa terrasse. . . . Sa maîtresse, à ses pieds, ramassait silencieusement les pages qu'il laissait tomber. Ses domestiques, la secrétaire, étaient invisibles derrière les vitres miroitantes, cachés quelque part à l'arrière-plan de la maison, *dans les coulisses d'une vie qu'il voulait éclatante, fastueuse et disciplinée comme un ballet.* Il avait cinquante ans *et ses propres jeux. Il était selon les jours un Maître des Cieux ou un pauvre auteur écrasé par un labeur dur et vain.* Il avait fait graver sur sa table à écrire: "Pour soulever un poids si lourd, Sisyphe, il faudrait ton courage." . . .

Il était beau avec des manières languides et cruelles de chat, des

---

34   Némirovsky, *Suite française*, 53.

35   Weiss, *Irène Némirovsky*, 166.

36   Philipponnat and Lienhardt, *La vie d'Irène Némirovsky*, 361.

37   On 532–33, Némirovsky characterizes him as "violemment collaborationniste" (fanatically collaborationist) because of his fear of communism and even "violemment nazi," out of both resentment against the workers who stole his meal and opportunism, since he will aspire to become the party's official writer.

mains douces, expressives, et un visage de César un peu gras. *Seule Florence, sa maîtresse en titre . . . aurait pu dire à combien de masques il pouvait ressembler, vieille coquette* avec ses deux poches livides sous les paupières et des sourcils de femme, aigus, trop minces.[38]

The writer Gabriel Corte was working out on his balcony. . . . His mistress was at his feet, silently picking up the pages that he kept dropping. His servants and his secretary were invisible behind glimmering window panes, hidden in the house somewhere in the background, behind stage in a life that he wanted to be dazzling, glamorous, and disciplined like a ballet. He was fifty years old and had his own games. On certain days, he pretended to be Master of the Heavens while on others he played the part of a writer overwhelmed with hard, thankless labor. He had had engraved on his writing desk: "In order to lift such a heavy weight, Sisyphus, it would take your courage."

He was handsome, with a languid, cruel catlike demeanor; soft, expressive hands, and the face of a rather heavy-set Caesar. Only Florence, his official mistress . . . could have revealed how many masks this old flirt, with his two lividly pocked eyes surmounted by sharp, overly thin, feminine brows, could don.

With his imperious watchword "Dedans ou dehors" (In or out), Sartre had intended to banish anything that might in any way imply some special epistemological capacity on the part of the novelist. These lines, however, show that Némirovsky does not merely content herself with gathering up and arranging elements that could be observed from the outside by a third-person narrator who would then deliver them in unadulterated linguistic form to the reader. On the contrary, she clearly intervenes in her narrative, emphasizing the traits that expose the decadent, almost pathological egotism of this high-society Parisian. In short, she has recourse to the indirect free style in order to convey her own value judgments.

But she goes even farther when her narrative voice imperceptibly slips inside the minds of her characters, beginning with Corte himself and proceeding on to those of his household. After having

---

38  Némirovsky, *Suite française*, 50–51; emphasis mine.

sketched Corte's portrait in broad strokes and placed it within a certain socioeconomic framework, Némirovsky exhibits him from the
sharply contrasting perspectives of his own self-awareness, his mistress's affective sensibility, his servant's opinion, and ultimately, in
chapters 14 and 15 of *Tempête en juin,* from the point of view of lower-
class people lacking all artifice and privilege. Némirovsky first delivers Corte's innermost thoughts in order to underscore his acute narcissism. Concerning his mistress Alice, who had "quelque chose de
bovine dans le regard"[39] (something bovine in her gaze), Corte avows:
"J'aime cela. Une femme doit ressembler à une genisse, douce, confiante et généreuse, avec un corps blanc comme de la crème, vous savez
cette peau des vieilles comédiennes qui a été assouplie par les massages"[40] (I like that. A woman should look like a heifer, gentle, trusting, and generous, with a creamy white body: you know, like the skin
you see on old actresses, the skin that has been softened by massages).
This one long sentence written in the indirect free style reveals that
even in the face of impending catastrophe, Corte continues to wal-
low in vanity. These same words also illustrate the full extent of the
privilege that Némirovsky has granted herself not only as an observer
knowing her characters from within and without, but also as a moral-
ist intent on articulating her analysis. When Florence announces the
arrival of the German planes that were wreaking havoc among the civilian population, Corte seems disturbed only by the interruption of
the exquisite states of the soul so carefully constructed by his writing:

—Ils ne me ficheront donc pas la paix?
    Il haïssait la guerre, elle menaçait bien plus que sa vie ou son
bien-être; elle détruisait à chaque instant l'univers de la fiction, le seul où
il se sentît heureux, comme le son d'une trompette discordante et terrible
qui faisait crouler les fragiles murailles de cristal élevées avec tant de
peine entre lui et le monde extérieur.[41]

"Won't they ever leave me alone?"
    He hated war. It was not only threatening his life and his well-being,

39  Némirovsky, *Suite française,* 51.        40  Némirovsky, *Suite française,* 51.
41  Némirovsky, *Suite française,* 53.

it was at every instant destroying his fictional universe, the only one in which he could feel happy. It was like the terrible sound of a dissonant trumpet that was causing the fragile walls of crystal that he had so painstakingly built up between him and the outside world to collapse.

As if to make Corte's refusal to face reality unequivocally clear, Némirovsky adds: "Il ne voulait rien voir. Il repoussait la réalité du geste effrayé et ennuyé d'un dormeur éveillé en plein rêve"[42] (He kept on refusing to see anything. He brushed reality aside with the worried, frightened gesture of someone awakened right in the middle of a dream). The narrator herself thus delivers this unambiguous verdict.

One indeed wonders whether it might just not be Némirovsky the narrator who is blowing this "trompette discordante et terrible" (terrible, dissonant trumpet) since she continues to defy any and all obstacles that might prevent us from seeing exactly how Corte appears in the eyes of others. His servant, for example, is totally unimpressed by his boss's blustery pretensions. As one who has long since lost any and all illusions about the compulsive habits and foolish impracticality of those he must serve, Marcel is in fact candidly convinced of his own superiority:

Il était bien temps de demander son avis. . . . Pour lui, il n'avait pas peur des Allemands. Il les avait vus en 14. . . . Lui, il aurait tout emballé, tout caché dans des caisses, tout mis à l'abri depuis longtemps. Il ressentait envers ses maîtres une sorte de dédain affectueux d'ailleurs, comme il en éprouvait pour les lévriers blancs, beaux, mais sans esprit.[43]

It was high time to ask his opinion. . . . As for himself, he was not afraid of the Germans. He had seen them in 1914. . . . If it had been up to him, he would have wrapped everything up, hidden it in crates, and put it away in a safe place a long time ago. Toward his masters, he moreover felt a sort of affectionate disdain, similar to what he felt for his hounds, who were white and handsome but without intelligence.

42   Némirovsky, Suite française, 53.
43   Némirovsky, Suite française, 55.

Thanks to the narrative voice giving us direct access to Marcel's inner reflections, we savor the rich irony of the situation. Relegated to backstage of his master's presumably glamorous life, thus reduced to a highly marginal and servile status within Gabriel Corte's smug self-awareness, the mere servant in turn despises the high-society Parisian novelist all while granting a highly condescending, if not dehumanizing, sort of affection. We find indeed that Marcel harbors for "ses maîtres" (his masters) the same sentiment that he feels for his dogs, "les lévriers blancs, beaux, mais sans esprit"[44] (his hounds, who were white and handsome but without intelligence). Thanks to this sudden reversal of perspectives, we readers can observe that both Gabriel Corte and Marcel take pleasure in seeing each other as beings without intelligence.

As if to shatter any remaining illusions about Corte's almost solipsistic egotism, Némirovsky gives his mistress Florence the privilege of putting his writings into the place they truly deserve in the context of the invasion that is threatening to destroy their very lives. Florence faces what must be considered as a dilemma far removed from all aesthetic or intellectual considerations: she must choose which items to keep and which to remove from a suitcase that stubbornly refuses to close:

—Vous arriverez peut-être à fermer ça, Julie?
—C'est trop bourré, Madame. C'est impossible.
Un instant, Florence hésita entre la boîte de fards et le manuscrit, puis elle choisit les fards et ferma la valise.
On fourrera le manuscrit dans le carton à chapeaux, pensa-t-elle. Ah non! je le connais, des éclats de fureur, sa crise d'angoisse, de la digitaline pour son coeur. Demain on verra, il vaut mieux tout préparer cette nuit pour le départ et qu'il ne sache rien. Puis on verra. [45]

"Maybe you can manage to close this, Julie."
"It's stuffed too full, Ma'am. It's impossible."

44   Némirovsky, Suite française, 55.
45   Némirovsky, Suite française, 56.

For a second, Florence hesitated between the box full of makeup and the manuscript, then she chose her makeup and closed the suitcase. We'll stuff the manuscript in the hat box, she thought. Oh no! I know him and his angry outbursts, his fits of anxiety, and the digitaline for his heart. We'll see tomorrow. It's better to get everything ready for the departure tonight without him knowing anything about it. Then we'll see.

Here again, we readers enjoy the privileged perspective afforded by the narrative voice that gives us direct access to the character's mind. We clearly understand that Florence is much more preoccupied with her makeup than with her lover's literary treasures.

Not only does Némirovsky mercilessly probe the nooks and crannies of her characters' murky minds, she also submits the social order to an equally implacable scrutiny. Here again, we find the same masterfully executed technique of reversing the narrative perspective. At the beginning of chapter 14 of *Tempête en juin*, Némirovsky situates her narration within Gabriel Corte's car. We thus find him roiling with humiliation and rage, totally repulsed by the inescapable social promiscuity occasioned by the civilian exodus. Némirovsky thus exposes the bigotry driving the indignation that, according to Hanna Diamond, a good number of bourgeois did indeed feel when circumstances forced them to rub shoulders with social groups whom they were accustomed to look down on.[46] So it is that the great Parisian novelist is obliged to share the plight of the commoners and lower-class people now scattered about over France's highways:

—Ces gens . . .
Il montra la voiture qui venait de les doubler. Florence regardait ses occupants: ils avaient passé la nuit d'Orléans auprès d'eux, sur la place: la carrosserie abîmée, la femme avec son enfant sur les genoux, celle dont la tête était enveloppée de linges, la cage d'oiseaux et l'homme en casquette étaient aisément reconnaissables.
Il frappa violemment à plusieurs reprises le petit nécessaire garni d'or et d'ivoire sur lequel il s'accoudait.
—Si des épisodes aussi douloureux qu'une défaite et un exode ne

46  Diamond, *Fleeing Hitler*, 22–25.

sont pas rehaussés de quelque noblesse, de quelque grandeur, ils ne méritent pas d'être! Je n'admets pas que ces boutiquiers, ces concierges, ces mal-lavés avec leurs pleurnicheries, leurs ragots, leur grossièreté, avilissent un climat de tragédie. Mais regarde-les! regarde-les! les voici de nouveau. Ils me sonnent ma parole! . . .
     Il cria au chauffeur:
     —Henri, accélérez un peu, voyons! Vous ne pouvez pas semer cette tourbe?[47]

"Those people . . ."
He pointed to the car that had just passed them. Florence looked at the people inside: they had spent the night next to them in Orléans, on the town square. The body of the car was damaged. The woman holding her infant on her knees, with its head wrapped in white cloth, the bird cage, and the man with the cap were easy to recognize.
     On several occasions, Corte struck forcefully the little toiletry kit decorated with gold and ivory on which he was resting his elbow.
     "If episodes as painful as a defeat and a mass exodus are not uplifted by something noble and grand, they do not deserve to exist! I can't accept that these shopkeepers, these concierges, these sloppy people with their whining, their gossip, their crass manners debase an atmosphere of tragedy. Just look at them! Look at them! Here they are again. My gosh, they drive me crazy! . . ."
     He shouted out to his driver:
     "Good grief, Henri, speed up a little! Can't you give that riffraff the slip?"

We will have more to say about the highly demeaning use of "tourbe" (literally, "peat," but figuratively "rabble," "riffraff," or perhaps "trash" when referring to people) in chapter 4. The changing perspectives created by Némirovsky's narrative voice will subsequently have us view Corte through the eyes of the people in the other car just as this passage has us consider them through Corte's eyes. However, we must take care not to overlook the marked asymmetry of attitudes. Corte looks down on these unrefined common folk and seemingly cannot find enough contemptuous things to say about them. He according-

47  Némirovsky, *Suite française,* 117.

ly refuses to acknowledge the many friendly words and gestures that they offer him. To his despair, they even display their own capacity to contemplate and comment on the sad spectacle of the civilian exodus:

Gabriel frémit de répulsion et détourna la tête, mais la femme effective-
ment lui souriait et tentait de lier conversation. . . .[48]
Elle aperçut enfin le regard fixe et glacé de Gabriel. Elle se tut.[49]

Gabriel shuddered disgustedly and looked the other way, but the woman actually kept on smiling and trying to start a conversation. . . .
She finally noticed that Gabriel was staring coldly straight ahead. She stopped talking.

As if to underscore his absolute refusal to share anything whatsoever, including a common human misery, with these fellow travelers that the circumstances have imposed upon him, the Parisian novelist strikes an impassible pose. For her part, however, the working-class woman shows her perception of Corte's cold gestures. Yearning for human contact, she tacitly avows her sensitivity, and with it, her vulnerablility. Corte's blatant disdain for her thus comes as a slap in the face that finally reduces her to silence.

Némirovsky's text leads us to believe that, in addition to his un-willingness to lend any material assistance, it is precisely the moral violence of Corte's flat refusal to acknowledge a common humanity or even to recognize the existence of his social others that provokes the rough confiscation of the little treasure trove of food that he had managed to lay his hands on by paying off the owner of a restau-rant in Paray-le-Monial. Thanks to the frank observations provided through the privileged eyes first of his mistress Florence and then of his servant Marcel, Némirovsky has already stripped away Corte's ex-travagant pretensions, thus giving us the full measure of his appar-ently boundless egocentric fantasies. She now proceeds to strip away, at least for a brief instant, his material privilege at the very moment when he was already savoring it in his mind:

48   Némirovsky, Suite française, 118.      49   Némirovsky, Suite française, 118.

—Je ne sais pas du tout ce qu'il y a dedans, murmura Gabriel du ton détaché et rêveur qu'il prenait pour parler aux femmes, aux femmes convoitées et jamais possédées encore. Non, pas du tout . . . Mais je crois sentir une odeur de foie gras. . . .

Au même instant, une ombre passa entre Gabriel et Florence, arracha le panier qu'ils tenaient, les sépara d'un coup de poing.[50]

"I have no idea of what there might be inside," murmured Gabriel in the noncommittal, dreamy tone of voice that he used when talking to women, that is, to women that he lusted after but had not yet slept with. "No, no idea . . . But I think I'm getting a whiff of foie gras. . . ."

At the same moment, a shadow slipped between Gabriel and Florence, snatched away the basket that they were holding, and separated them by slugging them with his fist.

Although this daring heist of Corte's precious food basket may appear as a sort of poetic justice in the eyes of the reader, there is, on the level of narration, more going on here than a dramatic and fairly amusing turnabout. Once again, Némirovsky brings about a striking reversal of perspectives as she subjects the conceited Parisian aesthete to the gaze of the very people whom he so viscerally despises. From a description of these working-class Parisians articulated from without through the discourse of Gabriel Corte, her text abruptly switches to a presentation elaborated from within by these proletarians themselves.

Némirovsky thus gives an active first-person voice to those who in Corte's view of things should not have any say whatsoever in important matters. Since we find their observations scattered throughout chapter 15 of *Tempête en juin* and at times separated by Némirovsky's narrative interventions, we shall gather these comments together before proceeding to an extended analysis. The text thus bears citing at length, beginning with the remarks of the young woman for whom the rather tasteful act of petty larceny was committed:

50  Némirovsky, *Suite française*, 122.

—Tu n'aurais pas dû faire ça, soupira la femme qui tenait un enfant nouveau-né dans ses bras. . . .

—Non, tu n'aurais pas dû . . . ça me gêne, c'est malheureux d'être forcé à ça, Jules!

L'homme petit, chétif, le visage tout en front et en yeux, avec une bouche faible et un petit menton de fouine, protesta:

—Alors, quoi? faut crever?

—Laisse-le, Aline. il a raison. Ah! la la! dit la femme à la tête bandée. Qu'est-ce que tu veux qu'on fasse? Ces deux-là, ça ne mérite pas de vivre, je te dis! . . .

—Mais tu les a bien eus, Jules, dit-elle à son frère, ça je t'assure, je ne te croyais pas capable de ça!

—Quand j'ai vu Aline qui tournait de l'oeil, et ces salauds chargés de bouteilles, de foie gras et tout, je ne me connaissais plus.

Aline, qui paraissait plus timide et plus douce, hasarda:

—On aurait pu leur demander un morceau, tu ne crois pas, Hortense?

Son mari et sa belle-soeur s'exclamèrent:

—Penses-tu! Ah! la la! Non, mais tu ne les connais pas! Mais ils nous verraient crever pire que des chiens. Tu penses! Je les connais, moi, dit Hortense. Ceux-là, c'est les pires. Je l'ai vu chez la comtesse Barral du Jeu, une vieille rombière; il écrit des livres et des pièces de théâtre. Un fou, à ce que disait le chauffeur, et bête comme ses pieds. . . .

Ils recommencèrent à parler de Corte. Ils pensaient avec satisfaction à l'excellent dîner qu'ils avaient mangé à sa place. Tout de même, ils le jugeaient à présent avec plus de douceur. Hortense, qui chez la comtesse Barral du Jeu avait vu des écrivains, des académiciens et même, un jour, la comtesse de Noailles, les fit rire aux larmes en racontant ce qu'elle savait d'eux.

—Ce n'est pas qu'ils soyent méchants. Ils ne connaissent pas la vie, dit Aline.[51]

"You shouldn't have done that," sighed the woman who was holding a newborn child in her arms. . . .

"No, you shouldn't have done it . . . It bothers me, it's miserable to have to resort to that, Jules!"

51  Némirovsky, *Suite française*, 124–28.

The scrawny little man whose eyes and forehead dominated his face, which featured a diminished mouth and a little weasely chin, protested:

"So you're telling me we should just croak?"

"Leave off, Aline. He's right. My goodness," said the woman with the bandaged head. "What do you expect us to do? I say people like those two characters don't deserve to live. . . ."

"But you really did 'em in, Jules," she said to her brother, "Boy, I tell you, I didn't think you were up to a stunt like that!"

"When I saw Aline about to faint, and those bastards loaded with champagne, foie gras, and all the rest, I was beside myself."

Aline, who seemed to be more timid and gentle, ventured to say:

"Don't you think we might have asked them for a bite to eat, Hortense?"

Her husband and sister-in-law exclaimed:

"Ha! Fat chance! You don't know these people! They'd just as soon see us croak more pitifully than dogs. Fat chance! I know these people," said Hortense. "Those two are the worst. I saw that guy when I was working for an old battleaxe, Countess Barral du Jeu. He writes books and plays. His chauffeur says he's crazy and dumb as a doornail."

They went back to talking about Corte. They savored the excellent dinner that they had eaten in his place. Nevertheless, they were presently less harsh in their judgment of him. Hortense, who had seen a number of writers, members of the Académie Française, and even the Countess de Noailles one day, when she worked for Countess Barral du Jeu, made them laugh so hard they cried by telling them what she knew about those people.

"It's not that they're mean. They just don't know the real world," said Aline.

There is a consummate irony in these passages. We see that those whom the famous Parisian man of letters had considered to be lacking any sense of "noblesse," "grandeur," or dignity in the face of the "tragédie" that was unfolding ultimately show a significant measure of moral scruples and even a certain ethical refinement at a time when, as was the case for countless refugees who had precipitously fled their homes in May and June 1940, they find themselves in dire straits.[52]

---

52  Cf. Diamond, *Fleeing Hitler*, 5–12.

Having recently given birth and now experiencing acute hunger pangs, the young woman holding her baby in her arms would have every reason in the world to brush aside moral compunction and worry instead about her own precarious situation. Némirovsky nevertheless has her display the greatest ethical sensibility of all, as she not only regrets the theft, but even finds herself feeling a bit guilty. The woman with the bandaged head ("la femme à la tête bandée"), who had caused Gabriel Corte to shudder with repulsion and recoil in horror, returns the courtesy by relating her firsthand knowledge of his sensual excesses and practical clumsiness to her working-class companions, who in turn delight in the revelation of upper-class foolishness and decadence. To a certain extent, the rival discourses of socioeconomic class difference and resentment seem to mirror each other. Just as events lacking all nobility and grandeur "ne méritent pas d'être" (don't deserve to exist) according to Corte, so we see first Jules, then Hortense declaring that these "salauds chargés de bouteilles, de foie gras et tout" (bastards loaded with champagne, foie gras, and all the rest) and who "verraient [les gens du peuple] crever comme des chiens" (would just as soon see [us proles] croak like dogs) do not deserve to exist: "ça ne mérite pas de vivre"[53] (people like that don't deserve to live). Eventually, however, these truculent charges give way to a more dispassionate, almost understanding philosophical perspective.

Within the characters' discourse as in the broader context of the narrative, ethics go hand in hand with aesthetics. Corte invariably wants to transform the event into an aesthetic object, thus seeking to dominate history by appropriating it to his own artistic ends. The working-class people with whom we find him constrasted, however, are scarcely in a position to afford the luxury of detaching themselves from the overwhelming historical ordeal. Némirovsky's irony reaches its peak when we realize that it is not the famed Parisian novelist with his presumably elevated views, but rather one of these proletarians who displays a thoroughly human wisdom worthy of

---

53  Némirovsky, *Suite française*, 124–25.

Montaigne. Holding her newborn child in her arms and wielding a faulty subjunctive ("soyent" instead of "soient") along with an inelegantly elided negative ("connaissent pas" instead of "ne connaissent pas"), the woman who appears as the humblest and most vulnerable nevertheless continues to express her misgivings about the gastronomical heist, and finally delivers her own cogent assessment of people like Corte: "Ce n'est pas qu'ils soyent méchants. Ils connaissent pas la vie"[54] (It's not that they're mean. They just don't know the real world). The indispensable role of Némirovsky's narrative technique in delivering this withering assessment of Corte's egocentric aestheticism cannot be overemphasized: we savor the irony thanks precisely to the changing perspectives that literally turn Corte's inflated illusions inside out. When the young working-class woman imparts her lesson of humanity to a major figure of the Parisian literary scene, we immediately gauge both the enormity of his intellectual hubris and the injustice of his social pretensions.

### Narrative, History, and Philosophy

More than any other narrative, *Tempête en juin* conveys the pathos of the countless individual tragedies while at the same time integrating them into a vast fresco of the civilian exodus of May–June 1940. Therein lies without question a considerable part of the dramatic power rightly felt by those reading Némirovsky's text some sixty-five years after the fact. She has sketched uncompromisingly satirical, yet at the same time subtle and nuanced, portraits of Parisian and provincial aristocrats and bourgeois as well as "les petites gens" ("the little people," in other words, farmers, workers, and servants). The particular contribution of her historical tableau does not reside merely in the accuracy and wealth of detail (which are in both cases considerable) of her representation of the various social classes that composed the French populace in 1940. The power of her representation is considerably augmented by the comparisons and contrasts that her nar-

---

54 Némirovsky, *Suite française*, 128.

rative inevitably establishes between one scene and the others that follow. As the narrative develops, the radical inadequation of each individual consciousness to the reality of the historical event becomes progressively more apparent. *Tempête en juin* thus juxtaposes a wide variety of attitudes and behaviors adopted by various personages in response to the particular socioeconomic and historical situation that they must face. In so doing, Némirovsky's text reveals the logic that, as Emmanuel Lévinas explains in one of his most important essays, "L'Ontologie est-elle fondamentale," is implicitly (if unwittingly) enacted in each case:

la compréhension de l'être ne suppose pas seulement une attitude théorétique, mais tout le comportement humain. Tout homme est ontologie. Son oeuvre scientifique, sa vie affective, la satisfaction de ses besoins et son travail, sa vie sociale et sa mort articulent, avec une rigueur qui réserve à chacun de ces moments une fonction déterminée, la compréhension de l'être ou la vérité.[55]

the comprehension of being not only supposes a theoretical outlook, but all of human comportment. Every human being is an ontology. For each human being, scientific achievement, emotional life, work and satisfaction of needs, social life, and death articulate this comprehension of being or the truth, with a rigor that reserves a specific function for each one of these activities.

Long before Jean-Paul Sartre, it was Lévinas who had explained the significance of Husserl's phenomenology and Heidegger's radical ontology for the French intellectual world. The above-cited passage emphasizes the degree to which twentieth-century philosophy found itself henceforth preoccupied with historicity. Before being encapsulated in the abstract formulations of philosophical discourse, the responses given by ordinary people to the basic questions of human existence receive their first articulation in the words and deeds of their everyday lives.

---

55  Emmanuel Lévinas, "L'Ontologie est-elle fondamentale?" in *Entre nous* (Paris: Grasset et Fasquelle, 1991), 13.

One of the essential tasks for Lévinas and others was accordingly to reveal the philosophical implications of the public and private matters that take place right before our eyes. It is to that very end that Alain Finkielkraut has devoted his remarkable essay on modernity, *Nous autres, modernes*. Charged with providing instruction in philosophy to the students at the highly prestigious École Polytechnique, an institution that touts itself as being at the cutting edge of science and technology, Finkielkraut decided to give them an awareness of the ontological presuppositions underlying life in the contemporary world: "je cherche d'abord à tirer au clair la métaphysique, c'est-à-dire le rapport fondamental à l'être qui se manifeste dans la sensibilité, les façons d'agir, de faire, les moeurs, les habitudes caractéristiques de notre temps. . . . Ce n'est pas *la* philosophie, c'est *leur* philosophie que je m'efforce d'apprendre à mes élèves"[56] (I seek first of all to define the concept of metaphysics, that is, the fundamental relationship to being that manifests itself in the sensitivity, in the modes of action and doing, in the mores and the habits that are characteristic of our time. . . . It's not philosophy *in itself* that I strive to teach my students, it's *their* philosophy). Current events therefore take on philosophical significance, while philosophers focus on history developing right at their doorstep. Lévinas thus explains that the philosophical enterprise can consist of "une attention radicale prêtée aux préoccupations pressantes de l'actualité. *La question abstraite de la signification de l'être en tant qu'être et les questions de l'heure présente se rejoignent spontanément*"[57] (paying a radical attention to the pressing concerns of current events. *The abstract question of the meaning of being as being and the issues of the present hour overlap spontaneously*).

But that is not all. In France, the preoccupation with history is widely recognized as one of the seismic aftershocks of the war whose repercussions have also been strongly felt in the domain of literature, as Lévinas again emphasizes:

---

56   Alain Finkielkraut, *Nous autres, modernes* (Paris: Ellipses, 2005), 7–8.
57   Lévinas, "L'Ontologie est-elle fondamentale?" 13; emphasis mine.

L'existence historique qui intéresse le philosophe dans la mesure où elle
est ontologique intéresse les hommes et la littérature parce qu'elle est
dramatique. Quand philosophie et vie se confondent, on ne sait plus si
on se penche sur la philosophie parce qu'elle est vie, ou si on tient à la vie
parce qu'elle est philosophie . . . comprendre l'être, c'est exister. . . .
Penser ce n'est plus contempler, mais s'engager, être englobé dans ce
qu'on pense, être embarqué—événement dramatique de l'être-dans-le-
monde.[58]

The historical existence that interests the philosopher to the degree that
it is ontological interests human beings and literature because it is
dramatic. When philosophy and life fuse together, we can no longer tell
whether we are concerned with philosophy because it is the stuff of life
or whether we treasure life because it is the stuff of philosophy . . . to
comprehend being is to exist. . . . To think is no longer to contemplate,
but to commit oneself, to be enveloped in what on thinks, to be em-
barked—the dramatic event of being-in-the-world.

Némirovsky's representation of the defeat and the civilian exodus in
*Tempête en juin* corresponds perfectly with the inextricable interwin-
ing of literature, philosophy, and existence that Lévinas points to in
these lines. Her narrative derives in part from her personal involvement with history and in part from critical analysis made from outside and "above" the rush of events. Explaining why he had more or
less abandoned his activity as a novelist and taken up journalism,
Mauriac confided that "l'horreur du monde réel [l]'a chassé de la fiction"[59] (the horror of the real world drove [him] out of fiction).

For her part, Némirovsky manages to reconcile the two, skillfully
using the devices of fiction to narrate a very real event in a way that
exposes the human-all-too-humain egocentrism, its attendant social
oppression, and the violence of history. To adopt the terms of Lévinas, Némirovsky develops her characters in a way that reveals their
comprehension of being, the philosophy implicit in their words and
deeds. As distorted, fallacious, or perverse as it may be, the logic of

58   Lévinas, "L'Ontologie est-elle fondamentale?" 14.
59   François Mauriac, "Le Métier d'écrivain," *L'Express*, April 5, 1957, 19.

their life is thus made palpable in the text. By means of a narrative voice that expresses itself from within and without, she puts herself and her readers in the place of her characters, with the end result of revealing the radical inadequation of each particular point of view, "philosophy," or subjective experience with the overall movement of history that outstrips and surpasses each one. Thanks to the juxtaposition of these multiple experiences and situations, however, the narrative allows us to measure the gap separating subjective perception from historical reality.

By narrating the action—or more frequently, her various protagonists' perception of the action—from a variety of sharply contrasting perspectives, Némirovsky exposes the discrepancy between the conscious intentions of her characters and the actual unfolding of events. Her text thus calls attention to one of the dramas of human existence as formulated by twentieth-century philosophy. In the above-cited article, Lévinas stresses the disparity between lived experience and history, the self and being, conscientious intentions and the actual repercussions of our acts. He goes on to articulate his unsettling conclusion: our human responsibility far outstrips our capacity to master, direct, or even understand our own attempts to act in a deliberate manner:

Nous sommes ainsi responsables au-delà de nos intentions. Impossible au regard qui dirige l'acte d'éviter l'action par mégarde. Nous avons un doigt pris dans l'engrenage, les choses se retournent contre nous. C'est dire que notre conscience et notre maîtrise de la réalité par la conscience n'épuisent pas notre relation avec elle, que nous y sommes présents par toute l'épaisseur de notre être. *Que la conscience de la réalité ne coïncide pas avec notre habitation dans le monde—voilà ce qui dans la philosophie de Heidegger a produit une forte impression dans le monde littéraire.*[60]

We are thus responsible beyond our intentions. It is impossible to avoid inadvertant action by keeping a watchful eye on each act. We have a finger caught in the gears, and things turn out differently than we wanted. That is to say that our consciousness and our mastery of reality

60   Lévinas, "L'Ontologie est-elle fondamentale," 14–15.

by consciousness does not exhaust our relationship with reality: we are present in all the layers of our being. *Our consciousness of reality does not coincide with our dwelling in the world: that is what it was in Heidegger's philosophy that made a strong impression on the literary world.*

The same dilemma can be discerned in Némirovsky's depiction of the most prominent representatives of the upper class in *Tempête en juin.* What characterizes Mme Péricand, Gabriel Corte, Charles Langelet, and M. Corbin is their socioeconomic and psychological hubris. They display boundless confidence in themselves, their privileges, and their comforts, as well as in their supposed merits and superiority over all the people whose job it is presumably to serve them in one way or another. By virtue of their material wealth and social privilege, they have the habit of directing, controling, dictating, and dominating everything and everybody. As Némirovsky portrays them in the radically unsettling context of the civilian exodus of June 1940, however, they appear totally overwhelmed, stunned, physically vulnerable, confronted with their own weakness, failings, and incompetence. The tragic turn of events rudely confronts them with the brutality of a Hobbesian state of nature and the injustice of history, as the tidal wave of panic and chaos sweeps across France, unleashing all sorts of fears and irrational behaviors.

What Némirovsky depicts on an individual level holds true collectively as well. Historians have long decried the astounding incompetency, unpreparedness, and stubborn illusions harbored by the political and military elite of the so-called civilization Maginot[61] that caved in under the pressure of the Second World War. The narrative of *Tempête en juin* allows us to observe the collective disaster unfold in all its pathos on the most concrete, yet intimate experience of personal lives. In other words, Némirovsky has us see it on the same level as that on which the vast majority of people in France at the time found themselves totally confused by the erratic, incoherent, and often contradictory information supplied by authorities who in the end

---

61    The term is that of Stanley Hoffman, "Le Désastre de 1940," in *Études sur la France de 1939 à nos jours* (Paris: Éditions du Seuil, 1985), 31–32.

left them to cope with the chaos and mayhem with their own devices.[62] Like Michelet's *Histoire de France,* Némirovsky's narrative of the fall of France recounts and reconstitutes the events as their protagonists experienced them, as they themselves interpreted events at the time. With Némirovsky as with Michelet, we discover events from close up, as they unfold.[63]

In order to understand the Occupation years, stresses Henry Rousso, we must first look long and hard at the tremendous movement of panic that gripped millions of people in late May and early June 1940, leading them to flee precipitously out over the open countryside where they would end up tragically the most vulnerable first to the German invasion and then to the demagoguery of Philippe Pétain.[64] In a similar vein, Hanna Diamond stresses the close link between the severe, widespread trauma of the civilian exodus and the Vichy regime's subsequent exploitation of the theme of suffering.[65] In that light, we would do well to take stock of the historical as well as the philosophical and literary import of Némirovsky's narrative of the fall of France in *Tempête en juin.* We know that Sartre conspicuously situated his historical and ideological coming of age precisely in the context of France's defeat, which forced him to share the plight of a good number of his compatriots with whom he had previously refused to find anything in common. It is not inconceivable that, in her own specific way, Némirovsky experienced a similar awakening to questions of collective destiny. On the other hand, Némirovsky's representation of the May–June 1940 debacle discredits Sartre's peremptory and derisive dismissal of any narrative voice that situates itself alternately within and without. In *Tempête en juin,* Némirovsky's dramatically changing and often abruptly reversing narrative perspectives expose the limits, lacunae, distortions, illusions, and inadequation of each subjective experience and therefore provide a concrete

---

62   Cf. Diamond, *Fleeing Hitler,* 7–12, 24–33.

63   Cf. Petitier, "Introduction," 29.

64   Henry Rousso, *Le Régime de Vichy,* 11.

65   Diamond, *Fleeing Hitler,* 12.

illustration of human existence as analyzed by Emmanuel Lévinas. At the same time, the text provides a compelling take on one of the major upheavals of recent French history by focusing as did Michelet on the immediate experience of common people caught up in events that outstripped their capacity to make sense of what was happening.

CHAPTER 3

# EPIC SUFFERING

For a close paraphrase of Némirovsky's perspective on private lives and collective destiny during the May–June 1940 debacle, we can cite one of *Tempête en juin*'s major protagonists, Philippe Péricand, the priest who takes on the task of accompanying a group of delinquants and orphans to safety in the southern provinces. As he assumes leadership of these youth just before setting out on the journey, he seeks to create a sense of unity and cohesion with the following words:

Dieu seul . . . connaît le sort réservé à chacun de nous dans les jours qui vont suivre. Il est hélas infiniment probable que nous souffrirons tous dans notre coeur car *les malheurs publics sont faits d'une multitude de malheurs privés,* et c'est le seul cas où, pauvres ingrats aveugles que nous sommes, nous avons conscience de la solidarité qui nous lie, nous membres d'un même corps.[1]

Only God . . . knows what fate is in store for each of us in the days to come. It is, alas, extremely likely that we will all suffer in our hearts, for *collective tragedies are made up of a multitude of individual ordeals,* and that is the only case in which we poor, ungrateful, blind people are aware of the solidarity that binds us together as members of one same body.

---

1  Némirovsky, *Suite française,* 62–63; emphasis mine.

Philippe's words will soon prove ironically and tragically prophetic for his own plight, as he ends up suffering atrociously not only in his heart but in his body, savagely murdered by the very ones he hoped in every sense to save. On a broader scale, Némirovsky's narrative of the debacle shows how France's collective ordeal is composed of a multitude of individual tragedies and betrayals: for better or for worse, the various individual itineraries are, as Philippe observes, indeed intertwined into one variously shared public destiny.

## Solidarity and Satire of a House Divided

Numerous passages of *Tempête en juin*, and in particular the striking similes that allow us to visualize the multitude of private tragedies converging into a common public disaster, provide a highly concrete figuration of Philippe's eloquent abstraction. Far from simply "remembering" or "preserving" the past, Némirovsky's narrative gives an epic dimension to the traumatic events that at the time remained fragmented and incoherent for those experiencing them. Hanna Diamond and Richard Vinen both stress that, with the collapse of France's administrative and communicational infrastructure, the vast majority of people simply did not have the means to piece together any sort of global assessment of the rapidly evolving military and civilian debacle. People therefore had all the more reasons to focus on the urgent imperatives of their own situation.[2] Unfettered by the constraints of immediate experience, Némirovsky's narrative offers on the contrary a perspective far beyond the perceptions of any one individual swept up in the chaos. It is important to point out, however, that the resulting account of the event cannot really be considered as testimony, particularly since Némirovsky did not herself personally take part in the exodus but gleaned her information from various newspaper and eyewitness accounts:[3] *Suite française* is a literary composition that proves all the more valuable for pro-

2  Diamond, *Fleeing Hitler*, 29–31, 66, 68, and Richard Vinen, *The Unfree French* (New Haven and London: Yale University Press, 2006), 16.

3  Phipponnat and Liendhardt, *La vie d'Irène Némirovsky*, 341.

viding a synthetic understanding that would otherwise be lacking. Only such an Olympian overview can reveal the pattern traced by the countless individual itineraries joining together to form a larger historical event. Here, as is often the case, Némirovsky composes a dramatic traveling shot of the throngs fleeing Paris, then provides a veritable epic catalog of vehicles and their contents, and finally places an epic simile at the end as if to recapitulate with added emphasis the full scope of the mass exodus:

sans fin, par la route de Paris coulait un fleuve lent d'autos, de camions, de voitures de charretiers, de bicyclettes auquel se mêlaient les attelages des paysans qui abandonnaient leurs fermes et partaient vers le Sud en traînant derrière eux enfants et troupeaux. . . . Des gens couchaient [à Orléans] par terre dans les salles des cafés, dans les rues, dans les gares, la tête appuyée sur leurs valises. L'embouteillage était tel qu'il était impossible de sortir de la ville. Certains disaient qu'un barrage avait été établi afin de laisser la route pour la troupe.

Sans bruit, phares éteints, les autos arrivaient les unes derrière les autres, pleines à craquer, surchargées de bagages et de meubles, de voitures d'enfants et de cages à oiseaux, de caisses et de paniers à linge, chacune avec son matelas solidement attaché sur le toit; elles formaient des échafaudages fragiles et elles paraissaient avancer sans l'aide du moteur, emportées par leur propre poids le long des rues en pente jusqu'à la place. A présent elles fermaient toutes les issues; elles étaient pressées les unes contre les autres *comme des poissons pris dans une nasse, et de même il semblait qu'un coup de filet pût les ramasser ensemble, les rejeter vers un affreux rivage.*[4]

along the Paris highway was flowing an endless stream of cars, trucks, carts, and bicycles mixed together with the horse-drawn vehicles of farmers who were abandoning their farms and heading south, dragging children and livestock behind them. . . . People were sleeping on the ground with their heads propped up on their suitcases in the streets, the cafés, and train stations. The traffic jam was such that it was impossible to get out of the city. Some people were saying that a roadblock had been set up in order to leave the road clear for the troops.

4   Némirovsky, *Suite française*, 89; emphasis mine.

Without a sound and with their headlights off, cars kept on arriving one after another, bursting at the seams, overloaded with luggage and furniture, baby buggies and birdcages, chests and laundry baskets, each car with its mattress solidly attached to the roof. They seemed like fragile scaffolds advancing without the help of a motor, carried by their own weight down the sloping streets to the town square. They were at present blocking all the exits; they were crowded against each other *like fish caught in a trap, and likewise it seemed that they had all somehow been scooped up together in a fishnet and thrown up on an awful river bank.*

A quick glance at other such similes, which are Némirovsky's figure of choice throughout *Tempête en juin,* reveals that they often liken an event to the spectacle of panicked animals or to some natural disaster:

Ce n'était pas à proprement parler de l'inquiétude mais une étrange tristesse qui n'avait plus rien d'humain car elle ne comportait ni vaillance ni espérance, *ainsi les bêtes attendent la mort. Ainsi le poisson pris dans les mailles du filet voit passer et repasser l'ombre du pêcheur.*[5]

Heureusement pour les Péricand, il n'était pas un coin de province où il leur fût impossible de trouver quelque ami ou quelque parent, avec de grandes maisons, des beaux jardins et des armoires pleines. *Mais la panique grandissait, se répandait d'une ville à l'autre comme une flamme.*[6]

Cependant une foule grandissante *venait battre les murs de l'église comme un flot.*[7]

Les femmes pénétraient avec brusquerie, *se jetaient dans l'église comme dans un asile inviolable.* Leur surexcitation, leur fièvre étaient telle [sic] qu'elles semblaient incapables de demeurer immobiles. Elles allaient d'un prie-Dieu à un autre, s'agenouillaient, se relevaient, quelques-unes se heurtaient aux chaises d'un air craintif et effaré *comme des oiseaux de nuit dans une chambre pleine de lumière.*[8]

It wasn't strictly speaking worry, but a strange sadness bereft of all human courage and hope, *like that of animals expecting to die. Such is the fish caught in links of the net that sees the shadow of the fisherman coming and going.*

Luckily for the Péricands, this was not a little area in the provinces

---

5  Némirovsky, *Suite française,* 90.       6  Némirovsky, *Suite française,* 93.

7  Némirovsky, *Suite française,* 97.       8  Némirovsky, *Suite française,* 97–98.

where it was impossible for them to find some friend or relative with a large house, a pretty yard, and a good stock of food. *But the panic was growing, spreading from one town to another like a flame.* In the meantime, an ever-increasing crowd of people *came rolling up against the walls of the church like the sea.* The women entered hurriedly, *rushing into the church as if into some inviolable asylum.* Their extreme nervousness and their feverish movements were such that they seemed incapable of staying still. They kept on going from one prie-dieu to another, kneeling down, standing back up, with some of them bumping into chairs, looking *as fearful and wide-eyed as birds of the night in a room full of light.*

By likening the desperate throngs of refugees to animals or elements of nature caught up in some natural cataclysm, these similes dramatically underscore the collective nature of the disaster. Far from condescending, these images offer on the contrary a highly sympathetic portrait of the distressed refugees and ultimately heighten the sense of pathos and tragedy conveyed by Némirovsky's narrative.

We get a somewhat different sense of how myriad individual comportments converge into a collective paradigm a few pages later in the text when, using the third-person indirect free style, Némirovsky implicitly responds to Philippe's exhortations to his juvenile wards to be mindful of personal and public suffering. Skeptical of patriotic flourishes and true to Diamond and Vinen's previously cited observations, she depicts the people of Paris as totally preoccupied with the immediate well-being of those closest to them:

Qui pensait aux malheurs de la Patrie? Pas ceux-là, pas ceux qui partent ce soir. La panique abolissait tout ce qui n'est pas instinct, mouvement animal frémissant de la chair. Saisir ce qu'on avait de plus précieux au monde et puis! . . . Et seul, cette nuit-là, ce qui vivait, ce qui respirait, pleurait, aimait avait de la valeur! Rares étaient les gens qui regrettaient leurs richesses; on enfermait dans ses deux bras serrés une femme ou un enfant, et le reste ne comptait pas; le reste pouvait s'abîmer dans les flammes.[9]

9  Némirovsky, *Suite française*, 72.

Who was thinking of the trials and tribulations of their country? Not these people, the ones who were leaving this evening. Panic did away with all that was not instinct, the movement of an animal shuddering in the flesh. Grab what is most precious to you and then! . . . And that night, only that which was living and breathing, which had love and tears had any value! Rare were the people who missed their wealth; they clutched a wife or a child in their arms, and the rest didn't matter; the rest could go up in flames.

The immediate answer to Némirovsky's rhetorical question is clear and explicit: as is always the case in such traumatic episodes of history, the common people of France are much too urgently caught up in protecting themselves and their loved ones to give much thought to the plight of their nation. But when we compare this commentary not only to the above-cited observations from Philippe but also to the actions relentlessly spotlighted by this same narrative voice, the irony is multiple. Némirovsky immediately proceeds to focus on the Péricands, who dangerously delay their own departure by trying to carry along everything conceivably valuable. They clearly count among the "rare" people fearful of missing their riches, but they are hardly alone. Charles Langelet thinks only of preserving his precious porcelain, while Gabriel Corte gives absolute priority to perpetuating the bubble of material and aesthetic narcissism with which he has managed to surround himself. In each case, Némirovsky juxtaposes her characters' acute sense of moral, aesthetic, or social superiority with a fundamental failure to face the dangers of the German invasion with solidarity and human decency: Mme Péricand abandons her invalid father-in-law Louis-Auguste Péricand in the chaos of a bombardment, Gabriel Corte hoards food and momentarily drives away his mistress, and Charles Langelet deviously steals gas and oil from a young couple who had trusted him to guard their car.

Given Némirovsky's stated intention to foreground the plight of the hapless crowds, it is not surprising that the most lamentable displays of cowardice come from the most privileged and pretentious. While clearly favoring the "little people" in French society, she nevertheless gives us a complex portrait of humanity. We find, for example, that, although genuinely moved by the spectacle of human suffering, the humble inhabitants of towns and villages in the provinces nevertheless easily yield to the imperatives of preserving their own moral and material comfort. In the same chapter (10) that strips away Mme Péricand's unctuous discourse of Christian charity to reveal the primacy of her bourgeois self-interest, Némirovsky provides an unblinkered view of local residents who find the streets, cafés, public squares, and train station of their small provincial town suddenly submerged by a tidal wave of refugees. The passage bears citing at length.

Les habitants étaient sortis sur le pas des portes et contemplaient ce spectacle avec une expression de profonde stupeur.

"Pauvres gens! Ce qu'il faut voir tout de même!" disaient-ils avec pitié et un secret sentiment de satisfaction: ces réfugiés venaient de Paris, du Nord, de l'Est, de provinces vouées à l'invasion et à la guerre. Mais eux, ils étaient bien tranquilles, les jours passeraient, les soldats se battraient, cependant que le quincaillier de la grand-rue et Mlle Dubois la mercière continueraient à vendre leurs casseroles et leurs rubans, à manger la soupe chaude dans la cuisine, à fermer le soir la petite barrière de bois qui séparait leur jardin du reste de l'univers. . . .

"Qu'ils ont l'air fatigués, qu'ils ont chaud!" répétaient les gens mais aucun n'avait l'idée d'ouvrir sa porte, d'inviter chez lui un de ces malheureux, de le faire pénétrer dans un de ces petits paradis ombreux que l'on apercevait vaguement derrière la maison, un banc de bois sous une charmille, ses groseilliers et ses roses. Il y avait trop de réfugiés. Il y avait trop de figures lasses, livides, en sueur, trop d'enfants en pleurs, trop de bouches tremblantes qui demandaient: "Vous ne savez pas où on peut trouver une chambre, un lit?," "Vous ne pourriez pas nous indiquer un restaurant, madame?" Cela décourageait la charité. Cette multitude misérable n'avait plus rien d'humain; elle ressemblait à un troupeau en déroute; une singulière uniformité s'étendait sur eux. Leurs vêtements froissés, leurs visages ravagés, leurs voix enrouées, tout les rendait semblables. Tous, ils faisaient les mêmes gestes, ils prononçaient les mêmes mots.[10]

---

10    Némirovsky, *Suite française*, 94–95.

The townspeople had come out on their doorsteps and were taking in the spectacle with a stark expression of stupefaction. "Poor folks. My Gosh, what a terrible sight!" they were saying with pity and a secret feeling of satisfaction: these refugees were from Paris, the North, and the East of France, whose provinces were fated to suffer war and invasion. They, on the other hand, had it easy: the days would pass, soldiers would fight while the hardware dealer on Main Street and Mademoiselle Dubois the haberdasher would continue to sell their pots and their ribbons, having hot soup in their kitchens, and in the evening closing the little gate that separated their yards from the rest of the universe. . . .

"They really look tired, they really are hot!" people kept on saying, but nobody thought of opening their door and inviting one of these miserable people into their home, of having one of them enter into one of these shady little areas of paradise that could be glimpsed in their backyards, with a wooden bench under the bowers, currant bushes, and roses. There were too many refugees. There were too many weary, livid, sweaty faces, too many crying children, too many trembling mouths that kept asking "Would you know where we can find a room, a place to sleep?," "Could you indicate a restaurant for us, ma'am?" That discouraged charity. This miserable multitude no longer had any human aspect; it resembled a routed herd; they all looked remarkably alike. Everything made them look the same: their wrinkled clothes, their ravaged faces, their hoarse voices. They all made the same gestures and pronounced the same words.

Némirovsky thus shows these petty bourgeois provincials clearly placing their continued comfort above the compassion that beckons them to open their homes to human misery. Although lacking the hypocrisy and arrogance of the socially prominent, they too are depicted as seeking the isolation of their own world and remaining oblivious to the suffering of others. They even greet their compatriots' suffering with a perverse sort of satisfaction.

Beyond such insights into the shortcomings of humanity displayed by persons of various socioeconomic origins, there is a larger, more important point for us to see here. Némirovsky's historical narrative subtly but poignantly exposes the collective collapse of France.

Though intimately and accurately portrayed as consumed by their own personal well-being—with the possible exceptions of the Michauds, Philippe, and Hubert—the various individual protagonists of *Tempête en juin* can nevertheless be seen as participating in and even contributing to the national disaster that is relentlessly unfolding. In spite of the lyrical strains voiced by several characters, Némirovsky's text ultimately represents their intersubjectivity, for their words and deeds have unsuspected echoes and repercussions that become evident to us as readers even—and in some cases especially—if unperceived by the characters themselves.

That Némirovsky is intent on portraying a national tragedy as such, and not just a series of anecdotal ordeals, becomes even more evident in chapter 27 of *Tempête en juin*. The narrative is pointedly set in "la reine des stations thermales de France"[11] (the queen of spas in France), an unmistakable euphemism for Vichy. As Némirovsky knew from her own visits, its renowned spas had since the late nineteenth century been a favorite rendez-vous for the upper echelons of French society, and in particular, administrative and military officials on vacation from their colonial posts. The number and quality of Vichy's hotels was indeed one of the prime reasons that the provincial town became the seat for the provisional government that was soon to become the eponym for the reactionary collaborationist dictatorship.[12] It is there that we once again find Gabriel Corte, now eagerly returning to the lavish luxury and prestige of one of his favorite vacation resorts. Némirovsky clearly identifies this cushy haven of privilege with the Vichy regime by having the Grand Hôtel's director mention that "l'on attendait d'un moment à l'autre l'arrivée du gouvernement"[13] (the members of the government were expected to arrive momentarily). The text then foregrounds all the comforts that allow the Grand Hôtel's elite clientele to escape from the hardships besetting the less fortunate people who are spilling out over the streets and even into the hotel lobby. While these hapless refugees

11   Némirovsky, *Suite française*, 239.        12   Cf. Diamond, *Fleeing Hitler*, p. 110.

13   Némirovsky, *Suite française*, 240.

are portrayed as desperately seeking the rudiments of sustenance and shelter, those as privileged as Corte can rejoice in an uninterrupted supply of coffee, cocktails, and whisky, along with unlimited hot and cold baths. The text emphasizes both Corte's joy at reclaiming his privileged status and the contrast with the plight of those not sheltered by their wealth:

> Dès leurs premiers pas sur le marbre du hall, les Corte se sentirent renaître: tout était calme. . . . On les reconnut, on les entoura. . . .
> Tout, autour de lui, s'accomplissait d'une manière discrète, ouatée, convenable. Il n'y avait plus de femmes accouchant dans un fossé, plus d'enfants perdus, plus de ponts qui retombaient en gerbes de feu comme des fusées, pulvérisant les maisons voisines, éclatant sous leur charge de mélinite mal calculée.[14]

As soon as they stepped into the marble foyer, the Cortes felt themselves coming back to life: everything was calm. . . . They were recognized, they were surrounded with attention. . . .

Everything in his presence was performed in a discrete, padded, proper manner. There were no longer any women giving birth in a ditch, no more lost children, no more bridges collapsing with bursts of fire like rockets, shattering neighboring houses, blowing up with the poorly calculated charge of melinite.

This conspicuous indifference to the tremendous suffering of the common people, some of whom we see summarily turned away by the Grand Hôtel, contrasts with the tawdry lack of generosity we saw among the townspeople depicted in chapter 10. While showing the latter yielding to a human-all-too-human self-interest, Némirovsky nevertheless accords them extenuating circumstances by indicating that the crush of refugees simply overwhelmed the modest moral and material resources of charity available from these bystanders.

No such alibi is to be found for the upper echelons of French society that *Tempête en juin* unmistakably associates with leaders of their devastated nation and situates in the Grand Hôtel in Vichy. Those

---

14  Némirovsky, *Suite française*, 240.

who charge that Irène Némirovsky never dared openly condemn Philippe Pétain[15] are missing the point. Némirovsky's intimate portrait of both the residents and the personnel of the Grand Hôtel unmistakably satirizes the occupants of the Hôtel du Parc in Vichy (i.e., Pétain and his followers).

If we ask with Némirovsky "Qui pensait aux malheurs de la Patrie?"[16] (Who was thinking about the trials and tribulations of their country?), we must unequivocally conclude that it is certainly not those whom see fearing that England might block shipments of whisky and serving the whims of their high-society clientele with a quasi-religious solemnity, even though they couch their discourse in terms of patriotic service, as does the director of the Grand Hôtel in his obsequious commiseration with Gabriel Corte:

—Moi j'ai failli perdre mes manuscrits, dit Corte.

—Ah! mon Dieu, quel malheur! Mais vous les avez retrouvés intacts?...

Un tel désastre.... Je suis suisse de naissance, français de coeur. Je comprends, répéta-t-il.

Et il demeura quelques instants immobile, le front baissé comme au cimetière lorsqu'on a salué la famille et qu'on n'ose pas se précipiter tout de suite vers la sortie.... Exagérant encore ses dispositions naturelles, il était arrivé à circuler silencieusement, comme dans une chambre mortuaire, et lorsqu'il dit à Corte: "Je fais monter les petits déjeuners?" ce fut sur un ton discret et funèbre comme s'il lui demandait en lui montrant le corps d'un parent cher: "Est-ce que je peux l'embrasser une dernière fois?"

—Les petits déjeuners? soupira Corte, revenant avec peine à la réalité quotidienne et à ses futiles soucis. Je n'ai pas mangé depuis vingt-quatre heures, ajouta-t-il avec un pâle sourire.

Ce qui avait été vrai la veille mais ne l'était plus, car il avait pris un repas abondant le matin même à six heures. Il ne mentait pas d'ailleurs: il avait mangé distraitement à cause de son extrême fatigue et du trouble où le jetaient les malheurs de la Patrie. Il lui semblait encore être à jeun.

15   See, e.g., Weiss, *Irène Némirovsky*, 170.
16   Némirovsky, *Suite française*, 72.

—Oh! mais il faut vous forcer, monsieur! Oh! je n'aime pas vous voir comme cela, monsieur Corte. Il faut prendre sur vous. Vous vous devez à l'humanité.[17]

"Such a disaster . . . I am Swiss by birth, French at heart. I understand," he repeated.

And he stood completely still a few moments, bowing his head as if at the cemetery when one has greeted the family, but doesn't dare rush for the exit right away. . . . Still exaggerating his natural inclinations, he had managed to walk around silently, as if in a funeral parlor, and when he said to Corte: "Shall I have your breakfasts brought up?" it was in a discreet, gloomy tone, as if he were asking him while indicating the body of a dear relative: "Can I kiss him one last time?"

"Breakfast?" sighed Corte, struggling back to everyday reality and its futile cares. "I haven't had anything to eat for twenty-four hours," he added with a dim smile.

That had been the case the day before, but was no longer so, for he had eaten a big meal that very morning at six o'clock. He wasn't lying, however: he had eaten absent-mindedly due to the extreme fatigue and confusion which the trials and tribulations of his country had occasioned in him. It seemed to him that his stomach was still empty.

"Oh! but you must force yourself to eat, Sir! Oh! I don't like to see you in such a state, Mr. Corte. You must keep your chin up. You owe yourself to humanity."

Némirovsky's rhetorical question ("Qui pensait aux malheurs de la Patrie?") echoes throughout the whole chapter as it does so unmistakably in this passage. The resulting irony undermines the ideological foundations of Pétain's National Revolution by exposing the arrogance and hypocrisy of the elite's extravagant lifestyle and the hypocrisy of their ostentatious patriotism. We should recall that Pétain never tired of injecting the thematics of sacrifice into his homilies ever since he had in his famous radio address of June 17, 1940, assumed leadership by announcing: " je fais à la France le don de ma personne pour atténuer son malheur. En ces heures douloureuses,

17    Némirovsky, *Suite française*, 241–42.

je pense aux malheureux réfugiés, qui dans un dénuement extrême, sillonnent nos routes. Je leur exprime ma compassion et ma sollici-tude" (I offer myself to France in order to ease her suffering. In this painful hour, my thoughts go out to the refugees in their misery, who are traveling along our roads in utter destitution. I extend to them my compassion and my solicitude). The preceding passage of *Tempête en juin* also mentions "les malheurs de la Patrie" (the country's tri-als and tribulations), only with stinging irony, since the reference is to Corte's momentary loss of appetite. The hotel director's fervent so-licitude in urging the writer to eat because he owed himself to hu-manity makes a mockery of the thematics of sacrifice. Corte, whom Némirovsky planned to portray as an opportunistic collaborator in a subsequent, never-completed volume entitled *Captivité,* is for his part content in this chapter of *Tempête en juin* to demonstrate his patriot-ic devotion by ordering piping hot coffee and by muttering "Pauvre France . . ."[18] when learning that his influential friend in the Nation-al Assembly has fallen from favor and hightailed it to Portugal.

Némirovsky takes another conspicuous swipe at self-serving as-sessments of the May–June 1940 debacle in chapter 28. There we find the banking magnates Monsieur Corbin and Monsieur le Comte de Furières meeting back in Paris after the signing of the armistice. In-censed at seeing their lucrative financial dealings and lavish lifestyles thrown into chaos by France's defeat, they dispense with effusive pa-triotism and lash out directly against those they hold responsible for the disaster. Predictably, they rail not against those in positions of power and authority, but against their supposed underlings, whose alleged selfishness and cowardice thwarted any chance of holding firm against the German invasion. Like Henry de Montherlant and so many others predisposed toward collaboration, Corbin snidely comments that the Germans' crisp discipline constrasts sharply with the sloppy demeanor of the French military. As could be expected, the Count simply passes the buck to all the civilians hampering the French army's maneuverability.

18   Némirovsky, *Suite française,* 247.

—Sans les civils, sans les paniquards, sans ce flot de réfugiés qui encombrait la route, il y aurait eu une chance de salut.
—Ah! ça, vous avez raison! Cette panique a été affreuse. Les gens sont extraordinaires. On leur répète depuis des années: "la guerre totale, la guerre totale...." Ils auraient dû s'y attendre, mais non! tout de suite la panique, le désordre, la fuite, et pourquoi? Je vous le demande? C'est insensé! Moi qui suis parti parce que les banques avaient reçu l'ordre de partir. Sans ça, vous comprenez....
... Et ce désordre, répéta-t-il, chacun ne pensant qu'à soi! Cet égoïsme.... Ah! ça donne une fière idée de l'homme![19]

"Without the civilians, with all those panicky fools, without that tide of refugees jamming the road, we would have had a chance to save the day."

"Boy, you're right, there! That panic was awful. People are incredible. For years they have been told about 'total war, total war.' They should have been expecting it. But no, right away, we get panic, chaos, flight. And for what reason, I ask you! It's crazy! As for me, I left because the banks had received the order to leave. Otherwise, you see...."

... "And the chaos," he repeated, "everyone thinking only of themselves! The selfishness.... Hah! that gives a proud picture of humanity!"

As is so often the case, Némirovsky uses her characters' own words to underscore the irony of their own righteous indignation. While Corbin here rails against selfishness and human weakness, we are told in no uncertain terms on the previous page that his "fureur patriotique"[20] has been spurred by the flight of his servants whom he suspects of having taken his new suitcases. In terms of humanity, he arguably presents the most tawdry example on display throughout the entire *Tempête en juin*. We first find him in chapter 5, obviously overwhelmed and flustered, boorishly squabbling with his kept mistress Arlette Corail, and capriciously ordering his employees about. Shortly after decrying his compatriots' supposed failure to stand firm in selfless service to their country in the above-cited passage,

19   Némirovsky, *Suite française*, 260–61.
20   Némirovsky, *Suite française*, 260.

he then avidly contemplates his prospective profits from a German takeover of the steel industry and peremptorily fires the couple that Némirovsky portrays as his most deserving employees, Jeanne and Maurice Michaud.

The Count fares little better in Némirovsky's implacable satire of the rich and powerful. He angrily imputes the unmitigated disaster both to the panic-stricken civilians mentioned in the words cited above and to the common soldiers under his command. Above all, the Count deplores their lack of motivation: "Que voulez-vous faire sans armes et avec des hommes gâtés, pourris, qui ne demandent qu'une chose, qu'on leur f... la paix"[21] (What do you expect us to do, with no weapons, and with men who are spoiled, rotten, who only want one thing: that you leave them the f*** alone"). It is no accident that these words echo closely the lyrics that Maurice Chevalier sung during "La Drôle de guerre" in the fall of 1939, notably for hundreds of French soldiers, as we see at the outset of Marcel Ophüls' *Le Chagrin et la pitié*.

> Les v'là tous d'accord,
> Quel que soit leur sort,
> Ils désirent tous désormais,
> Qu'on nous foute une bonne fois la paix!

> There they all agree,
> Whatever their fate may be,
> From now on, they all want
> To be left the hell alone [in peace]!

Like so many of his compatriots who found themselves mobilized in September 1939, the Count de Furières had grudgingly reported for duty, complaining that, having had to sacrifice several years of his youth to serving in World War I, this call to arms was now depriving him of the well-deserved happiness of his mature years. Just as ardently as they did, the Count clearly wished that history would just leave France in peace and him alone to pursue his banking interests

---

21  Némirovsky, *Suite française*, 260.

and his social life at the Jockey Club.[22] When we place the entire passage in the wider context first of *Tempête en juin* and then amid the ambiant discourses of the early Occupation years when Némirovsky penned her historical narrative, we quickly see that the irony extends well beyond moral and even social satire to strike another blow against the discourse of patriotism and military piety that undergirded Pétain's claims to authority. In their admiration for the Germans' supposed order and discipline, their outrage over the people's alleged moral weakness, and their smug refusal to take their responsibility as rich and powerful leaders for the absence of preparation and leadership, Corbin and de Furières appear in Némirovsky's novel as textbook examples of Vichy's hypocrisy.

Némirovsky had no need to name names: her text mercilessly satirizes the hollow moral and political pretensions of the "Vichyssois," to use a term that for both Némirovsky and her contemporaries designated those whom we now know as "Pétainists."[23] By likening Florence's meticulous vestimentary deliberations to those of an army officer leading his troops into battle, Némirovsky moreover mocks the aura of military heroism with which Pétain constantly cloaked himself and his regime: "d'un coup elle rallia toutes ses énergies éparses comme le chef d'armée qui, malgré son besoin de repos et constatant l'inefficacité de ses subalternes, reprend en main le commandement et, chancelant encore de fatigue, dirige lui-même ses troupes sur le champ de bataille"[24] (she gathered up at once all her scattered energies, like the military leader who, even though in need of rest and aware that his subordinates are ineffective, takes the command of his troops back into his own hands and, staggering with fatigue, leads his troops onto the battlefield himself). For us as well as for Némirovsky's contemporaries in the early 1940s, it is impossible not to think of Pétain when reading these allusions to a tired military leader burdened with bumbling subordinates. The simile moreover accentuates the ironic tenor of the passage by juxtaposing Florence's

22  Némirovsky, *Suite française*, 258–59.    23   See Rousso, *Le Régime de Vichy*, 109.

24  Némirovsky, *Suite française*, 243.

stereotypically feminine preoccupation with vanity and the supposedly virile virtues of a warrior, just as the discourse of Corte's mistress proceeds without transition from the solemn to the frivolous:

Voyez-vous, Julie, nous ne nous rendons pas bien compte de ce qui se passe. Ce sont des événements d'une portée incalculable, je vous le dis, incalculable. . . . La vie des gens sera changée cet hiver. Vous me sortirez le sac de daim gris avec le fermoir d'or, tout simple. . . . Je me demande de quoi Paris a l'air.[25]

You see, Julie, we don't really realize what is taking place. These are events of unimaginable dimensions—unimaginable, I tell you. . . . Life will be different for people this winter. Take out my gray suede leather purse, the plain one, with the gold latch. . . . I wonder what Paris looks like.

While neither as pompous nor callous as her masculine companion, Florence nevertheless partakes of the privilege that shelters her from the brunt of the historical catastrophe roiling the French nation. In depicting her as alternately sensitive to the collective tragedy and concentrated on her own beauty, Némirovsky once again shows that private lives remain inextricably linked to public destinies and vice versa.

We are now poised to appreciate the full implications of Philippe's grim assessment of what was about to transpire: Némirovsky's narrative repeatedly and poignantly shows that "les malheurs publics sont faits d'une multitude de malheurs privés"[26] (collective tragedies are made up of a multitude of individual ordeals) by underscoring the intersubjectivity of her various protagonists. The thematic and contextual interconnections lead back and forth to and from the thoughts, words, and deeds of one person or group and another as well as to and from the individual anecdotes and the major historical disaster engulfing them all. Although those caught up in the heat of the event do not perceive these connections, and although Némirovsky's text often shows such "solidarity" unwitting, often tragic, and at times even

25  Némirovsky, *Suite française*, 244.
26  Némirovsky, *Suite française*, 63.

perverse, we readers could indeed say that "nous avons conscience de la solidarité qui nous lie, nous membres d'un même corps"[27] (we are aware of the solidarity that binds us together as members of one same body).

In response to the question that ironically echoes throughout the various episodes of *Tempête en juin*, "Qui pensait aux malheurs de la Patrie?," we must in the end answer "Irène Némirovsky." In her biography of Chekhov, she indicates how writers should face the trials of their time. Likening the Europe of 1940 with the grim situation faced by Chekhov under the reign of Alexander III in Russia, she writes: "De même qu'à présent, le monde était divisé en bourreaux aveugles et en victimes résignées, mais tout était mesquin, étriqué, pénétré de médiocrité. On attendait l'écrivain qui parlerait de cette médiocrité sans colère, sans dégoût, mais avec la pitié qu'elle méritait"[28] (Just as it is today, the world was divided into mindless executioners and resigned victims, but everything was small-minded, chintzy, permeated with mediocrity. People were waiting for the writer who would speak about that mediocrity without anger, without disgust, but with the pity that it deserved). Here again, compassion takes precedence over didacticism, and once again Némirovsky's approach invites a parallel with Michelet, who according to Petitier considered the historian to be charged with a quasi-sacred function, that of rescuing from oblivion countless lives of those who otherwise would remain anonymous, lost in obscurity, or deliberately silenced out by oppression.[29]

### Lucid Compassion and the Agony of Defeat

Having observed in some detail Némirovsky's focus on the tawdry behavior of the rich and the powerful in the May–June debacle, it is important to specify what sort of "pitié" is being advocated here. Since *Tempête en juin* exposes turpitude, cowardice, and hypocrisy

27    Némirovsky, *Suite française*, 63.

28    Philipponnat and Liendhardt, *La vie d'Irène Némirovsky*, 340.

29    Petitier, "Introduction," 10.

without editorializing or giving any other overt expression of anger or disgust, but with dramatic juxtapositions and reversals of narrative point of view, it clearly measures up to her expectations of the writer narrating the ordeals of history. Némirovsky's pity for her times, or more precisely, what several commentators, and in particular Pascal Bruckner,[30] have termed her compassion for those thrown into the turmoil of World War II in France is similarly not explicitly stated but tacitly conveyed by several elements of her text. We have noted that *Tempête en juin* clearly confirms her stated intention to make the common people, "the crowd of those who suffer without understanding," the veritable "hero" of her narrative. It is hardly an accident that one of the prime qualities she attributes to these hapless throngs is that of pity, even amid the terror of the strafings and bombings to which they found themselves exposed out on the open road. Of the weakest and most vulnerable, Némirovsky thus writes:

Lorsqu'ils [Maurice et Jeanne Michaud] arrivaient sur une de ces hauteurs légères qui coupaient les routes de place en place, ils voyaient jusqu'à l'horizon, aussi loin que pouvait porter leur regard, une multitude confuse traînant les pieds dans la poussière. Les plus fortunés possédaient une brouette, une voiture d'enfant, un chariot fait de quatre planches montées sur des roues grossières qui portaient leurs bagages, étaient courbés sous le poids de sacs, de hardes, d'enfants endormis. Ceux-là étaient les pauvres, les malchanceux, les faibles, ceux qui ne savent pas se débrouiller, ceux que l'on repousse partout au dernier rang, et quelques timorés aussi, quelques avares qui avaient reculé jusqu'au dernier instant devant le prix du billet, les dépenses et les risques du voyage. Mais brusquement la panique les avait saisis comme les autres. Ils ne savaient pas pourquoi ils fuyaient: la France entière était en flammes, le danger partout. Ils ne savaient certainement pas où ils allaient. Quand ils se laissaient tomber sur le sol, ils disaient qu'ils ne se relèveraient plus, qu'ils crèveraient là, que mourir pour mourir, autant valait rester tranquille. Ils étaient les premiers debout lorsqu'un avion approchait. *Il y avait entre eux de la pitié, de la charité, cette sympathie active et vigilante que les gens du peuple ne témoignent*

---

30    Pascal Bruckner, "Elle s'appelait Irène," *Le Nouvel Observateur*, October 21, 2004.

*qu'aux leurs, qu'aux pauvres, et encore, en des périodes exceptionnelles de peur et de misère.*[31]

When they [Maurice and Jeanne Michaud] arrived at the top of one of these rises that crossed the roads every now and then, they saw stretching out all the way to the horizon, as far as their eyes could see, a muddled multitude of people dragging their feet in the dust. The most fortunate possessed a wheelbarrow, a stroller, or a cart that was made of four boards mounted on crude wheels and which carried their luggage. They were stooped under the weight of bags, tattered clothes, and sleeping children. These were the poor, the unfortunate, the weak, those who cannot manage on their own, those who always get pushed to the last row, along with a few timorous people too, and a few miserly people who had recoiled up until the last instant before the price of a ticket, the expense and risk of travel. But suddenly they had been caught up in the panic like the others. They didn't know why they were fleeing: the whole country was on fire, danger was everywhere in France. They certainly didn't know where they were going. When they flopped down on the ground, they kept saying that they wouldn't ever get back up, that they would croak there, that as long as they were going to die, they may as well take it easy. They were the first to get up when an airplane was approaching. *Among them, there was pity, charity, that active and vigilant sympathy that the common people only display with one another, with the poor, and even then, only in times of exceptional fear and hardship.*

In the midst of a commonly suffered ordeal, the solidarity displayed by these humble lower-class people stands in direct antithesis to the behavior of Corte, Langelet, Corbin, and Charlotte Péricand, whose panic and disarray are exacerbated by the presumption that they are entitled to exemption from such catastrophes. Not incidentally, this sad spectacle is narrated from the perspective of the Michauds, who along with the rest of the crowd were fleeing as best they could. Only a few paragraphs later in the text, Némirovsky, as we have seen, portrays Maurice contemplating the traumatic event with a singular combination of intellectual detachment and human compassion. Although not partisan according to the ideological fault lines of her

31  Némirovsky, *Suite française*, 100–101; emphasis mine.

time or ours, Némirovsky clearly "identifies" with the common people of France so prominently and sympathetically featured in *Tempête
en juin*.

The passage from chapter 11 cited above is emblematic in another
important way as well. For there, as in numerous passages throughout the narrative, Némirovsky gives us a visual overview of the tragedy
as it unfolds. We have on several occasions had recourse to the term
"epic" for a specific reason. In the end, there emerges from Némirovsky's historical narrative an irresistibly epic dimension, which is
created in no small part by such sweeping panoramas. These panoramas occur throughout *Tempête en juin*, notably at both the very beginning of the first chapter, where the narrator surveys a long series of
Parisians jolted from their slumbers by the latest alert,[32] and at the
end in the very last chapter, which gives us a traveling shot of the
snow slowing extending over both urban and rural landscapes.[33]
The same passages moreover often contain not only the epic similes
that we have already analyzed but also a sort of epic catalog of misery
listing series of vehicles, places, objects, and of course people swept
up in the tidal wave of the invasion.

### The Shock and Confusion of Defeat

Némirovsky's mockery of the discourse of military glory and her
implacable exposition of human weakness obviously place her narrative in diametric opposition to the glorification of a collective saga
and individual heroism traditionally ascribed to the epic. A crushing
defeat followed by a humiliating occupation made any such celebration absolutely out of the question. The epic dimensions of her *Suite
française* rather demonstrate her commitment to enable future generations of readers to understand these "malheurs de la Patrie" by
consigning them to her narrative. If we ask again "Qui pensait aux
malheurs de la Patrie?," the answer we get from Némirovsky's text is

32  Némirovsky, *Suite française*, 33–34
33  Némirovsky, *Suite française*, 298.

clear: it is the most vulnerable, those who witness the mayhem firsthand and suffer the brunt of its human and material destruction. These brave souls include not only Jeanne, Maurice, and Jean-Marie Michaud, but also the working-class woman Hortense Gaillard, whom we later find forced by dire financial need to work as a maid and a cook for the exquisitely fatuous aesthete Charles Langelet. Learning of the Germans' entry into Paris, she is shown to be overcome with irrepressible feelings of anger, sorrow, and shame, even though Némirovsky makes it clear that, true to her surname "Gaillard" (a French term commonly used to designate hardy, stout, cheerful, vigorous individuals), she was rarely prone to tears in spite of the many vicissitudes of her life.[34] Conversely, we find the rich and powerful quickly resuming their life of privilege and ease in spite of their pompous expressions of indignation. Such is the case not only for Gabriel Corte and his cohorts at the Grand Hôtel, who are delighted to find that for them nothing had really changed at all,[35] but also for Charles Langelet back in Paris, where he returns to his bar, lights up a cigar, and settles back into the good life.[36]

No such callousness is to be found in the passages narrated from the point of view of Némirovsky's fondest representatives of the common people, the Michauds. Two passages in particular foreground the reaction of the Michauds in order to offer an empathetic assessment of the historical disaster that has devastated the French nation. The first narrates the news of the armistice, which was by all accounts a dramatic development when on June 17, 1940, Pétain took to the radio to announce that "C'est le coeur serré que je vous dis aujourd'hui qu'il faut cesser le combat." (It is with a heavy heart that I say to you today that the fighting must cease). Avoiding the slightest allusion to the "Vainqueur de Verdun," Némirovsky instead filters our perception of the event through Maurice and Jeanne Michaud's reaction to the armistice agreement, which was finally signed on June 22, 1940:

34  Némirovsky, Suite française, 127.     35  Némirovsky, Suite française, 250.
36  Némirovsky, Suite française, 272.

On frictionnait la tête de Jeanne avec de l'essence de lavande quand le fils du coiffeur accourut pour dire que l'armistice était signé. Dans l'état de fatigue et d'accablement où elle se trouvait, elle comprit à peine la portée de cette nouvelle; ainsi au chevet d'un mourant lorsqu'on a pleuré toutes les larmes, il n'en reste plus pour son dernier soupir. Mais Maurice, se souvenant de la guerre de 14, de ses combats, de ses blessures, de ses souffrances, sentit un flot d'amertume monter dans son coeur. Toutefois il n'y avait plus rien à dire. Il se tut.

Ils demeurèrent plus d'une heure dans la boutique de Mme Josse et sortirent de là pour se rendre chez eux. On disait que les pertes de l'armée française étaient relativement peu élevées mais que le nombre des prisonniers atteignait deux millions. Peut-être Jean-Marie se trouvait-il parmi ces derniers? Ils n'osaient espérer rien d'autre.[37]

Jeanne was having her head massaged with lavander-scented cologne when the hairdresser's son ran in to say that the armistice had been signed. Being fatigued and overwhelmed, she scarcely understood the significance of this news; just as it is when people have shed all their tears standing by someone's deathbed, and then have no more to cry when the dying person breathes his last. Maurice, on the other hand, remembered the First World War along with its battles, his wounds, and his suffering: he felt a tide of bitterness rise up in his heart. There was nevertheless nothing else to say. He remained silent.

They remained in Madame Josse's shop for over an hour, then left to go home. It was said that the French Army's losses were relatively low, but that there were as many as two million prisoners. Perhaps Jean-Marie was among them? They dared not hope for anything else.

These lines are emblematic of Némirovsky's narration of the fall of France. As in other passages that we have studied, she foregrounds the way in which a momentous event is perceived by a particular person in a specific context: here it is the hair salon that serves as the rather incongruous setting for the news of the armistice. Némirovsky's text shows that the perception of this event, which was to have the most serious consequences, was contingent on the mindset of the observer at the time. Different observers can accordingly

37  Némirovsky, *Suite française*, 253–54.

be expected to have varying reactions to the same event, depending on their own social milieu, personal itinerary, and ideological baggage. Thus while the full implications of the agreement that France had reached with its archenemy remained entirely murky to Jeanne (just as they did for the vast majority of people in France),[38] Maurice relates the armistice to his personal experience of the previous war. Both remain first and foremost concerned about the fate of their son Jean-Marie, who had been mobilized to fight the invasion.

That Némirovsky empathized with their distress is again evident in her depiction of Jean-Marie Michaud taking stock of the debacle as he begins to recover from his battle wounds:

Si on avait dit à Jean-Marie qu'il se trouverait un jour dans un village perdu loin de son régiment, sans argent, dans l'impossibilité de communiquer avec les siens, ne sachant pas s'ils étaient en bonne santé à Paris, ou comme tant d'autres ensevelis dans un trou d'obus au bord d'une route, si on lui avait dit surtout que, la France vaincue, il continuerait à vivre et même connaîtrait des moments heureux, il ne l'aurait pas cru. C'était ainsi pourtant. La plénitude même du désastre, ce qu'il avait d'irréparable contenait un secours, comme certains poisons violents fournissent leur antidote, tous les maux dont il souffrait étaient irrémédiables. Il ne pouvait pas faire que la ligne Maginot n'eût pas été tournée ou enfoncée (on ne savait pas au juste), que deux millions de soldats ne fussent prisonniers, que la France n'eût été battue. Il ne pouvait pas faire marcher la poste, le télégraphe ou le téléphone, ni se procurer de l'essence ou une voiture pour arriver jusqu'à la gare distante de vingt et un kilomètres, où d'ailleurs les trains ne passaient plus car la ligne avait été détruite.[39]

If someone had told Jean-Marie that one day he would find himself lost in a village far from his regiment, without money and without any means of communicating with his family, not knowing whether they were safe and sound in Paris or whether, like so many others, they were buried in a crater created by shelling on the roadside, and if someone had above all told him that, after France had been defeated, he would continue to live and even enjoy moments of happiness, he would not have believed it. But

38  Diamond, *Fleeing Hitler*, 102, 110–11.    39  Némirovsky, *Suite française*, 284.

that's the way it was. The fact that the disaster was so extensive and caused such irreparable damage paradoxically had a bright side, just as certain deadly poisons provide their own antidote: all the causes of his suffering were irremediable. Nothing he could do could change the fact that the Maginot Line had been avoided or breached (people didn't know exactly), that two million soldiers had been taken prisoner, and that France had been defeated. It was impossible for him to make the postal services, the telegraph, or the telephone functional, or to get gas and a car in order to reach the train station that was twenty-one kilometers away, where moreover trains were no longer running because the rail lines had been destroyed.

Using the indirect free style to deliver Jean-Marie's assessment of France's defeat, Némirovsky articulates the anxieties common to the majority of the French population: the trauma of civilian casualties, the bewilderment at the total futility of the Maginot Line, and the accompanying collapse of what had on paper been the most powerful army in Europe, the two million prisoners of war, and the severe disruption of transports, communications, and supplies. The haunting memories of World War I and the preoccupation with the fate of the two million prisoners of war alluded to in the above cited passages do not simply convey the mind-set of Némirovsky's characters of choice: these were the prime concerns of the French populace in general.

Némirovsky's portrayal of the May–June 1940 debacle once again illustrates the fact that mutual affinities of novels and historical narratives are particularly prominent in France. Petitier underscores the considerable cultural impact of Michelet's *Histoire de France* by pointing out just how closely related it was to the artistic projects of the literary giants Balzac, Zola, and Proust, who in writing their works aimed to capture daily life to the point of competing with reality.[40] Speaking somewhat hyperbolically, Tzvetan Todorov has stated that in many instances he could learn as much about the human condition from one of Balzac's novels as from the social sciences.[41] We

40  Petitier, "Introduction," 10.

41  Tzvetan Todorov, *Devoirs et délices d'une vie de passeur: Entretiens avec Catherine Portevin* (Paris: Éditions du Seuil), 115.

could, mutatis mutandis, make the same observation with respect to the empirical tenor of Némirovsky's *Suite française:* when one compares the concrete details incorporated into her narrative with the results of the most recent historical research into the May–June 1940 exodus in France, one can only be struck by her novel's factual and analytical fidelity to the historical event.

The first paragraphs of the novel focus on anxious Parisians awakening to air raid sirens and artillery fire. Their city having already been bombed, they remain skeptical of good and bad news, and totally confused: "'On n'y comprend rien', disaient les gens"[42] ("It doesn't make any sense," people kept saying). Hanna Diamond emphasizes that it was indeed impossible for the overwhelming majority to have a clear perception of the situation precisely because the civilian and military authorities did not trust the general public to know the truth, and so either kept the public in the dark or gave contradictory reports.[43] So it is in Némirovsky's narrative. The upper-class characters such as Corte and the Péricands decide to flee after being tipped off by insiders. As was indeed the case for most people living in Paris, Jeanne and Maurice Michaud only realize that an exodus is imminent when they see trucks being loaded in front of government ministries.

*Tempête en juin* accurately depicts the departure of all as being precipitous, improvised, and ultimately chaotic, with train stations quickly overwhelmed and roads clogged. The disorderly rush and discomfort of this spontaeous evacuation was just the beginning of the nightmare that would bring about untold suffering entailed by the separation of some ninety thousand children from their parents and the deaths of one hundred thousand refugees.[44] Setting out over the open road on foot alongside countless others, the Michauds contrast sharply with Langelet and Corte. Némirovsky's satiric depiction of the latter's disgust at finding themselves literally rubbing up against the commoners that they despised as vulgar underlings re-

42    Némirovsky, *Suite française*, 34.

43    Diamond, *Fleeing Hitler*, 29–31, 66, 68.

44    Diamond, *Fleeing Hitler*, 143.

flects the momentary social leveling occasioned by the extreme conditions that often stripped away the artifices and pretensions of privilege in French society of the time.[45] All find themselves exposed to bombing and strafing by German planes; almost all suffer from a dire lack of basic necessities such as food, water, shelter, and medical care. Némirovsky's panoramas of these highly vulnerable civilian convoys point to the varied, often makeshift means of transportation, including everything from pushcarts and bicycles to horse-drawn buggies and automobiles, whose crudely affixed mattresses testified to the refugees desperate, largely futile, attempts to preserve themselves and their belongings.

Diamond confirms that, under these traumatic circumstances, rumors and fears such as those related to Charles Langelet by the young couple from whom he steals gas and oil were rampant, and that the occurrence of thievery among refugees became frequent amid the collapse of familiar social structures and constraints.[46] Léon Werth's narrative, of which we will have much more to say in chapter 4, concurs in reporting widespread acts of looting among refugees themselves. While Diamond observes that, as we see the Michauds doing in *Tempête en juin,* most people nevertheless displayed a large measure of goodwill and courage under all the duress, it was also the case that provincials, as we have seen in several previously cited passages from Némirovsky's narrative, did eventually became numb to demands for food and shelter, as both their moral and material resources were put to severe strain.

Némirovsky does not show the significant numbers of foreigners and Jewish refugees that we know participated in the May–June 1940 exodus, nor does she deal with key military and political decisions. She does, however, show the tendency to try to make sense of the 1940 invasion by referring back to the legacy of World War I. While Némirovsky does not make the slightest allusion to the acts of looting committed by French soldiers, Diamond tells us that most

45   Diamond, *Fleeing Hitler,* 73–74.
46   Diamond, *Fleeing Hitler,* 74–77.

French soldiers did indeed act like the ones we find in *Tempête en juin*, generally helpful, but silent about the military situation.[47] Most importantly, Némirovsky's text reveals the gaping chasm separating the intensity of the uncontrolled, rapidly unfolding historical event and peoples' pathetic and largely futile efforts to control their destinies and make sense of the situation. Although somewhat anecdotal and fragmentary on the level of each individual episode, the various chapters nevertheless add up to provide a global representation of the debacle whose accuracy is confirmed by the most recent historical scholarship.

Observing that *Suite française* dwells on the personal trials and tribulations of its characters without any explicit reference to de Gaulle or Pétain, Jonathan Weiss suggests that Némirovsky once again failed to connect her narrative to the urgent historical issues of *her* time.[48] Instead of demanding that Némirovsky further the ideological and didactic priorities of *our* time, however, we have everything to gain by understanding her *Suite française* in its own narrative terms. In so many critical ways, Némirovsky's narrative conveys the pathos of the May–June 1940 catastrophe. By faithfully representing the priorities and cares widely shared by the French people at the time of the debacle, *Tempête en juin* makes us attentive to the personal ordeals often ignored in historical accounts dwelling on military action and political developments. As Richard Vinen aptly puts it:

Historians tend to see France in the summer of 1940 as part of a bigger story, one that involves the battle between the Germans and the Allies or one that involves the collapse of French democracy. The majority of the French people, however, thought of this period in terms of much more personal dramas of displacement and separation.[49]

Némirovsky's historical narrative offers a sympathetic view of the French people's collective experience. To borrow Philippe's terms

47   Diamond, *Fleeing Hitler*, 72.

48   Weiss, *Irène Némirovsky*, 167.

49   Richard Vinen, *The Unfree French* (New Haven and London: Yale University Press, 2006), 44.

once again, her novel strikingly reveals just how "les malheurs publics sont faits d'une multitude de malheurs privés" (collective tragedies are made up of a multitude of individual ordeals), thus creating an awareness "de la solidarité qui nous lie, nous membres d'un même corps" (of the solidarity that binds us together as members of one same body). Whereas Jonathan Weiss mockingly characterizes Némirovsky as "un écrivain de nulle part" (a writer from nowhere) and "une déracinée" (a person without roots or an uprooted person) having fled from her native Russia and unsuccessfully sought citizenship in France all while allegedly forsaking her Jewish roots,[50] *Suite française* unequivocally situates her as an author narrating the cataclysmic defeat and occupation of France from within the national community. Paradoxically, it is precisely by portraying her desired compatriots' frequent failure to recognize and practice the solidarity that willy-nilly linked them all together as members of one common body politic that she expressed an ardent "volonté de vivre ensemble" (will to live together) with the French people in whom, like Michelet, she saw "la réalité fondamentale de la nation"[51] (the fundamental reality of the nation).

### Remembering Chaos and Humiliation

Having analyzed how Némirovsky undermines Vichy's manipulative interpretation of the May–June 1940 debacle all while advancing a compassionate representation of France's collective tragedy, we can now more fully appreciate the significance of her *Tempête en juin* in terms of history and memory. The fact of the matter is that Némirovsky's intense focus on the exodus faithfully translates the very preoccupations of the early years of the Occupation which have ironically been forgotten amid the strident calls of the "duty to remember" of our own era. Hanna Diamond pointedly observes that although a rich, abundant body of testimony is readily available, the

50   Weiss, *Irène Némirovsky*, 8.
51   Petitier, "Introduction," 16.

exodus of the eight to ten million people who frantically set out to escape the Nazi invasion has only received cursory attention from both historians and the public. Although unprecedented in both scale and specific nature, the event is not included in narratives of victimhood. The hundred thousand people who lost their lives during the exodus have no memorial, and unlike the Resistance, collaboration, or the Holocaust, the exodus has no place in commemorations or museums. Contrary to the innumerable accounts of resistors, collaborators, and Holocaust victims, narratives of the exodus have neither been publicly valued or cultivated, which may go a long way in explaining why its protagonists have rarely spoken of the event.[52]

There are several other major reasons why public memory of the exodus has been scant and irregular, even though the massive flight of civilians in May–June 1940 was the most far-reaching, widely shared event of the war in France (as opposed to involvement in the Resistance or collaboration, which in reality concerned a small minority of the entire population). First, it does not fit into the binary schemes of collaboration versus resistance that have been privileged ever since the legacy of Robert O. Paxton's *Vichy France: Old Guard, New Order* and Marcel Ophül's *Le Chagrin et la pitié* shattered the domination of public memory by the Gaullo-communist "myth of resistance" in the early 1970s and ushered in an era of relentless probing that has continued up until the present. As Tzvetan Todorov has observed, militants for memory most often wish to narrate the past of their nation or social group either from the perspective of conquering heroes or from that of innocent victims.[53] Rarely do we find a tragic narrative of history. The story of the millions of people fleeing in panic, terror, and total disarray is neither suitable for any heroic narrative nor is it instrumental for any specific group seeking to advance its status as victims.

Most historical accounts have thus neglected the tidal wave of

---

52   Cf. Diamond, *Fleeing Hitler*, 205–10.

53   Tzvetan Todorov, *Mémoire du mal, tentation du bien* (Paris: Robert Laffont, 2000), 154–59.

confused, disoriented, and vulnerable civilians and preferred to focus
on the interplay of military force, ideology, and political figures. The
oversight is in part due to the fact that the underlying importance of
the exodus was not readily and dramatically apparent, since it was
not seen by historians as affecting the end result of defeat and occupation.[54] Yet Hanna Diamond has vividly demonstrated that what
happened on the civilian or "humanitarian" level was in fact critical,
even if it cannot be read in the traditionally privileged frames of reference. The civilian debacle was in the first place exceptional in scope,
drama, and severity: the shocking spectacle deeply impressed all
who witnessed it, notably the eloquent socialist and statesman Pierre
Mendès France, whose calm yet moving recollection of the infernal
sights that he had observed during the exodus marks *Le Chagrin et
la pitié*. More importantly, the exodus was a critical development occurring in a pivotal moment. It touched the nerve and fabric of the
French nation: at the heart of the momentous event were ordinary
people preoccupied with immediate, pressing concerns and dangers
touching them and their loved ones. That some hundred thousand of
these people died during the exodus enables us to gauge the severity
and scope of the chaos and suffering.

It is crucial to remember that the arrival of Pétain to power as
premier coincided with the highest point of the trauma that had so
thoroughly fragilized the nation on all levels: countless individuals feared for their present and future well-being, while the supply,
transportation, and communication networks essential to keeping
them sheltered, fed, and in contact with each other were severely disrupted if not totally dysfunctional. Separated from loved ones, in dire
need of basic supplies and medical attention, abandoned or left largely to their own makeshift devices by civilian and military authorities, both those exposed to danger and hardship on the roads, rail-
ways, and bridges and those observing their ordeal were desperate
for some sort of order, protection, and "normalcy."[55] Not surprising-

54   Diamond, *Fleeing Hitler*, 208.
55   Cf. Diamond, *Fleeing Hitler*, 12.

ly, they were soon to become easy prey for Vichy's paternalist propaganda that harped on the virtues of rural simplicity, family values, and traditional hierarchies while attributing the disaster to communists, Jews, moral decadence, and the supposedly scheming, corrupt politicians of the Third Republic. Diamond stresses that most people were confused from the beginning to the end of the disaster, largely because they lacked reliable information. In the face of the Nazi *Blitzkrieg* unleashed on May 10, 1940, French government and military leaders prevaricated, not trusting the population's reaction to the truth of the disastrous situation, and then repeatedly issued conflicting orders. The end result was that it was most often impossible for civilians either to make sense of the situation or to make informed, rational decisions. This lack of access to reliable facts only heightened their longing for figures of authority and order.[56]

Hanna Diamond's devastating, yet nuanced analysis of the May–June 1940 civilian exodus in France leads us to a fuller appreciation of Némirovsky's *Tempête en juin*. On one level, the latter's fictional narrative has clearly contributed to a rekindling of interest in an unjustly neglected event. From the callous, contradictory directives issued by the banking magnate Corbin, to the narcissistic egotism of the Parisian aesthetes Corte and Langelet, to the alternately pious and panicked pratter of the self-righteous uppercrust Catholic Mme Péricand, *Tempête en juin* relentlessly exposes the lack of preparation and planning, the persistent denials of reality, the determination to cling to self-interested perceptions, and the often chaotic improvisations that only compounded the unfolding disaster for millions of people in France. Némirovsky conspicuously skewers the hypocrisy of rhetorical bravado that is almost invariably followed by opportunistic, unprincipled pursuit of the narrowest of individual interests. *Tempête en juin* underscores words and deeds of cowardice and turpitude that expose the many preexisting divisions and sharp tensions that can be seen as rife among the protagonists and their respective cohorts. In the end, these often ridiculously trivial rancors and suspi-

---

56   See Diamond, *Fleeing Hitler*, 29–31, 66, 68.

cions adumbrate the many deep ideological fault lines and social tensions undermining French society in 1940.

More importantly, Némirovsky focuses precisely on the very aspects of the drama that were both foremost in the minds of those who experienced the event and critical for determining public reaction to the creation and first initiatives of the Vichy regime. Because she uses the indirect free style to follow the changing, episodic perspectives of a number of protagonists, her perspective on the exodus is in one sense anecdotal and limited. Ultimately, however, *Tempête en juin* elaborates an overarching narrative, for the numerous individual views ultimately provide a mosaic that reveals an overlapping of individual experiences and the interrelation of seemingly isolated occurrences. At the same time, the text foregrounds the contingency of each individual perspective and the inadequation of subjective consciousness with respect to the historical event. Thus exposing the discrepancy between perception and reality, Némirovsky encourages skepticism toward tendentious interpretations of the catastrophe and maintains a critical distance from such discourse. We should not underestimate the importance of such intellectual independence, which historians now consider to be one of the earliest forms of resistance: denying the very foundation of Vichy's discourse was a means of opposing its National Revolution.[57] Vercors's *Le Silence de la mer*, the book hailed as one of the first and most powerful expressions of the Resistance, focuses intensely on the psychological and the intellectual refusal of the Nazis' attempt to hide the brutality of their enterprise under a smokescreen of cultural refinement. Vercors also draws attention to Vichy's calls for polite cooperation with those who had defeated and occupied France. As we shall see more clearly in the following chapters, Némirovsky's *Suite française*, though written and published in highly different circumstances, nevertheless contains elements that dissipate many illusions about the true nature of Vichy discourse and even the German presence on French soil.

57   See Jean-Pierre Azéma, *De Munich à la libération, 1938–1944* (Paris: Seuil, 1979), 119–26, and Henry Rousso, *Les Années noires: Vivre sous l'occupation* (Paris: Gallimard 1992), 58–59.

# CHAPTER 4

## ACCOUNTING FOR DISASTER

*Tempête en juin* and Its Contemporaries

The specific contributions of Némirovsky's narrative of the May–June 1940 debacle, including not only its strengths, but also certain limitations, come into sharper focus when we compare *Tempête en juin* with several other prominent narratives of the defeat and exodus also written during the early years of the Occupation by authors who occupied distinctly different, yet highly significant, positions in the French intellectual arena of the time: René Benjamin's *Le Printemps tragique*, Antoine de Saint-Exupéry's *Pilote de guerre*, Marc Bloch's *L'Étrange défaite*, and Léon Werth's *33 jours*. The curious notion that the traumatic events of 1940 still remain cloaked under some sort of taboo simply will not withstand scrutiny.[1] In his 1940 diatribe "Le Solstice de Juin," Henry de Montherlant foregrounded the debacle with copious and conspicuous, albeit highly distorted, examples of civilian and military humiliation. Writing in radically different conditions for a much different public and for opposite motives, Antoine

---

1  Christopher Lloyd, "Irène Némirovsky's *Suite française* and the Crisis of Rights and Identity," *Contemporary French Civilization* 31, no. 2 (2007): 169, cites Julian Jackson, *The Fall of France*, to this effect.

de St.-Exupéry dwelled extensively on the traumatic aspects of the defeat in his *Pilote de guerre*. Marcel Ophül's universally acclaimed documentary *Le Chagrin et la pitié* has been hailed by Henry Rousso as one of the first and most important works that shattered pious myths and set in motion the probing and investigation of the 1970s, 1980s, and 1990s in France. Now frequently studied on both sides of the Atlantic, the film conducts a painful dissection of the debacle that extends over two full hours of newsreel footage and interviews.

But even as early as 1951, *Jeux interdits (Forbidden Games)*, the highly acclaimed film by René Clément, offered the general public a close-up of the panicked, fearful, selfish infighting that pit the French against themselves under the German onslaught. In the early 1980s, the journalist and historian Henri Amouroux provided lengthy, detailed accounts of virtually every aspect of the civilian and military catastrophe in his highly popular radio series *Les Français sous l'Occupation* (The French under the Occupation) broadcast over France's best-known public radio channel France-Inter as well as in the very first volume, *Le Peuple du désastre,* of his well-known *Grande Histoire de l'Occupation*. The sensationally public and popular tabloid *Paris-Match* featured a cover story on the May–June 1940 debacle in 1990. More recently, in addition to the above-cited historians who stress the importance of understanding the debacle in a general approach to Vichy and the Occupation, Jean-Louis Crémieux-Brilhac has provided a two-volume account of *Les Français de l'An 40*.

Given the considerable historical and cultural attention devoted to the event, it is hard to escape the impression that claims of shattering some supposed "taboo" are simply the most recent iteration of the old saw clearly designated as such by Éric Conan and Henry Rousso in 1994: even after the full extent of Vichy collaboration and complicity in the Holocaust had been revealed and studied in detail by countless books, articles, and documentary programs, the media kept clamoring for the truth to at last be told while at the same time claiming to pull off scoop after scoop. Whatever one advances in praise or criticism of Irène Némirovsky's *Tempête en juin*—and we will continue to argue that the work engages the events of its time in an exceptionally rich and powerful manner—it is simply not possible to claim that it breaks some taboo. It is, however, necessary to examine contemporaneous narratives of the fall of France to fully appreciate the specificity of her contribution.

## René Benjamin: *Le Printemps tragique*

In publishing *Le Printemps tragique* in 1940 only a few months after the calamitous events, René Benjamin was one of the very first to focus on the exodus. While Philipponnat and Lienhardt cite *Le Printemps tragique* as one of Némirovsky's sources for her account of the debacle,[2] even the most cursory reading of Benjamin's rambling hodge-podge of vaguely philosophical musings, curiously salacious provincial gossip, and highly contrived eyewitness accounts leads one to wonder how Némirovsky could have seen such a text as anything but a foil to her own project. Indeed, apart from their common historical setting, almost everything sharply distinguishes Benjamin's text from Némirovsky's. Whereas Némirovsky eschews didacticism, Benjamin unabashedly spells out the ultra-Pétainist morals of the story. His first-person, highly anecdotal, and loosely knit account of his stay in the Tours region during the spring and summer of 1940 serves as a pretext for incessant antimodernist diatribes against urbanism and technology as well as for Pétainist scoldings on the salutary benefits of the French nation's supposedly well-deserved defeat and suffering. On top of all that, we also get an unequivocal eulogy for a distinct social and moral hierarchy, with Pétain leading the way, seconded by the traditional aristocratic elite, and bolstered at the base by the unshakable virtues of a respectfully obedient peasantry. Supposedly attuned to the vital rhythms of nature, the virility of blood and soil is presented by Benjamin as the military and agrarian antidote to the deleterious effects of Third Republican democracy and industrialization.

Not surprisingly, Benjamin's Vichyssois scheme of things proves

---

2   Philipponnat and Lienhardt, *La vie d'Irène Némirovsky*, 342.

to be highly unambiguous. Although a handful of characters are given the podium on occasion, the first-person narrator orchestrates, arranges, and sharply focuses all the various scenes and dialogues in *Le Printemps tragique*. There are no ironic reversals of perspective, nor does the discourse of one character ever undercut that of another. All the elements in the text are carefully composed to point in the same direction: Pétain and the ideology of the Révolution Nationale. Benjamin's heavy-handed attempt to teach the lessons of history in *Le Printemps tragique* stands in direct antithesis to the multiplicity of narrative perspectives that are so prominent in *Tempête en juin*. Némirovsky's art of the novel is crucial, as we have seen, not only for underscoring the contingency of each character's discourse, but also for undermining Vichy propaganda.

The multiplicity of narrative points of view in Némirovsky's text is moreover indispensable for her compassionate depiction of the common people. By revealing how various groups and individuals perceive each other, and by emphasizing their physical vulnerability and moral contingency, *Tempête en juin* points to their interdependence and common humanity. We have the creation of a veritable community of suffering instead of exploitation of fear and pain to whip people into submission. On that level, the opposition to René Benjamin's Pétainist narrative could not be more complete. *Le Printemps tragique* depicts the common people—and in particular petty bourgeois city dwellers (sociologically identical to the Michauds)—as the epitome of all that is wrong with France. Benjamin misses no opportunity to heap scorn on their anxiety and suffering, indicating that they have not only brought it on themselves but that they are also the cause of the disastrous defeat. The most telling episode is doubtless the passage featuring one of Benjamin's main protagonists, Fiamma, who predictably proves to be true to the flaming ideological purity not so subtly suggested by her name. Finding the throngs of desperate refugees in and around Tours, she snifflingly observes that people have forgotten the vital importance of pain and hardship, which have been masked by modern pleasures and conveniences. She later excoriates the disorderly appearance of a group of severely wounded refugees comprised mainly of the elderly, women, and children. Fiamma then commands them to line up with humility and respect unless they intend to be treated by a veterinarian: if unable to walk, then they are to crawl. For his part, the narrator pompously pronounces that "[l]e malheur c'est l'ordinaire de l'existence humaine"[3] (misfortune and misery are the common lot of human existence). But instead of evoking compassion and understanding, René Benjamin presents pain, death, and destruction as part of the natural organic order designed to purge and strengthen the race.

Benjamin repeatedly engages in haughty denunciations of the supposedly self-indulgent masses and expresses his regrets for the years of decadence and decline that have sapped France's vitality. Interestingly, the narrator of *Le Printemps tragique* asks the same question as Jeanne Michaud: "Pourquoi faut-il que ce soit toujours les mêmes qui souffrent?" (Why does it always have to be the same ones who suffer?) The answer that he hastens to provide is highly indicative of his slant on the May–June 1940 debacle, for he focuses on the aristocratic elite, "quelques grands esprits qui n'ont cessé de defendre ce pays" (a few great minds who have unfailingly continued to defend the country), not the common people left in the dark, abandoned.[4] Here again, the antithesis with *Tempête en juin* could not be more complete: as we have amply demonstrated in both her stated intentions and her textual realization, Némirovsky empathizes first and foremost with little people as well as with the confused, terrorized crowds driven to desperation by the violence and chaos of the invasion. She depicts suffering and death not as medicinal but on the contrary as scandalously senseless and tragic, reserving contempt and mockery precisely for those who claim that their presumed superiority should insulate them from such an unsettling spectacle.

Némirovsky's sympathetic portrayal of the common people caught up in the tragedy of May–June 1940 takes on even greater significance when we observe just how uncommon it was at the time. René

---

3    René Benjamin, *Le Printemps tragique* (Paris: Plon, 1940), 186.
4    Benjamin, *Le printemps tragique*, 239–40.

Benjamin's text is in that regard revealing. In his famous speech of June 17, 1940, Marshal Pétain had made an ostentatious verbal display of sympathy for the refugees: "En ces heures douloureuses, je pense aux malheureux réfugiés, qui dans un dénuement extrême, sillonnent nos routes. Je leur exprime ma compassion et ma sollicitude" (In this painful hour, my thoughts go out to the refugees in their misery, who are traveling along our roads in utter destitution. I extend to them my compassion and my solicitude). His highly paternalistic "compassion" and "solicitude" quickly yielded over to increasingly stern admonitions and authoritarian scoldings that gave little evidence of either compassion or even understanding of the distress and suffering of the great majority of the French populace.[5]

### Saint-Exupéry: *Pilote de guerre*

Even among those who looked for ways to continue the fight against Nazi Germany after the armistice, there was often little interest in the plight of the millions of civilian refugees who had spilled out over France's roads in the heat of the debacle. Antoine de Saint-Exupéry's *Pilote de guerre* offers both a significant contrast with Némirovsky's *Tempête en juin* and a curious affinity with Benjamin's *Le Printemps tragique* in a way that parallels Saint-Exupéry's hopeless attempt to reconcile de Gaulle and Pétain during the Occupation.[6] Written during Saint-Exupéry's extended stay in the United States, where he had come in hopes of persuading the Americans to join in the fight against Hitler, *Pilote de guerre* seeks first and foremost to galvanize military opposition to the Germans by honoring those such as Saint-Exupéry himself who had risked their lives in a desperate attempt to impede the invasion and defeat of France. His narrative clearly rejects the armistice and the Vichy policy of collaboration, and his intensely introspective contemplations are infinitely more

---

5  Cf. Diamond, *Fleeing Hitler*, 192–93.

6  Cf. C. E. Nettlebeck, "Saint-Exupéry, Antoine de," in *Historical Dictionary of World War II France* (Westport, Conn.: Greenwood Press, 1998), 323–24.

nuanced and complex than the smug prononouncements found in *Le Printemps tragique*. Saint-Exupéry's narrative technique, however, centers the elements of the text on the first-person narrator who filters all descriptions and dialogues through his own meditations. The egocentrism of his narration corresponds in turn to the social and intellectual hierarchy implicitly but unmistakably favored by his presentation of the May–June 1940 debacle.

On the one hand, when conjuring up his fondest memories of France at peace, Saint-Exupéry invariably recalls idyllic scenes of the rural, Catholic, artisanal French society steeped in custom, tradition, and obedient quietude. When, on the other hand, it comes to describing the exodus of civilians who have precipitously gathered a few belongings and fled their homes only to find themselves encumbering military supply lines, exposed to enemy fire, and overwhelming the already meager or exhausted resources of other towns and villages, Saint-Exupéry's exasperation and outright disgust are palpable in the language of his text. Exalting the thrilling challenges and grave dangers of his own role as a pilot, he seems to consider himself as an elite warrior of the skies. Judging by his text, he has little patience for the common people, whom he designates in revealing terms, as we find in the following account of his encounter with one group of refugees:

Nous avons trempé dans *la tourbe* lente qui lentement traversait ces villages:
—Où allez-vous?
—On ne sait pas.
Jamais ils ne savaient rien. Personne ne savait rien. Ils évacuaient. Aucun refuge n'était plus disponible. Aucune route n'était plus praticable. Ils évacuaient quand même. On avait donné dans le Nord un grand coup de pied dans *la fourmilière*, et *les fourmis* s'en allaient. Laborieusement. Sans panique. Sans espoir. Sans désespoir. Comme par devoir.[7]

---

7   Antoine de Saint-Exupéry, *Pilote de guerre* (Paris: Gallimard, 1942), 111; emphasis mine.

We plodded our way through the slow *bog* of people slowly going through these villages.

"Where are you going?"

"We don't know."

They never knew anything. Nobody knew anything. They were evacuating the area. There was no longer any refuge available. There was no longer any passable road. They kept on evacuating anyway. Somebody had given *the anthill* a big kick in the North of France, and *the ants* were going away. Laborioiusly. Without panic. Without hope. Without despair. As if by duty.

There is nothing fortuitous in Saint-Exupéry's use of *la tourbe* (interestingly, the same term used by Corte in contemptuously referring to the working-class people with whom he had to share the road) to refer to the refugees as both "mob" or "rabble" and "peat." For centuries, the French nobility associated common people with the demeaning image of the earth or the dirt they had to work and turn for food by calling them *roturiers,* or collectively *la roture,* a word derived from the Latin *ruptura,* associated with breaking the soil. The images of the anthill *(la fourmilière)* and ants *(les fourmis)* only reinforce the association of common people with the lowly soil. The highly pejorative terms used to refer to refugees in this passage are moreover emblematic of those we find throughout *Pilote de guerre,* which repeatedly associates refugees with images of tiny organisms or lowly animals with little intelligence:

Là-dessous sont les hommes. Des *infusoires* sur une lamelle de microscope. Peut-on s'intéresser aux drames de familles des *infusoires*?

Embouteillage des routes, incendies, matériels épars, villages écrasés, pagaille . . . immense pagaille. Ils s'agitent dans l'absurde, sous leur nuage, comme des *cloportes sous leur pierre.*[8]

. . . des chasseurs ennemies volant bas cracheront une rafale de mitrailleuses sur ce *lamentable troupeau.*[9]

J'éprouve un sourd malaise à me dire que tous ces travailleurs, toutes

8  Saint-Exupéry, *Pilote de guerre,* 108; emphasis mine throughout.

9  Saint-Exupéry, *Pilote de guerre,* 118.

ces petites gens, aux fonctions si bien définies, aux qualités si diverses et
si précieuses, ne seront plus, ce soir, que *parasites et vermines.*
Ils vont se répandre sur les campagnes et les dévorer.[10]
Et s'en vont ces *moutons sans berger.*[11]
Il s'agit *d'un immense troupeau* qui piétine, fourbu, devant l'abattoir. [12]

There below are the humans. *Diatoms* on the slide of a microscope. Is it
possible to take interest in the family problems of *diatoms?*
Jammed highways, fires, equipment shortages, pulverized villages,
chaos . . . monumental chaos. They scurry around ridiculously underneath their cloud, like *pill bugs under their rock.*
. . . low-flying enemy fighter planes will spew machine gun bursts
over this *pathetic herd.*

It is unsettling for me to muse that all these workers, all these
lower-class people with such precisely defined jobs, with such diverse
and valuable skills, will this evening be no more than *parasites and
vermin.*
They are going to spread out over the countryside and devour it.
And so these *unshepherded sheep* are going away.
We are dealing with a *huge herd* that is wearily marking time just
outside the slaughterhouse.

Seeing Saint-Exupéry qualify the refugees as "parasites" and "vermin," one can hardly be surprised to find that he presents these confused, desperate civilians—and not the military leaders—as the very
embodiment of the disaster that has befallen France: "Arrachés à
leur cadre, à leur travail, à leurs devoirs, ils ont perdu toute signification. . . . Ils sont la défaite"[13] (Torn away from their surroundings,
their work, their responsibilities, they have lost all meaning. . . . They
are the defeat). Such disdainful condescension clearly situates Saint-
Exupéry's depiction of the civilian exodus closer to Benjamin's narrative than to Némirovsky's.

10  Saint-Exupéry, *Pilote de guerre*, 119.    11  Saint-Exupéry, *Pilote de guerre*, 122.

12  Saint-Exupéry, *Pilote de guerre*, 123.    13  Saint-Exupéry, *Pilote de guerre*, 124.

## Marc Bloch: *L'Étrange défaite*

We get a dramatically different perspective from the renowned Annales school historian and Resistance martyr Marc Bloch, whose keen analysis of the May–June 1940 debacle was posthumously published as *L'Étrange défaite*. Whereas René Benjamin unambiguously exhibits Vichy's contempt for the ideals and institutions of democracy and Saint-Exupéry derides the scheming incompetence of the politicians in charge of leading the French nation, Bloch's narrative provides us with what is doubtless the most erudite and impassioned defense of the French Republic in its darkest hour, without overlooking its deficiencies. In his methodical assessment of the defeat, however, Bloch gives priority to the role of the military and the government while considering the humanitarian catastrophe presented by the massive exodus of civilians fleeing the terror and mayhem of war as a decidedly secondary, if tragic, result of strategic and institutional failures.

Although not insensitive to the acute suffering (particular involving children) that he had himself witnessed as a soldier deployed in a number of areas, Bloch's account of the exodus focuses more on the failure of the poorly prepared French populace to stand firm and support the war effort. In his view, the defense of the nation should have prevailed over civilians' unrealistic and even selfish expectation of immunity from the dangers and destruction of warfare. Thus favoring lucid analysis over empathy, Bloch concentrates on understanding the exodus as a serious distraction from what should have been a vigorous counteroffensive. Harking back to the legacy of the French Revolution, Bloch argues that when the Republic is in danger, all must participate in the war effort: "personne, dans la cité menacée, n'échappe à la levée en masse, à ses gênes ni à ses risques. Là est la seule voie claire. Le reste n'est que sensiblerie—ou lâcheté"[14] (when the republic is in danger, nobody is exempted from military service, or from its discomforts or from its risks. That is the only way that

---

14    Marc Bloch, *L'Étrange défaite* (Paris: Gallimard, 1990), 164.

clearly makes sense. The rest is merely mawkishness or cowardice). In the final analysis, Bloch dismisses the preoccupation with the plight of civilians as misplaced and counterproductive sentimentalism. He nevertheless seeks not to stigmatize the fleeing masses but to put the phenomenon into historical perspective. The astute historian thus observes that the 1940 campaign differed radically from World War I in that lines were not fixed and that the war was quickly carried to people and places that had escaped destruction in 1914–1918. At the same time, he points out that modern sensibilities had lost touch with the grim facts of military conflict. On the one hand, contemporaries had forgotten that for centuries warfare had claimed more lives among the civilians in the countryside and in rural villages than among soldiers. On the other hand, observes Bloch, people had been warned by newsreel images of the Spanish Civil War, the invasion of Poland, and "the rape of Nanking" that were widely screened in the cinema halls of the late 1930s. People were left frightened without being prepared to act sensibly in case of war. The most acute and damaging failures were the cases of "administrators" pleading that their city not be defended. While Bloch realizes that these local officials were led by the harsh memories of the previous war (in which he also participated as a soldier), he insists that as regrettable as they may have been, the slaughters of World War I were nevertheless a sacrifice that was necessary in order to preserve France's political independence and cultural autonomy. Declaring that "la nation armée ne connaît que des postes de combat"[15] (the nation at arms recognizes only combat positions) Bloch roundly denounces the government's declaration of cities with more than 20,000 inhabitants to be "open" (therefore undefended), which resulted in official orders to evacuate and the scandalous sight of firemen fleeing with their equipment and their possessions, leaving cities to burn.[16]

Instead of dwelling on the immense human tragedy, Bloch analyzes the exodus as just one more symptom of France's systemic failure to withstand the extreme duress and challenges imposed by the war

15   Bloch, L'Étrange défaite, 166.        16   Bloch, L'Étrange défaite, 161–66.

with Nazi Germany. Regardless of the final outcome, insists Bloch, "l'ombre du grand désastre de 1940 n'est pas près de s'effacer"[17] (the shadow of the great disaster of 1940 is not about to fade away). Tragically, he would be arrested, tortured, and executed for Resistance activity in 1944, and thus prevented from witnessing the Liberation of France and the Allied victory to which he had given his life.[18] Beyond the many technical malfunctions and strategic errors evident in both government and military leadership, Bloch, like the vast majority of his contemporaries of every stripe, sees the military defeat and civilian exodus as a catastrophic failure of the French nation that called for a thoroughgoing, unblinkered scrutiny of the entire set of its social attitudes, institutions, and behaviors. The title *L'Étrange défaite* itself points precisely to that urgent imperative: "Examen de conscience d'un Français" (A French citizen searches his soul). From educational practices to trade unions and newspapers, the familiar habits of everyday life were to be called into question.

Bloch's assessment of the debacle resembles Némirovsky's narrative of the exodus in that it casts a particularly harsh light on the bourgeoisie, who in the historian's mind had played a pivotal role in the catastrophe that had devastated France. Taking care to situate the "bourgeois" socially, culturally, and economically with what remains still today one of the most precise definitions of the widely used term, Bloch stresses that the French bourgeoisie felt threatened economically and socially not only by the worldwide crisis but also by the vociferous demands of the working class. Indignant at seeing workers gain access to leisure time and pleasure under the reforms of the Popular Front, much of the bourgeoisie harbored a bitter rancor against Léon Blum and a nostalgia for order, deference, and hierarchy.[19] While recognizing that there were a few representatives of "les couches populaires" (the common or lower-class people) among the commanding

17    Bloch, *L'Étrange défaite*, 207.

18    See Carole Fink, *Marc Bloch: A Life in History* (Cambridge and New York: Cambridge University Press, 1989).

19    Bloch, *L'Étrange défaite*, 194–98.

officers, Bloch nevertheless observes that the majority were tied to the bourgeoisie and shared their social prejudices and intellectual paralysis, thus leading them to despise the Left and even Roosevelt:

L'école, la caste, la tradition avaient bâti autour d'eux un mur d'ignorance et d'erreur. Leurs idées étaient simples. . . . Ainsi, un groupe de jeunes chefs, recrutés entre les plus intelligents, n'ouvrait jamais un quotidien qui reflétât, si peu que ce soit, les opinions professées, à tort ou à droit, par la majorité des Français.[20]

Schools, rigid social classes, and tradition had built a wall of ignorance and error around them. Their ideas were simple. . . . So it was that a group of young leaders recruited from the most intelligent groups were never reading newspapers that could to the slightest degree reflect rightly or wrongly the opinions expressed by the majority of French citizens.

From a somewhat different perspective, Bloch thus castigates the very same egocentrism and social bigotry that, as we have amply seen, Némirovsky so implacably satirizes in her narrative.

Marc Bloch moreover insists that the link between private lives and public destinies is inextricable and crucial for the viability of democratic institutions. This emphasis on the character and actions of ordinary people makes *L'Étrange défaite* particularly instructive for our understanding of Irène Némirovsky's historical narrative. Noting her intense focus on private life and morals, Némirovsky's biographers have presumed her to have a more or less Pétainist perspective.[21] *L'Étrange défaite*'s uncompromising account of the May–June debacle shows that, if totally distorted and unscrupulously exploited by Vichy propaganda, the issue of national character was also critical to persons of unimpeachable antifascist credentials. For it is not to return to some past order but on the contrary in hopes of making the French Republic a viable opponent of Nazism that Bloch stresses the importance of work, discipline, virtue, and sacrifice, and even speaks of punishment for the failure to transcend petty self-interest among unions and gov-

20   Bloch, *L'Étrange défaite*, 201.

21   See Weiss, *Irène Némirovsky*, 159–60, along with Philipponnat and Lienhardt, *La vie d'Irène Némirovsky*, 341–45.

ernment employees: "L'heure du châtiment a aujourd'hui sonné. Rarement incompréhension aura été plus durement punie"[22] (Today, the hour of punishment has come. Rarely has the failure to understand the situation been punished more harshly). Warning that shaking free of the Nazi stranglehold will not come without a great cost in terms of human life, Bloch explicitly stresses the necessity of sacrifice (which Philipponnat and Liendhardt immediately associate with Vichy): "Car il n'est pas de salut sans une part de sacrifice; ni de liberté nationale qui puisse être pleine, si on n'a travaillé à la conquérir soi-même"[23] (For there is no healing without a measure of sacrifice; nor can the freedom of our nation be entire if we have not worked to achieve it ourselves). Citing Montesquieu, Bloch recalls that the French Revolution and democracy emphasized the vital importance not of the basest instincts as do the Nazis but of virtue: "Dans un État populaire, il faut un ressort, qui est la vertu"[24] (In a government by the people, there must be a mainspring, which is virtue).

This preoccupation with the character and behavior of ordinary people links Marc Bloch's thoroughgoing "Examen de conscience d'un Français" with Irène Némirovsky's narrative of private lives caught up in a collective disaster. In Bloch's analysis, commitment to democratic values ultimately means that instead of viewing the common people as contemptible underlings incapable of knowing the facts and acting upon them (as is the case in the narratives of René Benjamin and Antoine de Saint-Exupéry), they are to be considered the flesh and bones of the nation (as in Léon Werth's *33 jours* as well as in *Tempête en juin*). Taking the common people seriously means not only that private lives and public destinies are intertwined, but also that a society's self-awareness is crucial for its decisions and actions. This collective self-awareness is based on intersubjectivity:

Or, de quoi est fait cette conscience collective, sinon d'une multitude de consciences individuelles, qui, incessament influent les unes sur les autres. Se former une idée claire des besoins sociaux et s'efforcer de la

22  Bloch, *L'Étrange défaite*, 172.          23  Bloch, *L'Étrange défaite*, 207.
24  Bloch, *L'Étrange défaite*, 208.

répandre, c'est introduire un grain de levain nouveau, dans la mentalité commune; c'est se donner une chance de la modifier un peu, et par suite, d'incliner, en quelque mesure, le cours des événements, qui sont réglés, en dernière analyse par la psychologie des hommes.[25]

Now, what makes up this collective awareness if not the awareness of a multitude of individuals who are constantly influencing each other. To form a clear idea of social needs and strive to spread that idea is to inject a bit of new yeast into the common mind-set; that is what gives people a chance to modify that mind-set somewhat, and then subsequently to change to a certain extent the course of events, which, in the final analysis, are governed by human psychology.

Bloch's exhortation anticipates the declaration of human freedom dramatically articulated in Sartre's paradoxical formulation: "Jamais nous n'avons été plus libres que sous l'occupation allemande"[26] (Never were we freer than under the German occupation). Bringing his immense erudition and intellectual acumen to bear on a recent event sharply circumscribed in time, the famed historian of the *longue durée* affirms that, when all is said and done, human beings are not the puppets of blind historical forces: they have the capacity to participate in, and thus influence, the course of events. The ideas and self-consciousness of individuals constructed and transmitted by public and private discourse are therefore crucial for the collective decisions and actions of the nation. Conversely, one of the factors contributing to the debacle, argues Bloch, was the widespread and demoralizing notion that France was as rotten and corrupt as certain newspapers had suggested.[27]

## Léon Werth: *33 jours*

Written shortly after the debacle in the summer of 1940, Léon Werth's *33 jours* offers what is doubtless the most detailed and astute

25   Bloch, *L'Étrange défaite*, 205.
26   Jean-Paul Sartre, *Situations III* (Paris: Gallimard, 1949), 11.
27   Bloch, *L'Étrange défaite*, 200.

eyewitness account of the civilian exodus, which he and his family experienced after precipitously leaving Paris on June 11, 1940. An assimilated Jew having distinguished himself as an author and art critic, Werth had been urged not to stay in what was sure to be a Nazi-occupied Paris by his best friend, none other than Antoine de Saint-Exupéry. Unlike the author of *Pilote de guerre* but similar to Némirovsky, Werth dramatically links private lives that have been so terribly disrupted and traumatized with public destinies that suddenly appear to be inscrutable, confusing, and ambiguous for refugees caught up in the chaos: "Et jamais les destins individuels ne furent, comme en cette guerre, plus étroitement liés à ce que nous appelons l'histoire. Notre vie est faite d'attente, d'angoisse et de longueur de temps"[28] (And never in what we call history were individual destinies more closely linked together as they were in this war. Our life consists of waiting, anxiety, and the tedious passing of time).

Far from deriding the refugees as cowardly, scatter-brained herds, as is the case in *Le printemps tragique* and *Pilote de guerre*, Léon Werth's narrative again confirms what Hanna Diamond has so convincingly argued: it was simply impossible for people to make rational plans and logical decisions because they had been systematically misinformed and prevented from expecting anything but victory. Once the military disaster was apparent, they did not have information that would have allowed them to avoid the panic, confusion, and mayhem encountered out on the open road. With the wildest sort of contradictory rumors still abounding even after the signing and implementation of the armistice agreement marking an end to the most traumatic aspects of the debacle, Werth still feels himself and his family to be prisoners of the situation, since they still have no access to any reliable means of transportation or communication.[29]

At the same time, however, Werth's account proves even more uncompromising than the stinging social satire and psychological perspicacity of Némirovsky's *Suite française*, in that his *33 jours* does

---

28  Léon Werth, *33 jours* (Paris: Magnard, 2002), 153–54.
29  Werth, *33 jours*, 154.

not omit the unethical, even criminal behavior on the part of a significant number of refugees. This factual honesty moreover corresponds to his keenly scrupulous attitude as a narrator. Although, as do both Benjamin and Saint-Exupéry, Werth carefully orchestrates the various components from the first-person perspective, he explicitly points out the inherent limits and contingencies of his narrative, stressing the difference between his text and what actually happened. He knows that he has left out certain information, some of which he would only acquire after the fact. Only later, for example, will he realize the total failure of the French military effort: he thought at the time that the movements that he had glimpsed were part of a plan to reinforce a line of defense on the Loire river. Nor could he and the others imagine that France would fall to the Germans. He realizes that, instead of merely chronicling what transpired from one day to the next, he has given a structured synthesis with a beginning and an end, thus transforming the action into a sort of play.[30]

In addition to this high degree of textual lucidity, Werth's unwavering fidelity to the experience of the exodus gives credence to his stated desire to serve as a witness giving testimony to the raw, unadorned reality of events.[31] If, on the one hand, the vast majority of refugees bore the discomforts and confusions of the first few days with a high degree of composure and occasional gestures of courtesy, on the other hand, the extended stress and fatigue combined with the traumatic exposure to strafing, bombing, and lack of food, water, and shelter eventually unleashed a number of highly undecorous and at times even shameful behaviors. Werth corroborates what we have already learned from both Irène Némirovsky and Hanna Diamond: with familiar, visible social contexts and constraints removed, ordinary people loutishly pursued their own advantage amid the panic and mayhem and even engaged in acts of looting and profiteering. Werth records a wide spectrum of behaviors on the part of both civilians and the military. While most French troops resemble those

30    Werth, *33 jours*, 51–54.
31    Werth, *33 jours*, 67.

depicted in *Tempête en juin* in that they assist and protect civilians all while remaining tight-lipped about the evolution of the military situation, others in *33 jours* can be seen hightailing it away from the front and pillaging abandoned homes and farms.

Even more unsettling than the instances of moral turpitude and duplicity visible among the *grands bourgeois* in *Tempête en juin* are the types of conduct and discourse that Werth witnesses on the part of French civilians no longer subjected to the traumatic dangers and anxieties of the debacle. Many scrounge for merchandise and valuables in the vehicles and personal effects abandoned by refugees strafed, stranded, and now left strewn over long stretches of roads. Others express overtly pro-German sentiments and condemn France's involvement in the war. Having received shelter from a crassly materialistic bourgeois household near the banks of the Loire river that all refugees were desperately wanting to cross, Werth sees his hostess offer champagne to the victors, and reports that a similarly minded bourgeois woman nonchalantly suggested that although France would now be a protectorate like Morocco, people would be no worse off and would carry on business as usual.[32] The most repulsive acts of profiteering and toadying to the Germans are observed among the bourgeoisie.

However, Werth does not refrain from mentioning that two women in a small farming village joined in celebratory dance with the German troops that had just overrun the French army and humiliated their nation. Nor does he hesitate to cast a harsh light on the political excesses that had undermined the war effort, including the folly of the anarchists who prior to the invasion had not cared if the Germans entered Paris, the bourgeois frightened by Léon Blum and eager for "order" similar to that offered by Hitler and Mussolini, the hesitation of pacifists to defend their country, and the chauvinist invocation of patriotism to rant over France's supposed failures. Far from the haughty elitism voiced by his friend Saint-Exupéry but similar to Marc Bloch (who was incidentally also his friend), Werth

32    Werth, *33 jours*, 102.

sees the May–June 1940 debacle as a moral and political failure well beyond a case of military inadequacy: "On est au fond. On a coulé à fond. C'est le moment de réinventer un patriotisme, de redéfinir un sens national. Belle occasion: les gens très bien n'en ont plus"[33] (We're at the bottom. We've sunk to the bottom. Now is the time to reinvent a patriotism, to redefine a sense of national belonging. A fine opportunity, for upper-class people no longer have any).

As a refugee himself (unlike both the soldier Marc Bloch and the military pilot Saint-Exupéry, who were directly engaged in military operations but distinctly apart from the masses of fleeing civilians), Werth is at times left pondering his own mixed emotions, mulling the stupidity of war, yet indignant to see how rapidly the French populace was accepting defeat and accommodating the Germans. He admits that he would have despised any nation that would have acted so submissively in the wake of a French victory.[34] Although without any illusions as to deep social and political divisions further weakening a now defeated nation, Werth eschews both scapegoating and autoflagellation, preferring instead to hold up his peasant host Abel Delaveau in the tiny village of Chapelon as an emblem of courage and dignity in the presence of the enemy. Struggling to contain his outrage as he relates the pro-fascist comments of a pharmacist who wants to blame the French Republic's schoolteachers and elected officials for the disaster, Werth persists in clinging to his notion of French integrity:

Je conte et résiste aux commentaires. Mais je constate que cette guerre a augmenté les haines politiques et que les partisans de l'ordre à tout prix, semblables en ceci aux révolutionnaires hypnotisés par les Russes, ne conçoivent cet ordre que sous des figures étrangères. Et je crois que la France, c'est Abel Delaveau et ce vieil instituteur.[35]

I tell my story and resist the temptation to provide commentary. But I do observe that this war has intensified political hatred and that, in one sense similar to the revolutionaries hypnotized by the Russians, those in favor of law and order at any price can only conceive of this law and order

33    Werth, 33 jours, 135.                    34    Werth, 33 jours, 156.
35    Werth, 33 jours, p. 138–139.

under the authority of foreign faces. And I believe that [the true face of] France is Abel Delaveau and this elderly elementary school teacher.

Abel Delaveau is a farmer who generously takes in Werth and his family during their flight from Paris. He not only gives them shelter, but hosts them as if they were close relatives, sharing his table and helping them get back on the road. We must hasten to observe that Werth emphatically does not hold up Abel Delaveau as an ideological emblem of the "return to the earth" and to traditional agrarian society, as would René Benjamin in support of Vichy's National Revolution. On the contrary, Werth has nothing but mockery and contempt for the reactionary ideology that immediately began to emanate from Pétain. Abel Delaveau appears instead as a model of honorable discourse and conduct amid the trying circumstances of a German occupation. As Burrin observes, the rapid defeat left a vast portion of French territory under the control of the Wehrmacht, the German army, with the result that millions of French people who had escaped occupation during World War I suddenly found themselves facing thorny options while navigating totally unfamiliar and uncharted ethical terrain.[36]

Indeed, the German soldiers described by Werth speak and act in a much more troubling manner than do those visible in Némirovsky's *Tempête en juin*. While many German troops do appear to conduct themselves in a relatively decent manner ("correct" is the French term that was most often used by civilians relieved to find them considerably less savage than rumor and propaganda had indicated), Werth describes a significant number of offensive and criminal acts on the part of the Wehrmacht. They come and take what they please, either through more or less disciplined "requisitions" or brutal pillaging. They summarily execute a group of French civilians who had lent a helping hand to soldiers defending their village. They also subject black soldiers ("tirailleurs sénégalais") to summary executions.

The most vexing issues, however, are raised after the military confrontations have ceased and France finds itself directly under the

36   Burrin, *La France à l'heure allemande*, 7–10.

thumb of the Germans. As a veteran of World War I, Werth had engaged in close combat with German forces. He nevertheless finds
himself unsettled by the omnipresence of these enemy soldiers now
appearing as proud conquerors and unopposed masters of the situation:

Ils sont près de nous, contre nous et autour de nous. Ils sont hors de la
maison et dans la maison, où ils entrent quand il leur plaît.[37]
Et les Allemands sont partout. Leur vie est superposée à celle du
village, en surcharge. On ne peut pas plus les éviter qu'on évite un trajet
de fourmis dans une allée de jardin.[38]

They are next to us, up against us, and around us. They are outside and
inside the house, which they enter when they please.
And the Germans are everywhere. Their daily life is superimposed
on that of the village, as an overload. You can no more avoid them than
you can avoid an ant trail on a path in the yard.

After the shock of military invasion, the French populace now experiences the invasive presence of the enemy in their villages, farms, and
courtyards. As Wehrmacht convoys thunder through town squares
and bucolic landscapes, German soldiers bask in their victory, setting up camp where they please, feasting, singing, and sunbathing
with what in the eyes of local French inhabitants appears as provoca-
tively ostentatious exhibitionism. Impressed by their military order,
Werth like his compatriots finds himself simultaneously fascinated, puzzled, and disgusted by their strange displays of cleanliness,
arrogance, courtesy, and vulgarity: "Nous sommes sous la domination des canons et des shorts. L'oppression, ce sont des canons et des
shorts"[39] (We are under the domination of cannons and shorts. Oppression consists of cannons and shorts). Like many others, Werth
is exasperated by the violation of the personal, acoustic, and discursive space so important to French sensibilities (and as we shall see
in chapters 6 and 7, so key to the thematics of *Le Silence de la mer*):

37  Werth, *33 jours*, 124.          38  Werth, *33 jours*, 168.
39  Werth, *33 jours*, 142.

"Nous ne sommes même plus maîtres de notre silence" (We no longer have any controle even over our silence), he complains.[40]

As Werth repeatedly and unavoidably comes into contact with the Germans in these first few days of the Occupation, he continually questions his own conduct, sounding the limits of national and personal integrity, weighing humanitarian imperatives against moral and political compunction. What can be considered to lie within the boundaries of conventional social courtesy among strangers? What must be shunned as indiscrete, obsequious, self-interested, or cowardly? Werth's frustration in coming to terms with these thorny issues confirms Burrin's observations on the novelty of situation. Werth deplores the overriding institutional ambiguity, noting that "le mot 'occupation' n'a point pour nous une signification bien définie"[41] (the word "occupation" does not have any well-defined meaning for us at all), and goes on to bemoan the lack of laws governing the relations between civilians and enemy soldiers.[42] It is in this context of relations between the occupying enemy army and the local population that Werth identifies Abel Delaveau as a model of national dignity and personal integrity. Although Delaveau brushes aside nationalist prejudice and considers people of all lands as equally human, he firmly rejects complicitous fraternization with the invading army of Hitler:

Abel a beau me dire: "Pris à part, ce sont des hommes comme nous", il sent comme moi que toute acceptation de ce que l'ennemi ne peut exiger par contrainte laisse toujours à réfléchir.[43]

It doesn't make any difference that Abel keeps telling me "Taken individually, they are human beings like us." He nevertheless feels as I do that any acceptance of that which the enemy cannot demand by force always leaves us dubious.

The upright farmer's actions match his words. On the one hand, Werth observes him talking with German soldiers and complaining

40  Werth, *33 jours*, 151.          41  Werth, *33 jours*, 141.
42  Werth, *33 jours*, 166.          43  Werth, *33 jours*, 153.

that the whole lot of political leaders are scoundrels: "Daladier, Cham-berlain, Goering, Hitler, tous salauds . . ."[44] ("Daladier, Chamberlain, Goering, Hitler, they're all bastards . . ."). On the other hand, when a second group of soldiers tries to haul off what he believes to be one of his calves, Delaveau will have none of it: undaunted by a German's drawn revolver, he leaps into the German truck with a knife to set the animal free. Determined to regain mastery over what for him is most emblematic of his day-to-day livelihood, Delaveau conveys his posi-tion by sharing with Werth a previous encounter with a young Ger-man officer:

Abel m'avait conté une conversation qu'il eut avec un gradé allemand, un étudiant de vingt ans, la veille ou l'avant-veille de notre retour à Chapelon. "Tous les peuples, lui avait-il dit, sont responsables de la guerre. Mais Hitler c'est la guerre elle-même." Le jeune homme n'avait eu un sursaut que lorsque Abel prononça le nom d'Hitler. Et Abel, qui se méfie des beaux parleurs, mais qui aime l'éloquence, lui avait dit: "Vous ne pouvez rien contre moi. J'aime mieux mourir debout que vivre à genoux. . . ."
    Mais à moi, il me dit plus simplement: "Ils sont là. Il faut supporter, mais non s'abaisser."[45]

Abel related a conversation that he had had with a German officer, a twenty-year-old student, a day or two before our return to Chapelon. "All nations," he had told him, "are responsible for the war. But Hitler is war itself." The young man jumped [was totally startled] only when Abel pronounced Hitler's name. And Abel, who is wary of smooth talkers, but who likes eloquence, told him: "You can't do anything to me. I would rather die standing upright than live on my knees. . . ."
    But to me, he said in a more simple manner: "They are here. We have to put up with them but not abase ourselves."

We can now appreciate the full significance of Werth's choice of Abel Delaveau to represent France at its best. Far from the taciturn models of traditionalism lionized by René Benjamin and contrary to the im-

44  Werth, *33 jours*, 131.
45  Werth, *33 jours*, 133–34.

ages of bovine ignorance advanced by Saint-Exupéry, Werth's farmer proves to be politically savvy and ethically courageous in dealing with the Germans. Werth shows his socioeconomically humble rural hosts to be shrewd political animals with several other anecdotes as well, and thus makes a mockery of both stubborn upper-class prejudices and ideologically constructed Vichy stereotypes. At the heart of his preoccupation lie the unconvoluted, yet searing questions concerning the attitudes and behaviors to adopt under the German occupation that was just beginning in the murkiests of contexts.

The commonsense clarity of Abel Delaveau's determination to "supporter, mais non s'abaisser" (put up with them, but not abase ourselves) belies the many quandaries faced by French citizens now at the mercy of invading forces for the essentials of day-to-day sustenance. The pressing dilemmas of the common people in France are henceforth no longer ones of military valor or abstract political ideology: they rather concern the most mundane aspects of everyday life that in the context of the German occupation take on considerable ambiguity. Can one accept food, cigarettes, chocolate, and sometimes even fuel from the Germans, especially when one observes that these commodities come from French stockpiles captured or pillaged by the Wehrmacht? It is no wonder that France's legendary obsession with food became even more pronounced during the war and Occupation, when many people were often deprived of the most basic necessities, beginning with the acute shortages occasioned by the civilian exodus.[46] What in normal times constituted the basis of culinary pride and gastronomical pleasure became during the Dark Years a matter of survival overlaid with haunting issues of honor and dignity on both individual and collective levels. In a well-known sequence of Le Chagrin et la pitié, director Marcel Ophüls asks Émile Colaudon, known as "Colonel Gaspard," just what spurred him to join the Resistance. In response, Colaudon relates the humiliation and anger that he experienced when seeing Germans come into a restaurant and heartily enjoy steaks unavailable to the French who had nevertheless raised the cattle. The

46   Ousby, Occupation: The Ordeal of France, 1940–1944, 116–20.

highly coveted but off-limits food item was thus a metonymy for the injustice and oppression of the German occupation of France.

In the strange new context visible to Werth even at the very outset of the Occupation, normally trivial matters likewise often become charged with symbolism. Several anecdotes illustrate just how the smallest acts are revealing. Observing a German soldier returning a stolen egg, Werth sees evidence of a concerted strategy to spare France for the time being and to give the impression of benevolence: "Un homme et son peuple sont tout entiers dans l'acte le plus pauvre. . . . Derrière ce soldat, il y a toute la force du *Reich* et les yeux des soldats allemands, ainsi que me disait un paysan, sont 'pleins de victoire'"[47] (Individual human beings and the nation to which they belong are entirely present in the most trivial act. . . . Behind this soldier, there is the full might of the Third Reich and, as one farmer told me, the eyes of the German soldiers are "full of victory"). On another occasion, Werth relates the encounter of a German officer and a French woman. When the German politely beckons her to precede him and then, noticing her reticence, asks if she is afraid, she replies that she is not, but his uniform makes him an enemy. To the German's claim that it had been France, not Hilter, that had wanted the war, the French woman retorts that she has read *Mein Kampf.* Here again, Werth presents a brief verbal exchange as emblematic of a concerted propaganda campaign by the Germans aimed at selling themselves off as benevolent and peaceloving, while depicting the English as warmongers.[48] Admitting his dissatisfaction with his own friendly demeanor in dealing with the Germans, Werth goes on to explain why he continues to relate a number of seemingly minor incidents:

Et qu'on veuille bien songer qu'à chacun de ces contacts avec l'Allemand vainqueur quelque chose, si peu que ce soit, de notre dignité est en cause. Je plains ceux qui ne l'ont pas senti. Et s'il est quelque théoricien, en qui la présence de l'Allemand ne réveilla point un sens national, je lui réponds que je n'aime pas le prisonnier qui flatte son geôlier.[49]

47    Werth, *33 jours,* 166.          48    Werth, *33 jours,* 157–58.
49    Werth, *33 jours,* 168.

And people should remember that in each one of these contacts with the victorious Germans, something of our dignity, as slight as it may be, is on the line. I feel sorry for those who have not sensed it. And if there is some theorist whose sense of national identity is not awakened by the presence of the Germans, I reply to him that I do not like the prisoner who flatters his jailer.

While holding up the moderate stance of Abel Delaveau as a model for going on with the necessary tasks of everyday life without compromising one's dignity, Werth is nevertheless appalled to see so many of his compatriots giving themselves over to inappropriately friendly and sometimes servile fraternization with the troops that Hitler had sent to invade and overrun their country. Without taking a hardline stance, Werth would clearly prefer more of the proud silence observed after the defeat of 1870. Such a posture was now being cited as a model for present conduct:

Je pense aux récits qu'on nous a faits de la guerre de 1870, à la silencieuse et méprisante fierté à laquelle se heurtait l'ennemi. Véridiques ou non, ces récits ont la même signification. Ils témoignent en tout cas de ce que l'on voulait paraître.[50]

I think about the stories that people have told us about the war of 1870, about the silent, contemptuous pride that the enemy ran up against. True or not, these stories all have the same meaning. They testify in any case to the way that people were trying to appear.

Far from anecdotal, Werth's extended reflections on the acceptable boundaries of seemingly superficial conversation and social interaction with the German occupying forces find significant echoes in Jean Texcier's oft-cited "Conseils à l'occupé" (Advice to the occupied people) which, as was the case for *33 jours*, was written in the immediate aftermath of the May–June 1940 debacle.[51] Similar questions are also addressed two years later in Jean Bruller's (more commonly known by

50  Werth, *33 jours*, 161.

51  Cf. Burrin, *La France à l'heure allemande*, 199–200, and Laurent Douzou, *La Résistance française: Une histoire périlleuse* (Paris: Éditions du Seuil, 2005), 32–33.

his nom de plume "Vercors") *Le Silence de la mer,* the resistance novel clandestinely published and circulated in 1942. While conceding that a number of contacts with the ubiquitous German forces were inevitable, both warn that if the French people let themselves be lulled into complacency by the Germans' superficial courtesy and attracted by their offerings of music, they could ultimately find themselves insidiously drawn into complicity with the Nazi enterprise.

Léon Werth's detailed descriptions of interaction between ordinary French people and the tidal wave of German troops that had swept in to conquer and occupy their small towns and villages allow us to more accurately gauge Irène Némirovsky's depiction of the defeat and Occupation in her *Suite française.* Indeed, the strengths, but also the limitations, of *Tempête en juin*'s narrative of the civilian exodus become even more clearly defined when we situate it with respect not only to Werth's *33 jours* but to the other accounts that we have reviewed in the present chapter as well. Némirovsky has been sharply criticized, and even suspected of harboring Pétainist sympathies, for several reasons: focusing intensely on private lives and moral questions, omitting specific references to Jews and the Jewish question, failing to explicitly denounce Pétain, and maintaining friendships with right-wing personalities. A scrupulous comparison with René Benjamin, Antoine de Saint-Exupéry, Marc Bloch, and Léon Werth, who as we have seen offer some of the most noteworthy narratives of the debacle from widely divergent ideological perspectives, quickly reveals that these charges are both unfounded and anachronistic.

Let us first consider the oft-cited absence of any specific reference to Jews or the Jewish question in Némirovsky's narrative of the civilian exodus. Although Benjamin harps over and over on the familiar racist thematics of virility, degeneration, the soil, and tradition, he makes absolutely no explicit reference to Jews or even foreigners except for one stereotypical depiction of a befuddled, bumbling, and non-Jewish Belgian. Saint-Exupéry's nostalgia for traditional hierarchies and agrarian tradition gave him a certain objective affinity for the reactionary discourse of the National Revolution, yet his only allusion to the Jewish question in *Pilote de guerre* was to conspicuously foreground the stereotypically Jewish features of a Jewish friend and comrade in arms. For his part, Marc Bloch addresses the question of his Jewish identity by saying that he only refers to it when in the presence of anti-Semites and by stressing that he defines himself culturally and politically in terms of the French Republic. His eloquent declaration is both emblematic of the fervent adhesion of many assimilated French Jews to the French Republic and instructive for observers of today who tend to view the question of Jewish identity in a markedly different manner. It therefore bears citing at length:

Je suis Juif, sinon par la religion, que je ne pratique point, non plus que nulle autre, du moins par la naissance. Je n'en tire ni orgueil ni honte, étant, je l'espère, assez bon historien pour n'ignorer point que les prédispositions raciales sont un mythe et la notion même de race pure une absurdité particulièrement flagrante, lorsqu'elle prétend s'appliquer, comme ici, à ce qui fut, en réalité, un groupe de croyants, recrutés, jadis, dans tout le monde méditerranéen, turco-khazar et slave. Je ne revendique jamais mon origine que dans un cas: en face d'un anti-sémite. Mais peut-être les personnes qui s'opposeront à mon témoignage chercheront-elles à le ruiner en me traitant de "métèque." Je leur répondrai, sans plus, que mon arrière-grand-père fut soldat, en 93; que mon père, en 1870, servit dans Strasbourg assiégé; que mes deux oncles et lui quittèrent volontairement leur Alsace natale, après son annexion au IIe Reich; que j'ai été élevé dans le culte de ces traditions patriotiques, dont les Israélites de l'exode alsacien furent toujours les plus fervents mainteneurs; que la France, enfin, dont certains conspireraient volontiers à m'expulser aujourd'hui et peut-être (qui sait?) y réussiront, demeurera, quoi qu'il arrive, la patrie dont je ne saurais déraciner mon coeur. J'y suis né, j'ai bu aux sources de sa culture, j'ai fait mien son passé, je ne respire bien que sous son ciel, et je me suis efforcé, à mon tour, de la défendre de mon mieux.[52]

I am Jewish, if not by religion—which I do not observe, no more than I do any other religion—at least by birth. I draw neither pride nor shame for that, being, I hope, a good enough historian to know that racial predispositions are a myth and that the notion of a pure race is a particularly flagrant absurdity when people claim that it applies, as is the

---

52  Bloch, *L'Étrange défaite,* 31–33.

case here, to what was in reality a group of believers who had been recruited earlier from the Mediterranean world of Turko-Khazars and Slaves. I never stake a claim to my origins except in one situation: when I am facing an anti-Semite. But people who will be opposed to my testimony may perhaps seek to undermine it in calling me a "mutt." I will calmly reply that my great grandfather was a soldier in 1793; that, in 1870, my father was in the army during the siege of Strasbourg; that he and my two uncles voluntarily left their native Alsace region after it had been annexed by the Second Reich; that I have been raised to revere patriotic traditions, which the Israelites of the Alsatian exodus had always kept up the most fervently of all; and that, finally, while certain people would gladly conspire to have me expelled today from France, and perhaps (who knows?) will succeed, France will, whatever may transpire, remain the homeland in which my heart is rooted. I was born here, I have drunk at the wellsprings of her culture, I have made her past mine, I breathe easily only under her skies, and I have, in turn, strived to defend her to the best of my ability.

It is important to observe that Bloch places these famous words at the very outset of his attempt to account for the disaster in the chapter named "Présentation du témoin" (Introduction of the witness) in which he shows his credentials and defines his perspective. To paraphrase, he was essentially stating: "Yes, I am Jewish, but that does not detract from my testimony, which I make as a French citizen, as a veteran of World War I as well as of the recent conflict, and as a seasoned historian." His main point is to insist that being Jewish is incidental with respect to his analysis of the May–June 1940 debacle. While he does deplore the failure of most French people to understand the grave threats posed by Nazism, Bloch does not make the slightest reference to either Jews or the Jewish question in all the rest of *L'Étrange défaite*. The example of Léon Werth's *33 jours* also proves highly instructive. Even though he joined the massive exodus out of Paris precisely because he had been warned by his best friend Saint-Exupéry to beware of the Nazis, Werth makes no mention whatsoever either of his own status as a Jew or of the plight of Jews in general. Like Bloch, Werth simply does not filter everything through Jewish identity: he instead thinks of himself first and foremost as a French citizen who just happens to have a Jewish family heritage. The fact of the matter is that even for such Jewish intellectuals as Marc Bloch and Léon Werth, the Jewish question as such was neither central to their thinking nor a priority in their historical narratives. Looking back from our present-day perspective almost seven decades after the events, we now realize that anti-Semitic racism was central to the ideology, politics, and even military strategy deployed by the Nazis. We live in the wake of the Holocaust, whose cultural and intellectual aftershocks are still being felt. We have to keep in mind, however, that such was emphatically not the case in 1940 nor even in 1945 after the defeat of the Axis powers, when neither the terminology nor the intellectual framework for analyzing the unprecedented genocide (the term itself had to be invented) existed yet: it would take at least two decades to recognize the Holocaust as a specific historical monstrosity with highly unsettling and far-reaching implications. To put it succinctly, it is simply not realistic to expect pre-Holocaust writers such as Bloch, Werth, and Némirovsky to display the moral and intellectual priorities that are ours today.[53] The lack of reference to Jews and the Jewish question in Némirovsky's *Tempête en juin* as well as in Werth's *33 jours* does not point to indifference or insensitivity: it simply reflects the very differenct intellectual landscape of the early 1940s.

When it comes to avoiding anachronisms, comparing Némirovsky's narrative with Werth's *33 jours* and Bloch's *L'Étrange défaite* also proves to be invaluable for the matter of putting into proper perspective the emphasis on private lives, character, and morality. Far from removing *Tempête en juin*'s narrative from the most crucial historical issues of her time and ours, the intense focus on the plight of ordinary people in their private lives allows Irène Némirovsky like Léon Werth to testify to the tremendous collective suffering while at the same time exposing the total lack of organization and planning on

53    See Annette Wieviorka, "On ne disait pas qu'on était juif" (Interview), in *Les drames de l'été 1945. Les collections de l'Histoire*, no. 28 (July–September 2005): 36–39, and Renée Poznanski, "Vichy et les Juifs: Des marges de l'histoire au coeur de son écriture," in *Le Régime de Vichy et les Français*, edited by Jean-Pierre Azéma et François Bédarida (Paris: Fayard, 1992), 57–58.

the part of government and military leaders. Némirovsky's represen-
taton of the civilian exodus furthermore points to the socioeconomic
tensions and prejudices that Bloch and Werth identify as detrimental
to France's capacity to resist the Nazi onslaught.

Perhaps most important is Némirovsky's use of changing, multiple narrative perspectives to undercut Vichy's highly tendentious
versions of the disaster that brazenly attempted to profit politically
from the widespread shock and humiliation of defeat. A close comparison of Némirovsky's historical narrative with those of her contemporaries dispels suspicions of a supposedly Pétainist slant to her
thematics. We have seen that, like Némirovsky, Marc Bloch and Léon
Werth both focus on cases of moral weakness and failure in facing
the traumatic conditions of the German invasion and the ensuing debacle. We have indeed observed that Bloch and Werth find occasion
to praise steadfast virtue, rural simplicity, patriotism, and military
honor. Instead of betraying some supposed sympathy for Vichy, however, Bloch and Werth, like the author of *Tempête en juin*, confront
these issues precisely because they have such crucial ramifications
for the life, autonomy, and integrity of the nation.

In terms of its overall representation of the exodus, Werth's narrative is closest to Némirovsky's in its sensitivity to the preoccupations of the people who lived through these events. The contrast with
Saint-Exupéry's disdainful paternalism is striking, all the more so in
that the two were close friends. At the same time, Werth's text lacks
the panoramic, omniscient perspective offered by *Suite française*. Because it focuses on the experience and commentary of one central
narrator, *33 jours* therefore does not convey the epic sense of collective suffering. And as could be expected from such a nonfictional text
cast as an eyewitness account, Werth's narrative is much more "prosaic," lacking the many ironic juxtapositions and reversals so crucial
to the piquant social satire found in Némirovsky's *Tempête en juin*.

The latter is not with out its own shortcomings, however. Whereas Bloch and Werth stress the extent to which individual, private behaviors bear heavy consequences for public life in a critical moment
of history, it is true that Némirovsky seems interested in public af-

fairs and history mainly to the extent to which they weigh heavily on personal destiny. Though she does very effectively communicate the collective pathos of the various individual ordeals, we find little indication in *Tempête de juin* of the many ways in which the French found their national identity and honor violated by invading German troops even after battlefield cannons had been silenced. Nor do we have any scenes of French soldiers running, hiding, surrendering, or looting. In that sense, Némirovsky does not explicitly connect the dramatic scenes of private lives to the larger and inescapably political dimensions of history beyond the immediate context of the civilian exodus in the way that Bloch and Werth so effectively do. Nevertheless, the assumption that a preoccupation with moral issues indicates a tie with Vichy ideology is a projection of present-day ideological divisions, since it is clearly unwarranted and unjustifiable within the context of the early 1940s.

Although it must be remembered that Némirovsky is writing as a novelist, not an essayist or historian, the ongoing question of private lives and public destinies—in other words the problem of history posed in the most personal manner—will be at the center of *Dolce*. Like Léon Werth, who also penned his observations shortly following the traumatic events of May–June 1940 and like Jean Bruller (Vercors), who penned the most famous portrayal of ambivalent Franco-German encounters in *Le Silence de la mer,* and even Jean-Paul Sartre, who brilliantly dissected the unsettling ambiguities of daily contacts among the French and their German conquerors in "Paris sous l'Occupation," Némirovsky is led to probe the same unavoidable questions: To what extent are German soldiers to be considered fellow human beings and to what extent must they be regarded as enemies, representatives of an oppressive regime incompatible with the values of the French Republic? In her seething narrative of sleepy provincial town occupied by German troops, Némirovsky elaborates a highly nuanced answer which, if analyzed carefully, turns out to be closer to the way in which the majority of people in France approached the historical upheavals and ordeals of their time, and in fact closer to our contemporary sensibility than might at first blush be apparent.

CHAPTER 5

## OCCUPATIONAL HAZARDS

### Sweet Dreams and Bitter Memories

Given the traumatic events and divisive discourses occasioned by
Hitler's conquest and occupation of French territory, there is no little audacity in Némirovsky's choice of *Suite française* and *Dolce* as titles. These musical terms would normally suggest a set of artful, del-
icately elaborated musical compositions in the French style and some
sweetly lyrical but perhaps wistful or plaintive adagio. They readily conjure up to the mind's eye many images[1] of *la douceur de vivre*
championed and immortalized by eighteenth-century French paint-
ers, writers (Voltaire and Diderot, among others), and revolutionaries
(e.g., Saint-Just) intent on decreeing the happiness of the world,[2] or
at least that to be enjoyed by the French bourgeoisie along with a few
progressive aristocrats.

1 One inevitably thinks of Watteau's misty *Pèlerinage à l'île de Cythère;* or the carefree, if
mannered, eroticism offered by Boucher and Fragonard, or the domestic bliss displayed
by the paintings of Chardin; or, to return to the domain of music, the ordered, yet supple
harmonies of Rameau.

2 Happiness as theme and political as well as cultural project is foregrounded in Saint
Just, "Sur le mode d'exécution du décret contre les ennemis de la Révolution," available at
http://royet.org/nea/1789-/1794/archive/discours/stjust_decret_ennemies_revolution-
03-03-94.htm.

In analyzing Némirovsky's representation of the German occupation in the small provincial town of Bussy and its surrounding countryside, however, we would first do well to measure the distance between the full semantic resonance of the title *Dolce* and the traumatic, if at times insidiously disguised, character of the German occupation of France as so aptly described by Philippe Burrin, who writes:

L'occupation étrangère est une intrusion, brutale, massive, dans les cadres familiers d'une société. Elle impose une autorité et exige une obéissance que ne fondent plus la tradition ou le consentement. Elle dérange les réseaux et les routines de la vie collective, elle place groupes et individus devant des choix auxquels les circonstances donnent de la gravité. En juin 1940, une défaite stupéfiante fait passer sous domination étrangère les deux tiers de la France. . . . Les Français vivent à présent sous la botte de l'Allemagne nazie. Les troupes ennemies campent sur leur sol, circulent dans leurs rues, entrent et sortent de leurs maisons. Elles régentent leur vie quotidienne, dérangent même l'ordre du temps. . . .

Pour l'immense majorité, que faire, sinon subir, plier devant la force triomphante, ajuster son comportement en conséquence?[3]

A foreign occupation is a brutal, massive intrusion into the familiar settings of any society. It imposes an authority and demands an obedience that are no longer based on tradition or consent. It upsets the networks and routines of community life, it places groups and individuals with choices to which circumstances lend considerable gravity. In June 1940, a stupefying defeat caused two-thirds of France to fall under foreign domination. . . . The French were now living under the thumb of Nazi Germany. Enemy troops were camping on their soil, going up and down their streets, entering and leaving their homes. These troops set the order of everyday life, and even upset the order of time. . . .

For the vast majority, what could be done except to suffer them, to stoop before triumphant force, and to adjust one's behavior accordingly.

3   Burrin, *La France à l'heure allemande,* 7.

One wonders just what could be farther removed from the fanciful notions of happiness, either in the form of exquisite *farniente* of aristocratic leisure or even of the more modestly bourgeois project of cultivating one's garden than daily life under the German occupation as described in these lines. In the pages that follow, our analysis of *Dolce* will reveal that, in spite of its disarming title, Némirovsky's narrative vividly illustrates many of the stark historical realities and ambivalent French responses pointed out by Burrin. *Dolce* is a literary masterpiece that provides a powerful, incisive view of French provincial society during the early stages of the German occupation. While its portrayal may in several important ways be incomplete, and its implicit politics flawed, *Dolce* nevertheless proves uncompromising in its depiction of individuals caught up in social systems and historical developments that outstrip their ability to comprehend and master their own destinies.

We will continue to center our literary analysis not on biographical matters but on the literary representation of history, seeking first of all to explain what perspectives on the war, the German occupation, and French society this narrative presupposes, conveys, and implies. We shall also have occasion to compare those perceptions with those transmitted by the discourses of her time as well as with those provided by the last thirty years of historiography. Before issuing value judgments as to the pertinence or accuracy of Némirovsky's narrative, we must first clearly delineate its contours, carefully examine its content, and situate it with respect to the discourses of her time and ours, particulary with respect to several crucial themes that have been identified as pivotal in defining French attitudes and behaviors toward both the Vichy regime and Nazi Germany: individual liberty versus social imperatives, the situation of women, the discourse of the National Revolution, the image of the Germans, and, hardly to be forgotten, procuring the basic necessities of everyday life.

Though somewhat different in degree and form, these crucial questions are all present in another famous narrative also written during the first two years of the Occupation, Vercors's renowned *Le Silence de la mer*. The striking resemblance of the essential problematic of the two texts is neither coincidental nor superficial. Both Némirovsky and Vercors lay the thematic and figurative foundation of their narratives by describing the sudden arrival of a German officer who peremptorily, if politely, requisitions lodging in a rural bourgeois homestead. This sudden intrusion of the enemy in the most jealously guarded confines of a private French dwelling proves in many important ways to be emblematic of the German occupation and of the entire set of vexing problems pointed out by Burrin. When we furthermore observe that both narratives offer a highly detailed, nuanced, and even sympathetic portrait of a sophisticated and refined German officer intent on wooing his unwilling French hostess in the intimacy of her own house, the similarities between Némirovsky's *Dolce* and Vercors's *Le Silence de la mer* appear so compelling as to require thorough scrutiny. At the same time, however, critical analysis quickly reveals major differences in the development of character, plot, and thematics and therefore helps in defining the specificity of Némirovsky's literary project in representing the first phases of the Dark Years in France.

### Life in the Provinces

At first blush, Némirovsky's Bruno von Falk seems to present a mirror image of Vercors's Werner von Ebrennac: both German officers display their cultural refinement not only with elegant speech, lofty reflections, and ceremonious courtesy, but even more strikingly with their virtuosity as musicians and composers. And as indicated by their names, both come from prestigious aristocratic families. They moreover skillfully orchestrate these signs of civilization in a patient enterprise of seduction directed toward a cloistered, seemingly quiescent provincial young woman. We will have much more to say about the images of the Germans and the expression of romantic aspirations found in both texts. At this point, however, it is important not to let such strong similarities prevent us from recognizing a fundamental difference in the nature and function of each respective work's characters.

Némirovsky articulates a highly detailed portrait of her main characters' mind-set, lifestyle, and discourse while at the same time foregrounding the problematical and highly conflictual class structure and function of the rural society centered in the little provincial town of Bussy. *Dolce* focuses intensely on the drama of individual persons caught in the webs of a rigid and rancorous social order, with its codes, expectations, prejudices, long-standing feuds, unforgiving rules, and injustice. While the wealthy bourgeois (Mme Angellier and Lucile) and the entrenched aristocrats (the Viscount and Viscountess of Montmort) garner the most attention, Némirovsky does not fail to offer a detailed, nuanced portrait of the peasantry with Madeleine Labarie and her husband, Benoît. The war and the fight to the death between the Allies and the Axis do not visibly appear to define hearts and minds, even if the conflict encroaches on private lives. Conversely, characters do not for the most part consciously define themselves with respect to matters of nation and politics, but seem to involve themselves in the latter only to advance or defend their own interests.

All of Némirovsky's characters in *Dolce* thus display highly personal preoccupations stemming from their particular problems as individuals caught up in social situations and historical events beyond their control. Even for Bruno von Falk, who is nevertheless emblematic of the German forces that have defeated and are now occupying France, political concerns seem secondary and incidental, even when such concerns trump personal aspirations. The exact opposite is true in *Le Silence de la mer*. From the very outset, Vercors portrays the narrator and his niece as little more than generic representatives of their defeated nation who must now confront the German victor in their own living room. They are not even given names, and we are told virtually nothing of their individual lives or social status other than the inferences that can be gleaned from the narrator's sober description of the frugal, apparently reclusive, and almost ascetic existence that they have in their modest, albeit far from impoverished, provincial home. They adamantly refuse to engage in small talk or make friendly gestures to their uninvited German guest precisely because they give priority to their national identity as citizens of a defeated, occupied, and humiliated nation: to approach von Ebrennac as just another ordinary human being would be a cowardly betrayal and an attempt to escape the overriding historical reality.

A similar logic informs the conduct and voluminous discourse of Werner von Ebrennac, who speaks first of the German climate, landscapes, and politics before proceeding to compare and contrast the respective cultural achievements of France and Germany. When he does speak of his father, it is only in reference to World War I and the Weimar Republic. When he relates an anecdote about his fiancée pulling the legs off a mosquito, it is only to illustrate the supposedly innate cruelty of the German people as a whole. Even when he expresses his dreams of marriage, the themes of love and sexuality remain heavily invested with (highly fanciful) notions of national identity:

> Maintenant j'ai besoin de la France. Mais je demande beaucoup: je demande qu'elle m'accueille. Ce n'est rien, être chez elle comme un étranger,—un voyageur ou un conquérant. Elle ne donne rien alors,—car on ne peut rien lui prendre. Sa richesse, sa haute richessse, on ne peut la conquérir. Il faut boire à son sein, il faut qu'elle vous offre son sein dans un mouvement et un sentiment maternels. . . . Je sais bien que cela dépend de nous. . . . Mais cela dépend d'elle aussi. Il faut qu'elle accepte de comprendre notre soif, et qu'elle accepte de l'étancher . . . qu'elle accepte de s'unir à nous.[4]

> Now I need France. But I am asking for a lot: I ask that she take me in. It is nothing to be in her home like a foreigner, a traveler, or a conqueror. Then she gives nothing, for you cannot take anything from her. You cannot conquer her wealth, her great wealth. You must drink at her breast, she must offer you her breast with a maternal gesture and feeling. . . . I know well that it depends on us. . . . But it depends on her also. She must accept to understand our thirst, and she must accept to quench it . . . she must accept to unite with us.

This famous passage derives its dramatic tension precisely from its calculated ambiguity: speaking of union between France and Germa-

---

4   Vercors, *Le Silence de la mer et autres recits* (Paris: Albin Michel, 1951), 36.

ny, von Ebrennac aims at the same time to woo the narrator's niece. Vercors's German officer totally subsumes the romantic dreams of private lives into public stories. While Vercors takes care to reveal the totally illusory and potentially fatal deception of such a union of the two nations, the stylized discourse constitutes the very fabric of *Le Silence de la mer.* Highly literary and thus far removed from normal conversational exchanges, it maintains the entire narrative on the level of allegory.

It is precisely such stylized allegorization that allows the seemingly self-effacing narrator of *Le Silence de la mer* to symbolize the (now problematical) ideal of a people united in resistance to the Nazi invader. Vercors's narrative thoroughly shatters von Ebrennac's dream of Franco-German unity by having the young officer relate his conversations with Nazi military leaders in Paris, who reveal the genteel veneer of culture to be merely a ploy aimed to mask German plans to extinguish the flame of French culture and reduce France to servility in all domains. It is hardly a coincidence that immediately after von Ebrennac's dramatic revelation, we get the narrator's most lyrical exposition of the thematics of silence running throughout the text:

—Ils éteindront la flamme tout à fait! cria-t-il [von Ebrennac]. L'Europe ne sera plus éclairée par cette lumière!
Et sa voix creuse et grave fit vibrer jusqu'au fond de ma poitrine, inattendu et saisissant, le cri dont l'ultime syllabe traînait comme une frémissante plainte:
—Nevermore!
Le silence tomba une fois de plus. Une fois de plus, mais, cette fois, combien plus obscur et tendu! Certes, sous les silences d'antan,—comme, sous la calme surface des eaux, la mêlée des bêtes dans la mer,—je sentais bien grouiller la vie sous-marine des sentiments cachés, des désirs et des pensées qui se nient et qui luttent. Mais sous celui-ci, ah! rien qu'une affreuse oppression.[5]

"They will put out the light completely," he cried. "Europe will no longer be illuminated by that light!"

5   Vercors, *Le Silence de la mer*, 55.

And his empty, grave voice made his unexpected, dramatic cry resonate to the depths of my chest. The last syllable lingered like a trembling moan:

"Nevermore!"

Once again, silence fell over the room. Once again, but this time how much more somber and stiff it was! Certainly, amid the silences of yesteryear—as underneath the calm surface of the waters, the churning of creatures in the sea—I indeed felt underwater life churn with hidden feelings, with desires and thoughts that are denied and that struggle. But underneath this one, hah!, nothing but horrible oppression.

Vercors's narrative depicts the extended stay of a sophisticated, engaging, and loquacious German officer in a polite, but adamantly unresponsive French household in order to contrast the Nazis' attempt to camouflage their sinister project of cultural domination under the trappings of collaboration, on the one hand, with the hoped-for French resolve to maintain a united front of refusal, on the other.

Némirovsky's *Dolce* offers exactly the opposite perspective, taking pleasure in highlighting all that makes the rural agrarian society centered in the small provincial town of Bussy a veritable snake pit, or, to turn Vercors's central metaphor on its head, a sea of creatures seething with hidden feelings, desires, and thoughts that boldly assert their existence and engage not in a unified struggle against a common enemy, but in bitter internecine strife. Instead of the rather idyllic, if Spartan, image of domestic warmth and familial solidarity in the supposed quietude of the provinces, as implicitly suggested by *Le Silence de la mer*, Némirovsky lays bare the ancestral hatreds pitting one social class against another and underlines the implacable rivalries setting spouse against spouse and wife against mother-in-law within families. The sharp contrast between the thematics of *Dolce* and those of *Le Silence de la mer* in fact stems from Némirovsky's radically different perspective. If, as several commentators have charged, she seems unwilling or unable to envisage the larger ideological issues of the war such as those addressed by Vercors through von Ebrennac's discourse on culture in the form of literature and music, Némirovsky nevertheless displays an acute perception of the politics of class and the workings of culture in the sense of mores. Although not entirely consonant with the imperative of unified resistance as championed by Vercors (and of course Charles de Gaulle, among others), *Dolce*'s unblinkered images of the proverbial "house divided against itself" in occupied France is hardly without interest, and may even turn out to be closer to our contemporary understanding of the Dark Years than may at first blush appear evident.

### Prides and Prejudices

Némirovsky's focus on the markings, mind-sets, and manners of social class is evident from the outset of *Dolce*, which like *Tempête en juin* centers a large portion of the action and dialogue on the most privileged representatives of the bourgeoisie, namely, Madame Angellier and her daughter-in-law, Lucile. The prose wastes no time in calling attention to what is commonly recognized as the bourgeoisie's signature preoccupation: the preservation of the property that ensures social status and material comfort, as we see in the very first sentence of chapter 1: "Chez les Angellier, on mettait sous clef les papiers de famille, l'argenterie et les livres: les Allemands entraient à Bussy"[6] (In the Angellier household, they were locking up family papers, silverware, and books: the Germans were entering Bussy). We get a very concrete and unmistakable sense of "l'ordre bourgeois" and its attendant materialism, as through Némirovsky's indirect discourse Mme Angellier carefully inventories the foodstocks, the wine, the piano, and the shotgun that had been locked away. Everything is therefore emblematically "in order":

Elle [Mme Angellier] récapitula mentalement: les meubles du grand salon enlevés, les rideaux décrochés, les provisions entassées dans la cabane où le jardinier mettait ses outils—oh, les grands jambons boucanés couverts de cendre, le jarres de beurre fondu, de beurre salé, de fine et pure graisse de porc, les lourds saucissons marbrés—tous ses biens, tous ses trésors. . . . Le vin, depuis le jour où l'armée anglaise

6  Némirovsky, *Suite française*, 307.

s'était rembarquée à Dunkerque, dormait enterré dans la cave. Le piano était fermé à clef; le fusil de chasse de Gaston, dans une cachette inviolable. Tout était en ordre. Il ne restait qu'à attendre l'occupant.[7]

She went back over everything in her mind: the furniture had been removed from the main living room, the curtains had been taken down, the food supplies had been piled into the shed where the gardener kept his tools—oh, the big smoked hams covered with ashes, the earthenware jars of melted butter, of salted butter, of pure, fine lard, the thick, marbled salamis—all these goods, all these treasures. . . . Ever since the day when the English army had returned to their ships at Dunkirk, the wine lay buried in the cellar. The piano was locked; Gaston's shotgun was tucked away in an inviolable hiding place. Everything was in order. The only thing remaining was to wait for the occupying troops.

Mme Angellier clearly manifests a miserly predilection for counting up her treasures and fondly caressing them in her mind's eye ("oh . . . tous ses biens, tous ses trésors") (oh . . . all these goods, all these treasures). We later confirm that Mme Angellier derives her pleasure not from sensual enjoyment, since she herself never drinks the fine wine so lovingly stored away, but from the sense of possession itself and her devotion to family patrimony: "Mais le vin fait en quelque sorte partie de l'héritage et, à ce titre, est sacré, comme tout ce qui est destiné à durer après notre mort. Ce Château d'Yquem, ce . . . elle les a reçus de son mari pour les transmettre à son fils. On a enterré les meilleures bouteilles dans le sable."[8] (But wine is in a way part of our heritage, and as such is sacred, as is all that is destined to last after we die. This Château d'Yquem, this . . . she had received these bottles of wine from her husband to be handed down to her son. They had buried the best bottles in the sand.). In giving first priority to the preservation of wealth and status as reified in her prized possessions and not to the actual enjoyment of goods, Mme Angellier illustrates what sociologist Philippe d'Iribarne has identified as the archetypically bourgeois strategy both for escaping death and de-

7   Némirovsky, *Suite française*, 311.
8   Némirovsky, *Suite française*, 476.

struction by constructing a clean, neat, orderly, safe, and comfortable physical environment and for claiming an elite status by accumulating material signs of wealth and distinction.[9] Némirovsky moreover points out that the prime reason for Madame Angellier's bitter resentment against Lucile are crassly material. Her son, Gaston, had married in order to secure a handsome dowry and lucrative inheritance, but hopes of acquiring his father-in-law's considerable real estate holdings were dashed when Lucile's father squandered his fortune through bad business decisions.[10]

Far from anecdotal, the underpinnings of this marriage prove to be emblematic of the provincial bourgeoisie, as becomes evident when Némirovsky has us view the wedded couple through the eyes of Lucile. Her indirect discourse reveals the extent of her unhappiness: having married Gaston in order to please her father, she now finds herself stuck with a vulgar, repugnant oaf whom she never loved, described as "cet homme gras et ennuyé, passionné seulement par l'argent, les terres et la politique locale"[11] (this overfed, bored man, driven only by money, land, and local politics). Reminiscent of such well-known literary antecedents as Emma Bovary and Thérèse Desqueyroux, Lucile thus presents another example of a sensitive, intelligent woman trapped in a bourgeois marriage that condemns her to a life of stultifying provincial boredom. While, as we shall later explain at length, Némirovsky does not fail to give a particularly striking, nuanced development to the subjective aspirations of her central protagonist, she explicitly uses Lucile and her stereotypically philistine bourgeois husband as emblems of French provincial life.

Née et grandie à la campagne, elle n'avait connu du reste du monde que de brefs séjours à Paris, chez une parente âgée. La vie dans ces provinces du Centre est opulente et sauvage; chacun vit chez soi, sur son domaine, rentre ses blés et compte ses sous. Les longues ripailles, la chasse, occupent les loisirs. Le bourg avec ses maisons revêches, défendues par

9   Philippe d'Iribarne, *L'Étrangeté française* (Paris: Éditions du Seuil, 2006), 68–70.

10  Némirovsky, *Suite française*, 311.

11  Némirovsky, *Suite française*, 321.

de grandes portes de prison, ses salons bourrés de meubles, toujours clos et glacés pour épargner les feux, était pour Lucile l'image de la civilisation.[12]

Born and raised in the country, her only experience of the outside world was from a few short visits to Paris in the home of an elderly relative. Life in these provinces of the Région du Centre is lush and unrefined; everyone lives within the confines of their own home, on their own domain, bringing in their wheat and counting their money. Leisure time is spent hunting and indulging in gluttonous feasts. With its stern houses protected by large, prisonlike doors, its living rooms crowded with furniture, always kept closed and chilly to spare firewood, the little provincial town was the very image of civilization for Lucile.

This grim tableau of the bourgeois life in provincial France stands in stark opposition to the rather blissful (if rather sparse and incidental) images offered by *Le Silence de la mer*, and points to all that constitutes the specificity of Némirovsky's *Suite française* as a sweeping historical novel of epic scope, in contrast with Vercors's sharply aimed resistance narrative. Apart from a few oblique references to Vichy, Pétain, and those who shamelessly sell their soul for a plateful of lentils,[13] *Le Silence de la mer* makes no reference to any social or familial tensions beyond the niece's stern reprobation of her narrator-uncle's timid inclination to converse with the German officer.[14] Némirovsky, on the other hand, implacably exposes the seamy underside of social power and status as well as the sordid reality of family life. *Dolce* lets us observe "la vie sous-marine des sentiments cachés, des désirs et des pensées qui se nient et qui luttent" (underwater life [churning] with hidden feelings, with desires and thoughts that are denied and that struggle), but instead of opposing the French people and their enemy aggressors, these local conflicts pit husband against wife, wife against mother-in-law, bourgeois mother-in-law against aristocratic viscountess, and viscountess against tenant farmer.

---

12  Némirovsky, *Suite française*, 321.

13  As Werner von Ebrennac so aptly puts it. See Vercors, *Le Silence de la mer*, 56.

14  See Vercors, *Le Silence de la mer*, 29.

It is hard to reconcile such searing portrayals of bourgeois hypocrisy and rural class conflict in the French provinces with Jonathan Weiss's claim that Némirovsky let herself be hypnotized by an illusory façade of domestic bliss and bucolic serenity stemming from the Barresian cult of native soil and bloodlines.[15] We see on the contrary throughout *Suite française* that she takes pleasure in highlighting the acute enmities and injustices stemming from the entrenched structures and mentalities of social class in rural France. As is the case in *Tempête en juin,* Némirovsky uses the changing perspectives of her indirect free style to narrate from within and without, thus presenting the thoughts and deeds of her personages as constantly filtered through the contingencies of a number of particular observers. Vercors, however, gives us one narrator who shapes our perception in a unified, concerted, coherent way, eliminating ambiguity.

For her part, Némirovsky implicitly but incontestably refuses all systematic, doctrinaire ideological representations of society and mores, beginning with those of the so-called National Revolution touted by Vichy. Nothing could be farther from the schmalzy images of quaint little villages huddled around a reassuring church spire, replete with modest artisans quietly plying their trades and peasant farmers reverently sowing and reaping their fields gently nestled in the rolling splendor of unblemished rural landscapes, such as one so readily finds adorning Vichy propaganda posters of the early Occupation years. Némirovsky's caustic rendering of social life in the small provincial town of Bussy can instead be compared with that found in Clouzot's *Le Corbeau,* which outraged Vichy to no end. For in composing such an elaborate portrait of Lucile and making her plight the thematic and narrative nexus of *Dolce,* Némirovsky was not just providing her own more sensitive, psychologically complex, and intellectually sophisticated variation on the well-known themes of marital unhappiness and provincial suffocation: she was also engaging in fierce satire.

Though the text soft-pedals this aspect, we must never lose sight

15   Cf. Weiss, *Irène Némirovsky,* 42–44.

of the fact that, as the wife of a prisoner of war, Lucile immediately takes on heavy ideological connotations within the context of the Vichy propaganda that was inundating all areas of French public life in these Occupation years. The National Revolution tirelessly touted women as mothers, faithful companions, and provisory heads of households,[16] while Pétain, the "Vainqueur de Verdun" (Victor of Verdun) and the "médecin des soldats" (the soldiers' doctor) saw the almost two million prisoners of war whose absence weighed so heavily on the nation's morale and economy as one of the pillars of his legitimacy. In that light, Némirovsky's characterization of Gaston Angellier as an overfed, boorish lout, and of Lucile as a childless woman yearning to escape the prisonhouse of her bourgeois marriage in order to seek her own individual romantic and intellectual fulfillment is nothing less than iconoclastic. Nor is Lucile's the only marriage rife with sexual dissatisfaction, domestic fatigue, and class bitterness. In many ways, the situation of Madeleine Labarie within her farming household parallels that of Lucile. Like her bourgeois counterpart, the rural housewife finds herself attracted to the handsome, sophisticated young German officer lodging in her home, all the more since her marriage of reason to the rough-mannered, tough-talking Benoît has left her weary and despondent. Here again, in order to appreciate the ideological significance of such harsh images of a rural household in the context of the Occupation, we must recall the insistent efforts of Vichy propaganda to present farmers as icons of agrarian tradition, serenity, and moral rectitude, as we have already pointed out with respect to René Benjamin's *Le Printemps tragique*. Némirovsky will clearly have none of it, and makes a mockery of such ideological nostalgia in *Dolce*.

On the other hand, it is equally difficult to claim, as does Christopher Lloyd, that Némirovsky's narrative stems from a "preoccupation with the forces of history, mediated through fiction."[17] She focuses

---

16   Sarah Fishman, *We Will Wait: Wives of French Prisoners of War, 1940–1945* (New Haven and London: Yale University Press, 1991), 30–59.

17   Lloyd, "Irène Némirovsky's *Suite française* and the Crisis of Rights and Identity,"177.

not on national destiny and ideologies as manifest in the vicissitudes of military confrontations and political formations, but on the drama of individual existence facing the deeply ingrained prejudices of social class and long-standing rivalries of sex, money, and power that characterize the provincial universe of Bussy. Here again, the perspective of *Dolce* thus stands in sharp contrast with that of *Le Silence de la mer.* Vercors's depiction of the narrator, his niece, and their frugal life remains allegorical, representative of a desired national attitude—in other words, totally ancillary to his exhortation for the French people to collectively reject the sirens of collaboration. Némirovsky's narrative, however, zooms in for detailed, close-up views of her characters' distinctive mind-sets, lifestyles, and discourses, and ultimately on their highly problematical social interactions. Yet *Dolce* is not merely anecdotally concerned with the plight of Lucile, Bruno, Mme Angellier, Benoît, and Madeleine: the narrative repeatedly draws our attention to the economic structures, behavioral patterns, and thought processes constantly at work in everyday life, and vividly exposed by the dramatic context of the German occupation.

We detect Némirovsky's attention to all that stems from the *longue durée* of social life in the following description of Easter Sunday in Bussy:

Cependant, le bourg avait son air habituel de paix dominicale; les Allemands mettaient une note étrange dans le tableau, mais le fond demeurait pareil, songeait Lucile. . . .

Mais les plus jeunes, comme tous les dimanches, demeuraient sur la place à bavarder. Elles n'allaient pas perdre, à cause des Allemands, un après-midi de fête, de loisirs; elles avaient des chapeaux neufs: c'était le dimanche de Pâques. . . .

Comme tous les dimanches, le notaire se rendait au Café des Voyageurs pour y jouer au tarot; des familles revenaient de la promenade hebdomadaire au cimetière: presque une partie de plaisir dans ce pays qui ignorait les divertissements; on y allait en bande; on cueillait des bouquets parmi les tombes.[18]

18  Némirovsky, *Suite française*, 324–25.

Nevertheless, the town maintained its usual appearance of a quiet Sunday; the Germans added an unusual element to this picture, but the background remained the same, thought Lucile. . . .

As they did every Sunday, however, the young people lingered on the town square to chat. The girls were not about to forego their leisure time on this holiday afternoon because of the Germans. They had new hats and it was Easter Sunday. . . .

As he did every Sunday, the notary public was going to the Café des Voyageurs to play cards; families were coming back for their weekly walk over to the cemetery. It was almost a fun outing in this area that had no other source of entertainment: people went there in groups and picked flowers among the graves.

The prose foregrounds everything that constitutes a regular Sunday occurence, and explicitly presents these habits as the familiar background of a "tableau" to which the Germans merely added an unusual new note.

Similarly, in describing Benoît's brooding demeanor, Némirovsky explains his gruff manners in terms of gender, social class, and national identity: "Benoît était taciturne et revêtu comme d'une triple armure de pudeur, masculine, paysanne et française"[19] (Benoît was taciturn and girded with something like a three-layered sense of modesty: masculine, peasant, and French). While highly individualized, Benoît nevertheless remains explicitly emblematic of French peasant men. Lucile's husband, Gaston, whose character is only outlined for the purpose of elucidating Lucile's situation, is likewise referred to as a typical provincial: "il avait cet aspect de maturité précoce que donne au provincial son existence sédentaire, la nourriture lourde et excellente dont il est gavé, l'abus du vin, l'absence de toute émotion vive et forte"[20] (he had that aspect of premature aging that the sedentary lifestyle, the rich and abundant food with which he stuffs himself, the overindulgence in wine, and the lack of any strong or lively emotion lend to a man in the provinces). Whereas *Le Silence*

---

19   Némirovsky, *Suite française*, 341.
20   Némirovsky, *Suite française*, 322.

*de la mer* uses the stylized, self-effacing personages of the narrator and his niece only to put concrete, individual faces on the desired national attitude of dignified refusal, Némirovsky presents nationality as merely one of several major components within each highly developed character's identity.

In order to appreciate the significance of the glaring spotlight that Némirovsky casts on the highly conflictual social interactions among the various components of the provincial farming community centered in the little town of Bussy, we must once again compare her narrative to the most prominent discourses of the early Dark Years when *Dolce* was written. Vercors and de Gaulle called on the French to unite by exhorting them to join in resistance to their common German enemy. Vichy sought to create the impression of a wounded nation rallying around Pétain's "providential" dictatorship by scapegoating and excluding the so-called anti-French elements, in particular communists, Jews, Freemasons, and foreigners supposedly responsible not only for alienating the nation from its traditional Catholic and agrarian institutions but also for fomenting social strife and political dissension. One of the most famous propaganda posters featured a grandfatherly image of Marshal Pétain captioned "Etes-vous plus Français que lui?" (Are you more French than he is?), thus appealing to his putatively quintessential Frenchness as the incontestable foundation of national unity precluding rancorous social relations and political strife. Many other posters depicted the French nation as a house infested, divided, or undermined by nefarious outsiders and interlopers of all sorts.

Némirovsky presents suspicion, mistrust, and infighting not as foreign imports but as endemic and long-standing within all the various families and among the social groups that make up this not-so-quaint little region that she situates at the very heart of French territory. These centuries-old inimical grudges have been passed down from generation to generation and extend from top to bottom of the social ladder, as we clearly see when Némirovsky explains the virtual feud still simmering between the local aristocrats and their tenant farmers:

De père en fils, les Labarie étaient métayers sur les terres des Montmort. De père en fils, on se haïssait. Les Labarie disaient que les Montmort étaient durs aux pauvres, fiers, pas francs, et les Montmort accusaient leurs métayers d'avoir le "mauvais esprit." . . . C'était une manière de concevoir la pauvreté, la richesse, la paix, la guerre, la liberté, la propriété qui n'était pas en elle-même moins raisonnable que celle des Montmort, mais opposée à la leur comme le feu l'est à l'eau.[21]

Generation after generation, the Labaries had been sharecroppers on the Montmorts' land. Generation after generation, they had hated each other. The Labaries would say that the Montmorts were hard on the poor, proud, and devious, while the Montmorts would accuse their sharecroppers of having "a bad attitude." . . . It was a way of viewing poverty, wealth, peace, war, freedom, and property that in itself was no less reasonable that the Montmorts' view of things, but it was as opposed to theirs as fire is to water.

The aristocratic Montmort and the farmers of Labarie family are hardly the only social groups perpetuating this sort of domestic cold war. When the Viscountess comes to procure an illegal sack or two of wheat from Mme Angellier, Némirovsky describes the mutual contempt and suspicion that makes such visits a rarity occasioned only by necessity.[22]

Elsewhere we learn that, like the Viscountess, Mme Angellier treats her own tenant farmers with an authoritarian contempt and mistrust, even using informers to police their income and lifestyle. Although Mme Angellier concentrates more on maintaining tight economic control while the Viscountess exercises religious tyranny, the two of them represent a tandem monopoly of power:

Mme Angellier, tous les mois, visitait ses domaines; elle choisissait un dimanche pour trouver son "monde" à la maison, ce qui exaspérait les métayers; ils cachaient précipitamment, dès qu'elle apparaissait, le café, le sucre et le marc de café des fins de déjeuner: Mme Angellier était de la vieille école—elle considérait la nourriture de ses gens comme autant de

21   Némirovsky, *Suite française*, 363–64.
22   Némirovsky, *Suite française*, 377–80.

pris sur ce qui aurait dû lui revenir à elle-même; elle faisait d'aigres reproches à ceux qui prenaient, chez le boucher, de la viande de première qualité. . . . Mme de Montmort gouvernait son monde avec des principes analogues, mais comme elle était aristocrate et plus attachée aux valeurs spirituelles que la bourgeoisie âpre et matérialiste dont sortait Mme Angellier, elle s'inquiétait surtout du côté religieux de la question. . . . Aussi, des familles qui se partageaient le pays—les Montmort et les Angellier, la plus exécrée était encore la première.[23]

Madame Angellier visited her farms every month. She would always choose a Sunday in order to find "her people" at home, which exasperated the sharecroppers: as soon as she appeared, they would hurry to hide the coffee, the sugar, and the liqueur that would conclude the Sunday noon meal. Madame Angellier was of the old school: she considered these people's food as having been taken from that which should have been included in her share. She sharply reprimanded tenants who bought top-quality meat from the butcher. . . . Madame de Montmort applied similar principles in ruling over her people, but since she was an aristocrat, she was more attached to spiritual values than was the crudely materialistic bourgeoisie to which Madame Angellier belonged. She was therefore above all concerned with the religious aspect of the issue. . . . Moreover, of the two families that divided up this area, the Montmorts and the Angelliers, the former was still the most hated.

Just as Madeleine and Benoît Labarie are explicitly identified as emblematic of their social milieu (the peasantry), so Mme Angellier and the Viscountess are specifically representative of the two social classes that constitute the twin pillars of socioeconomic power in the Bussy area: the bourgeoisie and the aristocracy.

Némirovsky's prime focus is not, as Lloyd would have it, on the forces of history, but on the implacable mechanics of class politics. She conspicuously links all of the characters in *Dolce* to the socioeconomic origins that largely define their thoughts and guide their acts. That is why, even though the published version of her narrative carries no chapter titles, her manuscript notes offer two sets of titles that foreground the occupation or socioeconomique status of the person-

23  Némirovsky, *Suite française*, 396–97.

ages featured within them, including "Le Chemin des Pauvres" (The Poor People's Road), "Les Prolétaires" (The Working-Class People), "L'Amateur de Porcelaines" (The China Collector), "Employés et patrons" (Employees and Bosses) "La Banque" (The Bank), "Pêcheurs d'âmes ou M le curé" (Fishers of Souls or the Parish Priest), and "Le Soldat" (The Soldier). That she conceived of her plot in terms of social interaction is further evidenced by the following note that she wrote to herself: "Non! Pas trop de milieux différents au début!"[24] (No! Not too many different social milieus at the beginning!).

### Noble Hypocrisy and Ideological Subversion

The preeminence of social class in *Dolce* takes on even greater significance when we observe that Némirovsky has aligned her main characters (Mme Angellier, Lucile, the Viscountess, Madeleine and Benoît Labarie) with the three orders (bourgeois notables, aristocrats, the peasantry or farmers) that Vichy was advancing as the authentic foundation of a society that was to be structured not by the ideals of 1789, but by France's traditional hierarchies. The propaganda of the National Revolution suggested that harmful divisions had been artificially introduced into French society by the illusory notions of equality and democratic government, and that the resultant dissensions had weakened the nation and thus largely contributed to the catastrophic defeat of May–June 1940. The ever paternalistic Pétain accordingly proclaimed, "Je hais les mensonges qui vous ont fait tant de mal" (I hate the lies that have caused you so much harm), and urged his wayward children to turn away from politics and occupy themselves with the vocations naturally arising from their traditions and social origins. Such was to be the basis of a harmonious society once more obedient to traditional elites and piously joined in efforts to rebuild their broken country.

Némirovsky's depiction of the little provincial town of Bussy and

24   NMR 9085 and 9086, Fonds Némirovsky, IMEC (Institut Mémoires de l'Édition Contemporaine).

its surrounding rural community makes a complete mockery of Vichy's notions of a cohesive people at peace with itself and dutifully obedient to the traditional authorities of a rural agrarian order. When she narrates a meeting held to solicit contributions of foodstuffs for prisoners of war—in other words, an occasion that should have galvanized national unity and, at least for the moment, silenced all petty local rivalries—we quickly see that there is little love lost among either the different social classes or even members of the same class. On the contrary, the text underscores these social tensions by focusing on the prominent woman presiding at the occasion, the Viscountess of Montmort. We measure the depth of the latter's disdain for her compatriots of the Bussy locality from Némirovsky's explanation of how she has to steel herself for the ordeal of addressing these vulgar commoners who prove largely insensitive to her noble admonitions, doubtless incapable of attaining the lofty heights of altruistic generosity to which the Viscountess would lead them. We thus find her likening her role before these local housewives to that of a missionary sent among those having yet to glimpse the light of civilization:

Mais elle considérait que c'était un devoir, et qu'elle était chargée, elle, par nature, d'éclairer ces bourgeoises et ces paysans, de leur montrer la route, de faire lever en eux le bon grain.

—Vous comprenez, Amaury, expliqua-t-elle à son époux, je ne puis croire qu'il y ait une différence essentielle entre elles et moi. Elles ont beau me décevoir (elles se montrent si grossières, si mesquines, si vous saviez!), je persiste à chercher en elles une lumière.[25]

But she felt that it was her duty, and that, by her nature, she had been charged with enlightening these bourgeois and these peasants, showing them the way, and cultivating the good grain within them.

"You understand, Amaury," she explained to her spouse, "I cannot believe that there could be any essential difference between me and these women. Even though they keep on disappointing me (if you knew how crass and how petty they show themselves to be!), I persist in seeking out a light within them."

25  Némirovsky, Suite française, 350.

The lady doth protest too much, for the Viscountess's disclaimer and feigned self-abnegation in seeking some faint glimmer of understanding only highlights her contemptuous view of these women as being inferior by birth. These deep-seated prejudices become even clearer as she explains her undertaking in perversely theological terms, referring to the sacrifice of the Savior and wondering if her real calling should have been to be sent to save supposedly backward and ignorant peoples in the wilderness. In order to appreciate Némirovsky's ironic rendering of her speech, the passage bears citing at length:

Mais l'ignorance, mon ami, l'ignorance où elles se trouvent est effrayante. Aussi, au début de chaque séance, je leur fais une courte allocution pour qu'elles comprennent pourquoi elles sont punies, et (vous pouvez rire, Amaury) j'ai vu sur ces joues épaisses un éclair de compréhension parfois. Je regrette, achevait pensivement la vicomtesse, je regrette de ne pas avoir suivi ma vocation: j'aurais aimé évangéliser une contrée déserte, être le bras droit de quelque missionnaire dans la savane ou dans une forêt vierge. Enfin, n'y pensons plus. Là où nous avons été envoyées par le Seigneur, là est notre mission.[26]

"But their ignorance, my friend, the extent of their ignorance is frightening. And so, at the beginning of each meeting, I give them a short talk so that they might understand why they have been punished, and (you can go ahead and laugh, Amaury) I have sometimes seen a flash of understanding on their thick cheeks. I regret," the Viscountess pensively concluded, "I regret not to have followed my calling: I would have loved to bring the Gospel to some forsaken region, to have been the right hand of some missionary on the savannah or in a pristine forest. Well, let's not give it any further thought. Wherever we have been sent by the Lord, there is our mission."

Némirovsky elevates the Viscountess's discourse to such a pinnacle of melodramatic grandiloquence that we can almost hear the author echoing the Count's bemused snickers with gales of her own derisive laughter. In any case, it is virtually impossible to read these lines without hearing ironic strains of Pétain's rhetoric which so often pre-

---

26   Némirovsky, *Suite française,* 351.

sented "le Vainqueur de Verdun" in a sacrificial role in order to drive home his scoldings and admonitions.

Némirovsky's parody of Vichy discourse continues in the narration of the speech that the Viscountess delivers to the little assembly. Némirovsky heightens the comic effect by alternating citations of Mme de Montmort's pompous exhortations with descriptions of the nervous, wide-eyed, giggly schoolgirls, one of whom comically falls from her seat just as the Viscountess gravely recalls "les douleurs de la Patrie" (the suffering of our homeland). Frowning but undaunted, the high-minded noblewoman admonishes this select group to pray "à Dieu Tout-Puissant pour qu'Il prenne en pitié les malheurs de notre chère France!" (to God Almighty that He may have pity on the misfortunes and miseries of our dear France!). With its haughty condescension, religious allusions, and stern moralizations, the formulation here and throughout the rest of the Viscountess's speech is vintage Pétain, issuing from the lips of Némirovsky's most staunchly and unequivocally Pétainist character, who, as we have seen, sternly points to the defeat as divine punishment and later declares in closing that "Nous n'avons qu'une seule consolation: notre cher Maréchal"[27] (We have but one sole consolation: our dear Marshal).

Némirovsky relentlessly undercuts this Pétainist discourse from within and without, on the one hand, presenting Mme de Montmort's tremolos as highly overwrought and artificial, and, on the other hand, showing her preachy exhortations to be not only inconsistent with her own personal conduct but also comically incongruous in the midst of the various local people assembled to hear them. Mme Montmort's invocation of the deity is interrupted by the entrance of the local elementary schoolteacher, who has scandalized the Viscountess's perfectly Pétainist notion of a Catholic social order by maintaining an exemplary conduct all while disdaining any and all religious gestures, even refusing to have a religious funeral for her husband. Némirovsky first subverts the Viscountess's pious pretensions by pointing out the true reason for her indignation: the fear

27    Némirovsky, *Suite française*, 355.

that too many people would understand that religion was not a pre-requisite for ethical conduct. The author then heightens the irony by specifying that the presence of this ideological and social enemy only added to the Viscountess's rhetorical flourishes.[28]

At this juncture as throughout the entire chapter, perhaps the most devastatingly satirical of *Dolce,* the irony of situation is doubled by that of discourse. All while thinking to herself that she had paid eight hundred francs for her shoes and could have all the footwear she wanted thanks to the rationing tickets she could get through the mayor, who just happened to be her husband, the Viscountess en-courages the schoolgirls to pen letters, and then enjoins the petty bourgeois housewives and local farming women to practice charity not by giving money but by donating butter, chocolate, sugar, and to-bacco for the prisoners who had no family to send them packages. The text underscores the artificiality of the Vicountess's spirited in-tervention by directing our attention to both the form and the content of her speech:

Pensez, continua la vicomtesse *d'une voix vibrante,* pensez à la joie du pauvre abandonné lorsqu'il lira ces lignes où palpitera en quelque sorte l'âme du pays et qui lui rappellera les hommes, les femmes, les enfants, les arbres, les maisons de sa chère petite patrie, celle, comme l'a dit le poète, qui nous fait aimer la grande davantage. Surtout, mes enfants, laissez aller votre coeur. *Ne cherchez pas des effets de style:* que le talent épistolaire se taise et que parle le coeur. . . . Ah, le coeur, dit la vicomtesse *en fermant à demi les yeux,* rien de beau, rien de grand ne se fait sans lui. Vous pourrez mettre dans votre lettre quelque modeste fleur des champs, une pâquerette, une primevère . . . je ne pense pas que les règlements s'y opposent. Cette idée vous plaît-elle? demanda la vicomtesse *en mettant la tête un peu de côté avec un gracieux sourire:* voyons, voyons, j'ai assez parlé. A vous maintenant.[29]

"Just think," the Viscountess continued *in a trembling voice,* "think of the poor abandoned prisoner of war's joy when he reads these lines that in a

28  Némirovsky, *Suite française,* 352.

29  Némirovsky, *Suite française,* 353; emphasis mine.

way convey the heartbeat of our country and that will recall to his mind the men, women, children, trees, and houses of his dear little hometown, which, as the poet has stated, makes us love our country all the more. Above all, my children, speak from your heart. *Do not seek stylistic flourishes:* let your talent remain silent and speak from the heart . . . Ah, the heart," said the Viscountess *while half-closing her eyes,* "nothing beautiful, nor anything grand can be achieved without the heart. You can put in some simple flower from the fields, a daisy, a primrose. . . . I don't think regulations prohibit them. Does this idea meet your liking?" asked the Viscountess, *tilting her head a bit to one side with a graceful smile:* "Well now, I have spoken long enough. It's your turn now."

The Viscountess's own florid and rather maudlin preciosity stands in direct opposition to the unadorned sincerity she recommends to the schoolgirls. At the same time, her affected intonation and highly mannered delivery seem to reach excesses of gothic proportions. While clearly a caricature, these traits would not have appeared implausible to readers of the Occupation years, who were regularly treated to a number of highly public expressions of Pétainism that we now perceive as ludicrously sententious and affected: one only has to listen to a recording of the inane stanzas of "Maréchal, nous voilà!" (Marshal, here we are!) dedicated to Pétain. The servile, mawkish worship of the deified Marshall Pétain is readily apparent from the opening stanza and refrain:

> Une flamme sacrée monte du sol natal
> Et la France enivrée Te salue Maréchal!
> Tous tes enfants qui t'aiment et vénèrent tes ans,
> à ton appel suprême, ont répondu "Présent!"
>
> (refrain)
> Maréchal, nous voilà!
> Devant toi, le sauveur de la France,
> nous jurons, nous tes gars de servir et de suivre tes pas.
> Maréchal, nous voilà!
> Tu nous as redonné l'espérance. La Patrie renaîtra.
> Maréchal, Maréchal, nous voilà!

"Here We Are, Marshal!"
A sacred flame arises from our native soil
And an ecstatic France salutes you, Marshal!
All your children that love you and worship your years
Have answered "Present!" to your call!

(refrain)
Here we are, Marshal!
Before you, the savior of France
We who are your lads swear to serve you and follow in your steps.
Here we are, Marshal!
You gave us hope once again. The homeland shall be reborn.
Here we are, Marshal![30]

One can also point out the distinct tremolos in the voice of Georges Lamirand haranging the public as documented in both *Le Chagrin et la pitié* and *Weapons of the Spirit,* to realize that Némirovsky closely patterned the viscountess's speech after widely familiar examples of Vichy propaganda. How better to hold it up for ridicule?

Némirovsky not only parodies the tone and thematic register of Vichy discourse, she goes on to mock its ideological underpinnings, primarily by foregrounding the social class of each speaker and the attendant socioeconomic origins of the rancors evident in the various responses to the Viscountess's appeal. The emblematically petty bourgeois notary public's wife tartly recalls that not everyone is so privileged as Mme de Montmort, since unpropertied townspeople have problems getting badly needed eggs and milk, even when they have just given birth. The eminently peasant Cécile Labarie pipes up and gives everyone an earful, protesting against the insinuation of black marketeering in the country farms. When she alleges that the monied bourgeois women have been snatching up ration tickets for money, the Viscountess can only despair of such "ventres doués de parole" (bellies gifted with the faculty of speech). The notary public's

30  The text of the song can found under "Extraits de la chanson 'Maréchal, nous voilà!'" at www.hist-geo.com/Texte/Marechal-Nous-Voila.php. An audio recording of the entire piece is even available at the following (eulogistically Pétainist) website: www.marechal-petain.com/chanson/chansondetails.htm.

wife, all while recalling to herself that she has been seen taking two lamb legs from the butcher's within one week, snaps back that towns-people don't have the reserves of farmers who hoard their hams, sausages, and bacon. The wide disparity between the Viscountess's exhortations and the petty socioeconomic sniping between bourgeois and farm people produces a highly comical irony that totally subverts the Pétainist notions of traditional hierarchies and patriotic piety.

Sensing imminent disaster, Mme de Montmort summons all the fervor she can manage and urges the women to think higher than the vulgar concerns of eggs, milk, and pigs. She therefore plays her rhetorical ace cards by invoking "notre cher Maréchal" (our dear Marshal) and World War I veterans along with the prisoners of war now detained in Germany. She thus admonishes her feisty audience to remain "unies comme l'étaient les poilus dans les tranchées, comme le sont, je n'en doute pas, nos chers prisonniers dans leurs camps, derrière leurs fils de fer barbelés ..."[31] (united as were the World War I soldiers in the trenches, and as are, I trust, our dear prisoners in their camps, behind their barbed wire ...). The Viscountess's hortatory labors are not entirely in vain since Némirovsky depicts the local women as moved by the thought of their men, for whom they are struggling to preserve home and property. But even though we see them volunteering food, Némirovsky underscores their ongoing rivalries and mutual suspicions by noting that they whisper the nature and amount of their donations into Mme de Montmort's ear, not wanting to be overheard by the others:

Seulement, elles se méfiaient de la voisine; elles ne voulaient pas paraître plus riches qu'elles n'étaient [sic]; elles craignaient les dénonciations: de maison à maison on cachait ses biens; la mére et la fille s'espionnaient et se dénonçaient mutuellement; les ménagères fermaient la porte de leur cuisine au moment des repas pour que l'odeur ne trahisse point le lard qui crépitait sur la poêle, ni la tranche de viande interdite, ni le gâteau fait avec de la farine prohibée.[32]

31   Némirovsky, Suite française, 355.
32   Némirovsky, Suite française, 356.

The only thing was that they mistrusted their neighbors. They didn't want to appear richer than they were, and they were afraid of denunciations. From one home to another, people hid their goods. Mothers and daughters spied on each other and turned each other in. Housewives would close the door to their kitchens during mealtime so that the smell of bacon sizzling in the frying pan wouldn't give them away with their cut of forbidden meat and their cake made from prohibited flour.

We would do well not to underestimate the ideological implications of what may at first glance appear to be simply a humorous portrayal of petty provincial squabbling. This passage in fact touches on two of the most sensitive matters that concretely impacted virtually everyone on French territory and left nobody indifferent during the Dark Years: namely, denunciations and the ubiquitous obsession with food.

The spying and snitching referred to here concern the problems of ration tickets and black market activity, which were in fact serious enough in themselves, since violations could result in arrest and imprisonment. The cases of betrayal not only among economic competitors but even among friends, neighbors, and family members are now known to have been numerous and widespread, symptomatic of a veritable collective psychopathology unleashed by the rigors of the Occupation. Often involving accusations of Resistance activity or revelations of Jewish identity, denunciations could prove to be highly lethal to their victims. It is precisely because denunciation was such a disturbing reality that Clouzot's *Le Corbeau* touched such a sensitive nerve in 1943 as well as after the war: the film scandalized both Vichy and the Resistance even though it only told the story of malicious gossip conveyed by anonymous letters and made no reference to the war or the Occupation.[33] Some three decades later in the early 1970s, as the veil of historical prudery was beginning to be lifted off the stark realities of the Dark Years, both Marcel Ophüls' *Le Chagrin et la pitié* and Louis Malle's *Lacombe Lucien* shocked French audiences by conspicuously pointing to the denunciations that had ravaged French society during the Occupation. Any doubts that one might

33  Cf. Vinen, *The Unfree French*, 177.

have about Némirovsky's awareness of these denunciations and of their sinister implications about French behavior during the Occupation are definitively shattered by her explicit reference to them at one of the most dramatic junctures of the plot in *Dolce*, when Lucile reveals that Benoît has been hiding in the cellar. When Mme Angellier haughtily proclaims that "Les Français ne se vendent pas les uns les autres"[34] (French people do not sell each other out), Lucile points out that the local German command has been receiving piles of anonymous letters from French residents accusing their compatriots of all sorts of offenses, and that the Germans could easily imprison almost everybody if they acted on these denunciations.[35]

Similar observations must be made with respect to the matter of food. On the one hand, the stealthy attempts to hoard prize commodities and hide illegally acquired goodies from the overly curious eyes of neighbors and landlords may appear to contemporary eyes as silly as the food fights in *Astérix*. Yet it is precisely the hopelessly petty nature of these local women's priorities that makes a total mockery of the Viscountess's moral pretensions, and therefore of Vichy. There also a very serious aspect to this subject. In the French context, the subject of food concerns far more than culinary pleasure: it remains even now as it was then heavily invested with sensitive implications of a cultural and even ideological character, involving notions of power, status, refinement, privilege, patrimony, and national identity. France's legendary predilection for fine food and drink was only accentuated by the rigors of the German occupation, during which the vast majority suffered severe shortages of the most basic commodities while at the same time the Germans siphoned off huge amounts of agricultural goods for their own consumption.[36] Little wonder then, that when asked, in *Le Chagrin et la pitié*, what was his first priority during the Occupation, the pharmacist Verdier unhesitatingly replies "Manger!" (Eating!). Such intense investment of food

---

34   Némirovsky, *Suite française*, 479.

35   Némirovsky, *Suite française*, 479.

36   Cf. Ousby, *Occupation: The Ordeal of France 1940–1944*, 116–20.

with social and political connotations can also be found throughout Némirovsky's *Suite française*. We have already seen that the social class conflict between Gabriel Corte and the working-class people with whom the civilian exodus brought him face to face was brought to a dramatic head by a basket of delectable food and champagne emblematic of his highly egocentric notions of class privilege. Similarly, our analysis of Mme Angellier's inventory has already shown to what degree her prized foodstuffs and wines were invested with bourgeois signification and symptomatic of her miserly materialism. The mutually visceral hatred opposing the Viscountess and her tenant farmer Benoît Labarie is centered on a centuries-old dispute over hunting wild game and enjoying the fruits of the land.

By comically spotlighting the squabble over food occasioned by the Viscountess's Pétainist harang, Némirovsky implies that the infighting and class resentment in this thoroughly agrarian and Catholic corner of the country's heartland is neither a foreign import nor a result of 1789, but an enduring and quintessentially French trait of national character. Her narrative therefore demolishes the falsely nostalgic images of socioeconomic harmony and submissive patriotic devotion that were supposed to result from the National Revolution's return to the soil and traditional hierarchy. We moreover measure the radical divide between Mme de Montmort's ostensibly missionary aspirations and her utter contempt for her nonaristocratic compatriots when Némirovsky narrates the Viscountess's innermost thoughts and feelings at the close of the meeting:

la vicomtesse devait faire un petit effort pour serrer cette main dont le contact lui était physiquement désagréable. Mais elle dominait ce sentiment contraire à la charité chrétienne et, par esprit de mortification, elle se forçait à embrasser les enfants qui accompagnaient leurs mères; ils étaient tous gras et roses, gavés et barbouillés comme de petits porcs.

Enfin, la salle fut vide. L'institutrice avait fait sortir les fillettes; les fermières étaient parties. La vicomtesse soupira, non de fatigue, mais d'écoeurement. Que l'humanité était laide et basse! Quel mal il fallait se donner pour faire palpiter une lueur d'amour dans ces tristes âmes. . . . "Pouah!" se dit-elle tout haut, mais, comme le lui recommandait son directeur de conscience, elle offrit à Dieu les fatigues et les travaux de cette journée.[37]

the Viscountess had to make a bit of an effort to shake this hand that for her was physically unpleasant to touch. But she overcame this feeling that was contrary to Christian charity, and in a spirit of mortifying the flesh, she forced herself to kiss the children who were accompanying their mothers; they were all overfed and pink, stuffed and smudged like little pigs.

At last the room was empty. The schoolteacher had dismissed the little girls and the farming ladies had left. The Viscountess sighed, not with fatigue, but with disgust. How ugly and base humanity was! What great pains one had to go to in order to kindle up a glimmer of love in these sad souls. . . . "Yuck!" she said aloud to herself. But as her director of conscience had recommended, she offered the labors and fatigue of this day to God.

Physically palpable and verbally explicit, Mme de Montmort's disgust thus punctuates Némirovsky's implacable satire of Bussy's most prominent champion of Pétain and the National Revolution.

We can now more fully appreciate the significance of Némirovsky's thoroughly ironic narrative with respect to both the dominent discourses of her time and the conventional wisdom of our own. Here again, it is crucial to measure the radical disparity between her perspective and ours, her preoccupation and ours, her perception of events and ours. The fact that her text was only recently published and therefore read in the context of today, with all the knowledge that we now have and with our particular focus, tends to telescope contexts and blur perspectives. Our perspective is that of memory, of valorizing what has disappeared or what has been lost or destroyed. We justifiably want to know how and why the loss occurred and who perpetrated the destruction. Ours is an irremediably post-Holocaust, post-Paxtonian perspective. Némirovsky's references are the 1920s, 1930s, and 1940s. In many instances, our age wants to use the text to confirm or to convey notions that are now commonplace. While An-

---

37  Némirovsky, *Suite française*, 356–57.

gela Kershaw is certainly correct in observing that *Suite française*'s depiction of the Occupation "proves that resistancialism was false,"[38] her perspective nevertheless remains anachronistic, since "resistancialism" was a postwar phenomenon and not an issue for the early 1940s when Némirovsky was writing her novel. In claiming that *Suite française* shows Némirovsky not only to have overcome the "naivete" of thinking that she could as an author control the meaning of her text but even to have resigned herself to the supposed reality of social construction of meaning imposed by context, Kershaw fails to recognize the deliberately corrosive nature of *Dolce*'s social satire, which we have demonstrated to be a thoroughly conscious subversion of Vichy ideology.

Christopher Lloyd, who finds *Dolce* only "gently satirical," is nevertheless equally off the mark in viewing Némirovsky as an author preoccupied "with the forces of history."[39] Our analysis has shown that Némirovsky focuses not on history, but on the concrete structure and function of social class as visible in the small provincial town of Bussy as well as in myriad aspects of her characters' mind-sets, lifestyles, and discourse. Némirovsky captures the drama of individuals entangled in the webs of a hypocritical and seemingly inflexible social order, with its codes, expectations, prejudices, rancors, rigid rules, and injustice. Her narrative is artistically much bolder and more complex than Vercors's in that it does not present an idyllic image of provincial quietude, warmth, and familial solidarity. As is the case in *Tempête en juin, Dolce* scrutinizes with particular intensity the attitudes and behaviors of the wealthy and the privileged, that is, of property-rich bourgeois and aristocrats. The war and the fight to the death between the Allies and the Axis do not appear as defining hearts, minds, and lives, but only as encroachments on private lives. Conversely, characters define themselves only secondarily with respect to matters of nation and politics, mainly focusing on their own interests.

38  Angela Kershaw, "Finding Irène Némirovsky," *French Cultural Studies* 18, no. 1 (February 2007): 59–81, quote from 77.

39  Lloyd, "Irène Némirovsky's *Suite française* and the Crisis of Rights and Identity," 172, 177.

Némirovsky does not explicitly issue a call to resistance or deliver a direct indictment of Vichy policy (as opposed to discourse). *Dolce* nevertheless provides a valuable contribution to understanding the Dark Years both for her contemporaries and for us today. In the first place, her depiction of provincial life under the Occupation proves to be much closer than was Vercors's *Le Silence de la mer* to the actual concerns of the vast majority of French people who, without collaborating or resisting, tended to lay low and ride out the storm, watching out first and foremost for what they considered to be their own vital interests. The reality is that most French people did not construct their identities, articulate their feelings, or conduct their lives in rigid conformity to ideological constructs or fault lines central to our own contemporary efforts to separate collaborators from resisters. They were much more driven by exactly the sorts of social and psychological vectors that Némirovsky highlights. Her thematic emphases are indeed emblematic of the preoccupations of her time: food, prisoners of war, the absence of men, social rancor, interactions with omnipresent Germans, and local assertions of power and authority under Pétain and Vichy. The glaring omission is that of the Jewish question. Here again, however, Némirovsky resembles the vast majority of her contemporaries: largely absorbed by their own concerns, they (tragically and unacceptably, and for reasons including anti-Semitism) took little notice of Vichy's persecution of the Jews. We should remember that, like virtually all of those issuing calls to resistance in 1940 and 1941 (when both *Le Silence de la mer* and *Dolce* were written), Vercors, although Jewish himself, does not make the slightest allusion to the Jewish question.

Némirovsky's satire of this traditional agrarian social order, mindset, and behavior paradigms in the fictional town of Bussy does not directly provide us with a template for understanding the Vichy regime. It nonetheless provides an uncompromising close-up view of provincial life in the early Occupation years. By gauging the sharp divisions and deep-seated tensions mercilessly highlighted by Némirovsky's narrative, we are much better equipped to understand the virtual civil war created by the German occupation. By clearly exposing the fierce, unseemly rivalries of sex, cultural tradition, and socioeconomic class at work in Bussy, *Dolce* points to the gaping disparity between Vichy ideology and its schmalzy images of such a France, on the one hand, and the concrete reality French society, on the other. As we will see in the following chapter, Némirovsky's narrative also delivers a brutally frank portrayal of the French population's accommodation of the Germans and the attraction of many French women to the German soldiers in their midst.

CHAPTER 6

# PORTRAITS OF THE NAZIS AS YOUNG MEN

## Unwelcome Visitors

France's stinging defeat brought into full public view the Wehrmacht soldiers marching down the Champs-Élysées, relaxing in countless provincial Cafés de Commerce, and camping in farms and châteaux, in each case profoundly changing the visible texture of everyday life. Philippe Burrin points out that the presence of German troops in the most venerated sites in France's urban and rural landscapes also crept into the innermost nooks and crannies of the French mind, even into their dreams.[1] The extended stay of these uninvited guests who had overrun the French army, thrown the nation into chaos, and taken prisoner some two million of its men constituted the most tangible sign of France's humiliating defeat, its now precarious status, and its highly uncertain future. Having suffered the ravages of war in their proverbial own backyard, the French now found Hitler's soldiers taking quarter in their homes, even pulling up a chair at their dinner table. For the early phases of the German occupation of France as well as for our own times, one can hardly overemphasize the impact of the omnipresent German soldiers on the French imagi-

1  Burrin, *La France à l'heure allemande*, 198.

nation. It is no coincidence that Vercors uses the figure of the uninvited guest as the premise of *Le Silence de la mer* and as a metonymy for the Occupation in general. The image of the Germans in the eyes of the French proved to be psychologically unsettling and politically crucial for everyone, including Vichy, the occupying forces, the early Resistance movements, the Allies, and the French populace itself.

Némirovsky's depiction of the Germans accordingly constitutes a critical component of her narrative and carries powerful political implications. Once again, however, we must take care to avoid the hasty judgments and premature conclusions too often brought on by Manichaean approaches seeking to divide everyone into two absolutely opposite, mutually exclusive camps of resisters and collaborators, heroes and villains. In the historical context of the early Dark Years, as in the aesthetics of Némirovsky's novel, the issues prove on the contrary to be multiple while reality remains opaque and somewhat ambiguous. The value of *Suite française* as a literary text offering powerful and disturbing representations of the French experience of World War II up until June 22, 1941, comes precisely from a rich and at times problematical complexity. In order to appreciate Némirovsky's specific contribution to our current understanding of the war years in France, we must here again adumbrate methodically and in some detail the historical and discursive background for her novel while at the same time examining the specific textual contours of her representation of the Germans.

Némirovsky formulates the question of German identity with much more ambivalence than we are now accustomed to. On the one hand, a relatively high degree of ideological indeterminacy brings us back to the quandary we face in reading and deciphering Némirovsky's *Suite française* in general, particularly in view of the momentous and problematical nature of national identity for Némirovsky as a Russian Jewish émigré who was denied French citizenship, arrested by French gendarmes, and finally murdered by the Nazis at Auschwitz. Our now largely unequivocal perception of the Holocaust and of Vichy's criminal complicity with the Nazis makes it difficult to perceive the considerable measure of historical uncertainty and moral confusion that characterized French public opinion during the first half of the Occupation. Burrin points out that before the massive roundups of Jews and brutal repressions of the Resistance in 1942—in other words, before the events that, while foremost in our own minds, were unknown to Némirovsky as she wrote her novel—the French tended to waver in their attitudes and hesitate in their conduct.[2] While most strongly opposed collaboration with the Germans and fervently hoped for an English victory, they did not always favor armed resistance. The numerous material hardships of everyday life and the highly uncertain prospects for an Allied victory gave pause to the vast majority of people in France. Only a tiny minority actively resisted, and many early resisters continued to look favorably on Pétain.[3] What we thus might describe as a sort of wait-and-see survivalism translated into a certain amount of ambiguity in everyday contacts with Germans.

Just as Léon Werth bemoans the lack of clear rules and guidelines to govern appropriate interaction between German troops and French civilians,[4] so Burrin indicates that the French were for the most part left on their own, largely dependent on ancestral reflexes in reacting to these enemy troops that, although fabled to be cruel, now often appeared almost benign.[5] The fact of the matter was that in general the French populace remained frightfully ignorant of the specifics—not to mention the sinister implications—of Nazi ideology.[6] This lack of empirical knowledge meant that in attempting to forge their own image of the invader, they most often either reached back into the collective memory of previous German invasions or else relied on the rumors that became so wildly abundant during the chaos and confusion of the civilian exodus. On the one hand, fearing barbarians who massacred civilians, cut off children's hands, and left homes damaged and soiled with human waste, they could, on

2  Burrin, *La France à l'heure allemande*, 202.

3  Burrin, *La France à l'heure allemande*, 193–95, 203.

4  Werth, *33 jours*, 166.

5  Burrin, *La France à l'heure allemande*, 198.

6  Burrin, *La France à l'heure allemande*, 46–47, and Ousby, *Occupation: The Ordeal of France, 1940–1944*, 49.

the other hand, often find themselves relieved and even impressed to see disciplined, well-groomed columns marching in singing and approaching the local population with courtesy. The widely posted propaganda images showing a smiling young German soldier holding a child aimed to exploit France's vague, incoherent ideas about Hitler's real intentions: "Populations abandonnées, faites confiance au soldat allemand"[7] (Abandoned people, trust German soldiers).

Everything in *Dolce* suggests that, rather than benefiting from some superior source of information or privileged viewpoint on Nazi Germany, Némirovsky largely shared the confused, sometimes contradictory, perspectives of the local French population that she depicts in her novel. Her description of the Germans' entry into Bussy is on that score revealing. As she details the specific components of the Wehrmacht unit parading down the main street and into the center of this small provincial town, we share the perspective of the townspeople awed by the impeccable organization and impressive array of cannons, tanks, and horses. The rhythmic thud of boots marching in step serves as a suggestive metonymy both of the imposing presence of the German army and of the military domination that resulted in the French having to live "sous la botte des Allemands" (under the thumb of the Germans). Némirovsky thus punctuates her description with references to the ominous sounds of raw power: "Le bruit des bottes allemandes régna seul. . . . De grands chars gris de fer martelaient les pavés. . . . Ils étaient si nombreux qu'une espèce de tonnerre ininterrompu ne cessa de résonner sous les voûtes de l'église. . . . Lorsque décrut ce grondement d'airain, apparurent les motocyclistes entourant l'auto du commandant"[8] (The thud of the Germans boots reigned over all. . . . Big iron-gray tanks were pounding the cobblestones. . . . They were so many of them that a sort of uninterrupted thunder resounded unceasingly under the vaulted ceiling of the church. . . . When this brass rumbling died down, there

---

7   Cf. Burrin, *La France à l'heure allemande*, 27–28, 41. Némirovsky clearly describes this propaganda poster with detail at the beginning of chapter 2 in *Dolce*, 314.

8   Némirovsky, *Suite française*, 307–8.

appeared soldiers on motorcycles surrounding the commander's car). The thunderous German procession moreover stands in stark opposition to the plaintive notes of the harmonium, the muffled prayers, and the sighs of the women in the church.

Némirovsky further accentuates the Germans' smugly triumphant military display with the timorous apprehension of the local French population by contrasting the prancing horses and strutting soldiers with the furtive gazes of the elderly women who peer through shuttered windows and whisper misgivings about the Germans' rapacious brutality: "derrière chaque volet clos un oeil de vieille femme, perçant comme un dard, épiait le soldat vainqueur. Au fond des chambres invisibles des voix gémissaient"[9] (behind each closed shutter was an elderly woman peering at the victorious soldiers with eyes as piercing as a stinger. In the back of invisible rooms voices were moaning). This correlation between the image projected by the German occupying forces and the attitudes of the subjugated French citizens watching them is no accident. Just as *Tempête en juin* shows how accounts of the debacle vary considerably from one subjective viewpoint to another, so *Dolce* connects the images of the Germans to the particular identity and situation of their observers. Némirovsky therefore makes our view of the Germans coextensive with our understanding of the French personages in her narrative. Here again, the contrast with *Le Silence de la mer* is telling. Whereas Vercors makes von Ebrennac almost entirely allegorical, and thus emblematic of the German mind-set, manners, and culture, we almost always see the Germans in *Dolce* as filtered in various ways through the particularly shaded lenses of different French characters.

### In the Eyes of the Observers

The inaugural portrait of the Germans found in chapter 1 of *Dolce* in fact indicates that the characters' perceptions are filtered through the mind-set common to their own social group as well as through

9  Némirovsky, *Suite française*, 308.

their own specific experiences. On the one hand, Némirovsky juxtaposes the Germans' ceremoniously proud entry into Bussy with the defensive posture of the local residents huddled together in the church and hiding behind the shuttered windows. The French citizenry of this little provincial town thus responds to the intimidating force collectively projected by the Germans with their commonly shared fears of their foes' legendary barbarity:

Au fond des chambres invisibles des voix gémissaient.
   —On aura tout vu. . . .
   —Ça démolit nos arbres à fruit, malheur!
Une bouche édentée chuchota:
   —Paraît que ceux-là sont les pires. Paraît qu'ils ont fait du vilain avant de venir ici.[10]

In the back of invisible rooms voices were moaning.
   "Now we've seen everything. . . ."
   "They're ruining our fruit trees!"
A mouth with missing teeth whispered:
   "People say that these are the worst. They say that these soldiers did some really ugly stuff before coming here."

Némirovsky points to the generic nature of this response by leaving the voices unnamed and by having them repeat the expression "Paraît que" (People say that) commonly used to pass on rumors. On the other hand, she highlights the specifically bourgeois response to the overbearing presence of the Wehrmacht: "Le bourg s'emplit d'un bruit de bottes, de voix étrangères, du cliquetis des éperons et des armes. Dans les maisons bourgeoises, on cachait le beau linge"[11] (The town was filled with the thud of boots, the voices of foreigners, the clinking of spurs and guns. In bourgeois homes, people were hiding their fine linens). Then follows the previously discussed account of Mme Angellier's meticulous inventory and careful hiding of her most precious commodities, which depicts this quintessentially bourgeois personage as concerned first and foremost with the danger of pillaging.

10  Némirovsky, *Suite française*, 308.    11  Némirovsky, *Suite française*, 309.

Burrin, among others, observes that during the Occupation the various social classes thus reacted in collectively different manners to the Germans.[12] France's high degree of social stratification resulted in contrasting, often conflicting vital interests. With varying sensibilities drawing attention to different aspects of German behavior, we can hardly be surprised to find individuals from different milieus approaching the Germans in appreciably different ways in *Dolce*. Throughout her *Suite française*, Némirovsky foregrounds individuals struggling against the overwhelming forces of society and history that far outstrip her characters' capacity to control their lives. In order to gauge the significance of the highly nuanced and somewhat ambivalent individual responses to the Germans detailed in *Dolce*, we must first analyze how she depicts them both on a collective level and in relation to social origins. A quick survey of *Dolce's* second chapter turns up virtually all of the major components of the complex and often contradictory relations between the Germans and the local inhabitants.

On one level, *Dolce* depicts a notable disjunction between, on the one hand, the abstract rhetoric and the public demeanor that formed the collective façade of both French and German behavior, and, on the other hand, the concrete reality one found in everyday individual contacts between occupying forces and local residents. Once more, Némirovsky's fictional narrative of these first encounters corresponds to historical reality with remarkable nuance and detail. It is now widely known that, far from leaving the legendarily important first impressions to happenstance, the Germans took care to appear disciplined, courteous, and even benevolent to the French populace. Not wanting to devote numerous troops and resources to administering occupied territory at the very time when he was attempting to bring Great Britain to its knees and preparing to expand his conquests on other fronts, Hitler had every interest in assuaging fears and cultivating quiescence in France. The first official measure we find the Germans enacting in chapter 2 of *Dolce* is to post on the walls of public

12   Burrin, *La France à l'heure allemande*, 207.

buildings a certain number of warnings and propaganda posters. As we have already noted, the most prominent poster encourages the locals to trust these soldiers of the Wehrmacht: "Populations abandonnées, faites confiance aux soldats du Reich!"[13] (Abandoned people, trust the soldiers of the Reich!) These efforts to make the Occupation seem anodyne were not in vain. Even though the terms of the armistice agreement resulted in France having to pay some sixty percent of its economic production to Germany,[14] the French heaved a collective sigh of relief in seeing that they would not suffer a fate similar to Poland's and that German troops exercised relative restraint in their dealings with French civilians. As the well-known and often cited expression would have it, "ils sont corrects"[15] (they behave decently). Vercors has his narrator echo this widespread sentiment in *Le Silence de la mer*. Noting von Ebrennac's highly formal, if stilted, manners and use of French, he mutters "Dieu merci, il a l'air convenable"[16] ("Thank God, he seems well-mannered").

### Close Encounters of the Third Reich

Némirovsky represents the alternating apprehension and relief of these first encounters with considerably more nuance in chapter 19 of *Tempête en juin*, which reveals the chasm of disparity between local fears of "quelque vision de l'Apocalypse" (some vision of the Apocalypse) or "quelque monstre étrange et effrayant" (some strange and frightening monster) and the mundane demeanor of this first German, in reality just "un soldat comme les autres" (a soldier like the others) who asks for a light and for directions.[17] Since, as we learn in chapter 2 of *Dolce*, Bussy has seen two other contingents of the Wehrmacht, Némirovsky conveys the proverbial sigh of relief by show-

13    Némirovsky, *Suite française*, 314.

14    Ousby, *Occupation: The Ordeal of France, 1940–1944*, 66.

15    Ousby, *Occupation: The Ordeal of France, 1940–1944*, 54–55. Cf. Burrin, *La France à l'heure allemande*, 28–29.

16    Vercors, *Le Silence de la mer*, 23.           17    Némirovsky, *Suite française*, 164.

ing the locals literally proceeding with "business as usual," opening their shops to these men in uniform who were good customers often paying handsomely even for outdated articles. These initial portraits of both German occupying forces and local French citizens nevertheless prove to be more complex and ambivalent than those in *Le Silence de la mer*. Both French and Germans exhibit a discrepancy between their collectively projected demeanor and their individual dealings with each other. Underneath the outward display of implacable power and discipline, the soldiers marching into Bussy are seen to be eagerly surveying their surroundings in hopes of gauging what welcome might be in store for them. Even after their ostentatious entry, they continue to convey signs of dominant power by making their boots thud conspicuously on the cobblestones and by including more ominous warnings of *Verboten* and "Sous peine de mort" (Under the penalty of death) on the posters that accompany the previously mentioned image of benevolence toward the French. At the same time and in spite of their suspicions, they purchase merchandise respectfully without complaining or attempting to bargain. Even the Germans raucously drinking and flirting with the waitress in the local tavern stop well short of the much-dreaded acts of violence and destruction.

The residents of Bussy show a similar inconsistency between public posture and private interactions. On the one hand, they pretend to take no notice of these enemy intruders by presenting a façade of a closed, empty town, both in the very first encounter described in *Tempête en juin* and at the outset of *Dolce:*

Tout le village, derrière les portes fermées, par l'entrebaillement des persiennes demi-closes ou à la lucarne d'un grenier, le regardait [le premier Allemand] venir.[18]
Personne aux fenêtres.[19]

Behind closed doors, through blinds cracked slightly open, or from a skylight in the attic, the entire village was watching him [the first German] come.
Nobody at the windows.

18   Némirovsky, *Suite française*, 163.      19   Némirovsky, *Suite française*, 307.

On the other hand, they gladly open their shops and accept the Germans' money. Indeed, the shopkeepers appreciate the German taste for French goods, just as the waitress flushes with embarrassment and pleasure at her sudden wealth of masculine attention. In a later chapter, Némirovsky shows a husband take pride in a young German's unabashed admiration of his wife's legs, while almost everyone enjoys seeing the Germans' appetite for French food and drink.

Lucile, the central character of *Dolce,* scandalously fails to maintain her personal space separate from that of the German officer Bruno von Falk in several important ways that will warrant extended discussion in our next chapter. She is hardly the only person whose conduct does not conform to expected standards. As we have seen, Némirovsky indicates that behind the façade of closed windows and blinds, numerous eyes closely follow the German entry: "Mais derrière chaque volet clos un oeil de vieille femme, perçant comme un dard, épiait le soldat vainqueur"[20] (But behind each closed shutter was an elderly woman peering at the victorious soldiers with eyes as piercing as a stinger). In chapter 6, we find the local population fascinated by these Germans who continue to parade around the town singing. The text moreover underscores the specifically feminine interest in these strapping young Germans:

"Nos maîtres," disaient les femmes qui regardaient l'ennemi avec une sorte de concupiscence haineuse. (Ennemis? Certes. . . . Mais des hommes, et jeunes).[21]

Ces hommes grands, bien bâtis, avec leurs visages durs et leurs voix harmonieuses, les femmes les suivaient longtemps du regard.[22]

"Our masters," said the women who were looking at the enemy with a kind of hateful lust. (Enemies? Certainly. . . . But [they were] men, and young).

For a long time, the women kept their eyes on these tall, strapping men with harsh faces and harmonious voices.

---

20  Némirovsky, *Suite française,* 308.       21  Némirovsky, *Suite française,* 316.

22  Némirovsky, *Suite française,* 344.

The most glaring example occurs in the penultimate chapter (21) of *Dolce* when a good number of local people cheerfully lend fine linens and silverware for the Germans' outdoor banquet on the château grounds and then turn out in large numbers to take in the festivities, including both music and toasts with "Heil Hitler!" The text even specifies that "tout le pays était là"[23] (everybody in the surrounding area was there). The same is true for the departure of the German troops described in the final chapter. Once again, virtually the entire town of Bussy is there to see them off: "Il était tard, mais personne ne songeait à dormir. Tous voulaient voir le départ des Allemands"[24] (It was late, but nobody thought of sleeping. All wanted to see the Germans' departure). And while most are content to ogle, Némirovsky's text reports a significant amount of more wistful leavetaking: "Ça et là, dans l'ombre d'une porte, on entendait un murmure, un bruit de baisers . . . quelques adieux plus tendres que d'autres"[25] (Here and there, in the shadow of a doorway, you could hear a murmur, a sound of kissing . . . some farewells were more tender than others). There have clearly been a large number of close relationships highly compromising to official norms of national integrity.

Némirovsky sharpens her portrayal of the townspeople's double-dealing with the Germans by explicitly calling attention to the two-faceted nature of the French attitude: "Aux habitants des pays occupés, les Allemands inspiraient de la peur, du respect, de l'aversion et le désir taquin de les rouler, de profiter d'eux, de s'emparer de leur argent"[26] (Among the inhabitants of occupied countries, the Germans inspired fear, respect, aversion, and the mischievous desire to do them in, to take advantage of them, to grab their money). Contrasted with Vercors's image of the narrator and his daughter unified in resolute refusal to fraternize with even the most enlightened and refined of German soldiers, Némirovsky's depiction of the rather uneven practices in Bussy offers a much more faithful rendering of the range of behaviors that were actually observed during this early

23  Némirovsky, *Suite française*, 499.        24  Némirovsky, *Suite française*, 514.

25  Némirovsky, *Suite française*, 515.        26  Némirovsky, *Suite française*, 315.

phase of the Occupation. Philippe Burrin notes that even among populations known to be anticollaborationist and pro-English, one found locals interacting with Germans in a very friendly way, often calling them by their first name, particularly in shops.[27] Whereas *Le Silence de la mer* portrays the individual words and deeds of both French and German protagonists as totally aligned with the collective posture that was publicly expected, *Suite française* reveals the highly complex, often contradictory relationship between collective codes and individual attitudes and actions.

### Unwritten Protocols

At the same time, however, Némirovsky repeatedly points to the widely recognized, if unofficial, French code of conduct that required or at least expected French citizens to maintain their dignity and act with discretion in their contacts with the German occupation forces. As we have seen in detail, the trauma of the German invasion occasioned widespread chaos and mayhem among the civilian population, resulting in a crushing defeat and the implosion of the political institutions of the French Republic. The immediately ensuing Occupation period represented not only a visible intrusion of German soldiers over wide expanses of French territory, before the most cherished Parisian monuments, at the center of small provincial towns such as Bussy, and even into private homes: such encroachments were intimately felt in the French collective psyche as a violation of more or less sacred space. In this context, many writers decried the shameless behavior of those who gawked at German military displays or casually chatted with enemy soldiers not only as a failure to observe commonsense discretion but as a lack of collective self-respect. Athough the defeat left ordinary French people momentarily powerless to repell or even contest the presence of these intruders, they were nevertheless expected to maintain a sense of composure and national dignity with two very simple gestures intended to main-

27    Burrin, *La France à l'heure allemande*, 208.

tain a proper distance from the Germans: turning away their eyes and remaining silent.

Writing shortly after the armistice agreement had formalized the German occupation of French territory on June 25, 1940, François Mauriac articulated this imperative with compelling clarity in an article entitled "Ce Reste de fierté" (This remnant of pride): "'Ayez des yeux pour ne point voir.' C'est le mot d'ordre à donner aux Français devant l'occupation étrangère"[28] ("May you have eyes in order not to see." This is the watchword to be given to French citizens facing foreign occupation). What he had observed, however, indicated that far too many of his compatriots had failed to excercise such discretion. Hence his insistent appeal for them to help France regain its collective composure:

> On excuse ce premier mouvement de curiosité, ces figures excitées comme pour le Tour de France. Et c'est bien d'un tour de France qu'il s'agit, hélas! d'une ronde sans fin qui n'est pas près de s'interrompre. . . . Mais maintenant, vous avez compris. La correction qui s'impose à l'égard de ces visiteurs que nous n'avons pas invités doit aller de pair avec l'absence du regard, avec l'inattention de tout l'être.
>
> Que l'occupation de la France s'arrête à la surface, au pavé, au goudron des routes, qu'elle ne pénètre pas jusqu'au tuf, jusqu'au secret des sources et des âmes. Surtout qu'elle n'intéresse aucun coeur.[29]

One excuses this initial reaction of curiosity and these faces as excited as those following the Tour de France. Alas, we are indeed dealing with a Tour de France, with an endless lap that is nowhere near ending. . . . But now, you have understood. The good manners required in dealing with these uninvited guests must be of a piece with an empty gaze, with the inattention of our entire being.

Let the occupation of France stop at the surface, on the cobblestone, on the tar of the highway, let it not penetrate to the bedrock, to the secret of wellsprings and souls. Above all, may it interest not a single heart.

---

28  Mauriac, *Journal. Mémoires politiques*, 763.

29  Mauriac, *Journal. Mémoires politiques*, 763–64. Laurence Granger, who edited this new collection, also observes in her note 5 on 763 that Mauriac's watchword anticipates Vercors's *Le Silence de la mer*.

Mauriac's injunction makes it clear that ignoring the Germans' public military displays was necessary not only to refuse a servile voyeurism but even more importantly to help preserve hearts and minds from ideological contamination. Writing not in the Bordeaux region, but in Paris, Jean Texcier expressed identical concerns with his clandestinely circulated "Conseils à l'Occupé" (Advice to the occupied people):

Depuis que tu es "occupé," ils paradent en ton déshonneur. Resteras-tu à les contempler? Intéresse-toi plutôt aux étalages.[30]

Étale une belle indifférence; mais entretiens secrètement ta colère.[31]

Surveille tes barrages contre leur radio et leur presse. Surveille tes blindages contre la peur et les résignations faciles. Surveille-*toi*.[32]

Ever since you have been "occupied," they have paraded to your dishonor. Are you going to stand there watching them? Turn your interest to storefront windows instead.

Display a fine indifference; but secretly kindle your anger.

Monitor your barriers against their radio and their press. Monitor your shields against fear and facile resignation. Monitor *yourself.*

Having lost control over the public spaces of their national territory, the French were thus, according to Mauriac, Texcier, and, as we shall soon see, Jean Guéhenno, nevertheless expected to protect the integrity of their inner space, the realm of thought and feeling, by holding up a wall of indifference and inattention to the Wehrmacht's concerts and parades. This posture moreover corresponds to a collectively shared cultural tendency to conceive of liberty as the possibility of maintaining one's identity within a protected space created by setting up barriers to unwanted gazes and visitors.[33] We thus see this strategy enacted in the difficult context of the Occupation: the impossibility of erecting physical walls to keep the Germans out is compen-

---

30  Jean Texcier, *Écrit dans la nuit* (Paris: La Nouvelle Édition, 1945), 10–11.

31  Texcier, *Écrit dans la nuit*, 15.

32  Texcier, *Écrit dans la nuit*, 20.

33  Laurence Wylie and Jean-François Brière, *Les Français,* 3rd ed. (Upper Saddle River, N.J.: Prentice-Hall, 2001), 30–32, 97–98.

sated by putting up virtual partitions that create an intellectual haven for clear, resolute thinking.

Mauriac and Texcier's recoil from the groups of garrulous spectators that all too often rushed out to see the Germans illustrates a paradigmatic determination to preserve an island of independent thinking, national serenity, and self-respect. Their reactions are paralleled by the strikingly similar words of the prominent socialist and distinguished man of letters Jean Guéhenno, who recorded the singular turn of events during the Occupation period in his *Journal des années noires*. When the tidal wave of the invasion washes him ashore in Clermont-Ferrand, Guéhenno is appalled to see so many of his compatriots rush out on June 21 to watch the Germans entering the town center. That many of these thoughtless spectators were refugees having just traveled over six hundred kilometers in their attempts to flee the erstwhile dreaded Germans prompts a bitterly ironic commentary: "O bêtise. Le barbare d'hier n'est plus que la dernière attraction: on veut voir le cirque de Pinder"[34] (Oh what stupidity. Yesterday's barbarians are now only the latest attraction: people want to see the Pinder circus).

Vehemently refusing to let himself be drawn into any sort of insidious fascination, Guéhenno resolves on June 22 to shun them from his mind's eye when writing his diary: "Je ne veux rien écrire ici de ces hommes gris que je commence à croiser dans les rues. C'est l'invasion des rats"[35] (I do not want to write anything here about these men in gray whose paths I am beginning to cross in the streets. This is the invasion of the rats). Filled with anger and shame by the signing of the armistice agreement and by his compatriots' meek acquiescence, Guéhenno decides to hide his intense disapproval under a pall of silence: "Je vais m'enfoncer dans le silence. Il faut que je taise tout ce que je pense"[36] (I'm going to sink into silence. I have to hush up everthing that I am thinking). Guéhenno withdraws to

34    Jean Guéhenno, *Journal des années noires* (Paris: Gallimard, 1947), 14.

35    Guéhenno, *Journal des années noires*, 15.

36    Guéhenno, *Journal des années noires*, 16.

an inner realm of silence not to avoid conflict and keep out of trouble, but rather to create a sort of inviolable inner space within which he can continue to cultivate the ideals of intellectual liberty and human dignity that he views as the heart of his national identity. Hence his adamant refusal to be occupied: "Je me réfugierai dans mon vrai pays. Mon pays, ma France est une France qu'on n'envahit pas. . . . ce pays qui n'est qu'une idée, n'est pas envahi, ne le sera jamais"[37] (I shall take refuge in my true country. My country, my France, is a France that cannot be invaded. . . . this country is only an idea. It has not been invaded and never will be).

## Testing the Limits

*Dolce* attests to the existence of this demanding code while at the same time pointing to a full range of local reactions to the presence of the enemy forces occupying Bussy. On one level, the German presence is experienced as a violation of public space. In the cases of requisitioned lodgings, local residents seek, like Guéhenno, Texcier, and Mauriac, to preserve their personal domains from encroachment. The empty streets, closed doors, shuttered windows, and drawn blinds that Némirovsky describes in narrating the Germans' ostentatious entry into Bussy point to the widespread understanding of this mandate to preserve a minimum of integrity. When at a later juncture Lucile outrages Mme Angellier by asking about German lieutenant Bruno von Falk's injury and by watching the German soldiers as they march by, her indiscretion prompts Mme Angellier to invoke the code in explicit terms. "Vous n'avez donc aucun sens des convenances. Les Allemands doivent défiler devant des fenêtres fermées et des persiennes closes . . . comme en 70"[38] (You obviously have no sense of propriety. The Germans must parade before closed windows and shut blinds . . . as in 1870). Unmoved by such characteristically icy and often venomous reproaches from her mother-in-law, Lucile hedg-

---

37   Guéhenno, *Journal des années noires*, 16–17.

38   Némirovsky, *Suite française*, 434.

es her response by saying yes, but only the first time, when they come marching in to town. In practice, Lucile finds that the omnipresence of German soldiers in daily life makes absolute compliance unfeasible for her and virtually all of her compatriots, including Mme Angellier herself.

Unable to prevent the enemy soldiers from occupying public spaces or private dwellings, local people attempt to reestablish psychological distance by means of a linguistic gesture. We thus see Némirovsky's characters resorting to what Ousby observes to have been a widely practiced strategy: in order to signify a fundamental, irreconcilable difference between the French populace and the German occupiers, the former often refrained from designating the latter directly, preferring instead to speak of them as "ils," "ça," or "ces messieurs"[39] ("they," "that," or "these gentleman"). Both Madame Goulot, announcing the very first German arrival depicted in *Tempête en juin*, and Mme Angellier, urging Lucile to hide precious family heirlooms from the desecrating gaze of the enemy in chapter 1 of *Dolce*, use the same expression: "ils arrivent"[40] (they're coming). The Viscountess is even more emphatic, referring to the Germans as "ces messieurs" in her conspicuously indignant complaints about the Germans camping on the grounds of her château.[41] The resolutely insolent Benoît Labarie, however, makes no attempt to conceal his hatred, referring to the Germans as "les Allemands" and even "les Boches" when defying the Viscountess on her own property.[42]

The contrast between the more prevalent euphemistic third person or indefinite pronouns and Benoît Labarie's blunt designation of the Germans by their proper and improper name is emblematic of the noticeable class differences that Némirovsky highlights. Only the peasants are portrayed as consistently following the unwritten code by maintaining a proud, dignified demeanor and by refusing to cozy up to Hitler's soldiers. Finding their way back to their farms care-

39   Ousby, *Occupation: The Ordeal of France, 1940–1944*, 170.

40   Némirovsky, *Suite française*, 163, 310.     41   Némirovsky, *Suite française*, 378–79.

42   Némirovsky, *Suite française*, 448–49.

lessly blocked by bands of soldiers sauntering around the village center, the farmers simply pretend to ignore them and go out using side streets.[43] Hit hard by the Germans' requisition of their horses, they nevertheless remain stoically silent and inscrutable while enduring significantly greater suffering than any other social class: "Les paysans se taisaient. On avait pris les jeunes hommes; on avait pris le pain, le blé, la farine et les patates; on avait pris l'essence et les voitures, maintenant les chevaux. Demain, quoi? Certains d'entre eux étaient en route depuis minuit. Ils marchaient tête basse, courbés, visage impénétrable"[44] (The farmers remained silent. Their young men, their bread, their wheat, their flour, and their potatoes had been taken; their gas and cars, and now their horses had been taken. What would it be tomorrow? Some of them had been on the road since midnight. They were walking with heads down, stooped, their faces impenetrable). The only other two personages who display such dignified composure and who refuse to engage in chummy small talk are also representatives of the lower class as artisans. When the shoemaker's wife starts to converse with two German soldiers going out of their way to be friendly, she draws a curt rebuke from her husband and quickly complies: "Mais le sabotier dit à sa femme:—T'as pas besoin de causer avec eux. La femme eut honte. Elle continua sa besogne en silence"[45] (But the shoemaker said to his wife: "Yuh don't have to chat with 'm." The woman felt ashamed of herself. She went silently about her task). Even more striking is the gardener who had to bring food, tobacco, and beer to the Germans guarding their munitions depot:

Le jardinier lui donnait ce qu'il désirait, puis, appuyé sur sa bêche, il le regardait pensivement s'éloigner, et enfin il reprenait son travail avec un haussement d'épaules qui répondait sans doute à un monde de pensées, si nombreuses, si profondes, si graves et étranges qu'il ne trouvait pas de mots pour s'exprimer.[46]

43  Némirovsky, *Suite française*, 314.

45  Némirovsky, *Suite française*, 348.

44  Némirovsky, *Suite française*, 456.

46  Némirovsky, *Suite française*, 367–68.

The gardener gave him what he wanted, then, leaning on his shovel, watched pensively as the German went away, and finally resumed his work with a shrug of the shoulders that was doubtless given in response to a world of thoughts so numerous, so deep, so grave and strange that he couldn't find words to express himself.

Némirovsky's portrayal of the unassuming silence that guarded the gardener's powerful meditations parallels Vercors's famous description of the sea of emotions swirling beneath the taciturn faces of the narrator and his daughter.

Némirovsky's clearest delineation of the code of conduct required to preserve both national honor and individual dignity in the presence of victorious enemy troops appears when Madeleine and Benoît Labarie find themselves sharing their table with the German officer Kurt Bonnet who has requisitioned lodging in their farm home. Though highly educated and capable of cultural sophistication, Bonnet brazenly flirts with Madeleine and finds amusement in provoking his unwilling French hosts with an indiscrete query that rudely calls attention to the most sensitive of topics, the humiliating defeat suffered by the French at the hands of the Germans.

—Et que pensent les Français, monsieur, de l'issue de la guerre? demanda Bonnet.

Les femmes se regardèrent avec une expression scandalisée. Ça ne se faisait pas. On ne parlait pas avec un Allemand de la guerre, ni de celle-ci ni de l'autre, ni du Maréchal Pétain, ni de Mers-el-Kébir, ni de la coupure de la France en deux tronçons, ni des troupes occupantes, ni de rien qui comptât. Il n'y avait qu'une attitude possible: une affectation de froide indifférence, le ton par lequel Benoît répondit en levant son verre plein à ras bord de vin rouge:

—Ils s'en foutent, monsieur.[47]

"And what, Sir, do the French think of the outcome of the war?" asked Bonnet.

The women looked at each other with shocked faces. You just could not do that. You could not talk about the war with a German, neither about the recent war nor about the preceding war, nor about Marshal Pétain, nor about Mers-el-Kébir,[48] nor about France having been cut in two, nor about occupation troops, nor about anything that mattered. There was only one possible attitude: an affectation of cold indifference, the tone with which Benoît responded while lifting his glass full to the brim with red wine.

"The French, Sir, don't give a f***."

This seemingly simple exchange is in reality highly charged with powerful subtexts. Rather than merely making conversation and sounding out Benoît's opinions, Bonnet is in fact gloating over the Germans' presumed superiority and France's alleged guilt while at the same time rubbing his hosts' proverbial noses in the mess of their own defeat. For all their lack of the highbrow literary culture acquired from formal schooling largely characteristic of the bourgeoisie, these farming women display an unequivocal recognition of and devotion to national and personal honor: they are scandalized by Bonnet's invitation to engage in musings that would constitute a breech of protocol. "Ça ne se faisait pas" (You could not do that) clearly conveys both their lucid perception and firm resolution. Even though the German is holding formidable trump cards in terms of arms and military reinforcements, Benoît proves to be up to this risky round of psychological poker, not only seeing his adversary's cocky bid, but raising him one by ironically apposing "monsieur" to a highly vulgar, and in this context provocative, expression not to be used with strangers or in polite company: "Ils s'en foutent" (They don't give a f***).

## Drawing the Line

Bonnet's question indeed forces Benoît into the position of a diplomat speaking as a representative of the French nation. The answer

48   On July 3, 1940, fearing that the considerable resources of the French fleet would fall into German hands, British ships opened fire on the French battleships docked in the port of Mers-el Kébir (near Oran on the Algerian coast) after the French ignored their summons either to sail on to Allied ports or to scuttle their ships. Some 1,300 French sailors were killed, while most French warships there were captured or destroyed.

that Némirovsky puts on his lips fully agrees not only with Vercors but also with Mauriac, Texcier, and Guéhenno: the only acceptable response is a firm refusal to chat with the enemy on such grave matters concerning the nation. He in fact goes one step farther, hinting at his desire to settle military scores with the German intruder, for when Bonnet lets his decidedly indiscrete curiosity lead him to query about the empty bed, Benoît replies coolly that such beds serve to put up the wounded or the dead.

Némirovsky's narration of the cocky young Kurt Bonnet's stay in the modest homestead of Madeleine and Benoît Labarie moreover confirms our preliminary observation: the images of the Germans that emerge from her text are coextensive in complexity with those of the French personages that they encounter. Of all the local residents portrayed in *Dolce*, it is these two young peasants who appear to be the most attuned to the insidious moral threats posed by the outwardly benign presence of the soldiers for the Third Reich in their midst. And no one is more acutely aware of the dangerous ambivalence of her own sentiments than Madeleine. Once again, Némirovsky's characterization turns out to be much more problematical, much less idealistic, much richer, and much closer to the vexing reality of the way people actually lived through the occupation than Vercors's *Le Silence de la mer*. Writing as an artist, not as a militant for the Resistance, Némirovsky represents this peasant milieu with searing realism. Rather than presenting an icon either of some pure rustic authenticity (as in Vichy propaganda) or of unswerving solidarity of a family united against the intruders (as in *Le Silence de la mer*), she depicts the young married couple grappling with intense social jealousies and sexual tensions, as Benoît bitterly resents Madeleine's repeated refusal of his advances and her attraction to bourgeois refinement.

These sensitive marital conflicts are only exacerbated by the arrival of Kurt Bonnet: for both Madeleine and Benoît, the brash young German officer recalls the stay of the Jean-Marie Michaud, whose bourgeois culture had made a considerable impression. Though unsettled and attracted by Bonnet's distinguished masculinity, which contrasts favorably with Benoît's gruff speech and brusque manners,

Madeleine firmly refuses to put his connection with the hostile presence of the German army out of her mind. In all her intellectual simplicity, Madeleine eschews fraternization for reasons of a political, historical, and cultural nature. When Bonnet tries to bridge the national divide by pointing out the existing of French words in the German language and suggesting that his own name indicated French ancestry, Madeleine instinctively recoils from the danger of servility:

C'était étrange: elle ne haïssait pas les Allemands; elle ne haïssait personne, mais la vue de cet uniforme semblait faire d'elle, jusqu'ici libre et fière, une sorte d'esclave, pleine de ruse, de prudence et de peur, habile à cajoler le conquérant, quitte à cracher derrière la porte close: "Qu'ils crèvent!" comme le faisait sa belle-mère qui, elle, du moins, ne savait pas feindre, ni prendre des airs caressants avec le vainqueur, pensa-t-elle.[49]

It was strange: she did not hate the Germans; she hated no one, but the sight of this uniform seemed to make her, she who until now had been free and proud, a sort of slave, full of wiles, prudence, and fear, skilled at cajoling the conqueror, even if, once the door was closed, she spit out her anger: "Let them croak!," just like her mother-in-law, who for her part was incapable of faking it or pretending to be nice with the victors, thought Madeleine.

Sharply rebuffing Bonnet's advances, Madeleine feels remorse about even continuing to talk to him. Némirovsky depicts her repeatedly asking herself what words, deeds, and gestures are acceptable and which could appear cowardly or servile.

### Sex, Class, and Politics

The interaction between Kurt Bonnet and the Labarie couple confirms our initial observation: Némirovsky depicts her characters in dynamic relation to the mores and mentalities of social class, yet avoids reducing them to merely allegorical figures. While clearly emblematic of her peasant milieu ("la paysannerie"), Madeleine proves to be a complex, multifaceted character because we continually see

49   Némirovsky, *Suite française*, 337.

her not in isolation but in relation to her husband, her demanding role as a farm wife, her peasant upbringing, and recent events in her life. Némirovsky's sketch of Kurt Bonnet is equally rich and complex for precisely the same reasons. Instead of the highly stylized, allegorical representative of the German nation led horribly astray that we find in Vercors's presentation of von Ebrennac, Bonnet offers a flesh-and-blood image of a young man in uniform. Némirovsky portrays him in much greater detail and with a more sinister ambivalence than Vercors does von Ebrennac. In *Le Silence de la mer,* Von Ebrennac's attraction to the narrator's taciturn niece takes the form of sublimated devotion to an abstract ideal more akin to the tropes of Petrarchan conceits and courtly love than to the sexual realities of the Occupation years. Némirovsky's narrative offers a more frankly libidinal perspective. Not hesitating in his very first encounter with Madeleine to affirm with a suggestive smile that "L'homme est fait pour être un guerrier, comme la femme pour le divertissement du guerrier" (Men are made to be warriors, just as women are made for the warrior's entertainment) and trying to grasp her hands only a few instants later, Bonnet's bold advances are unequivocally sexual. The text makes it clear that, instead of arising from any political or idealistic motives, this young German soldier's arrogant flirtation is simply an expression of his youthful virility.

Interestingly, Némirovsky indicates that the same holds true for Bonnet's deeds as a soldier. Whereas *Le Silence de la mer* tells us virtually nothing about von Ebrennac's participation in the German army's previous campaigns except that he was wounded, *Dolce* details Bonnet's military behavior during various phases of the Wehrmacht's triumphant sweep over French territory. What we find on this level is a disturbing combination of discipline and cruelty alternating with highly selective acts of kindness. Némirovsky informs us that he had without compunction, and in some cases eagerly, carried out orders to shoot straggling French soldiers being marched back to Germany. Yet on other occasions, the same Kurt Bonnet had forbidden French farmers to carry their chickens upside down and had warmly thanked and richly rewarded an elderly French woman who had taken care of him during his bout with the flu. Curiously, Némirovsky explains Bonnet's behavior not in terms of national character or Nazi ideology, but as a by-product of adolescent impulsivity tinged with sadism:

Il [Bonnet] croyait qu'un homme digne de ce nom devait être de fer. Il s'était montré tel, d'ailleurs, dans la guerre, en Pologne et en France, et pendant l'occupation. Mais il obéissait beaucoup moins à des principes qu'à l'impulsivité de l'extrême jeunesse. . . . Il se montrait bienveillant ou cruel selon l'impression que lui faisaient choses et gens. . . . Il était cruel, mais c'était la cruauté de l'adolescence . . . on ne s'apitoie pas sur les souffrances d'autrui: on ne les voit pas, on ne voit que soi. Dans cette cruauté il entrait un peu d'affectation qui venait de son âge autant que d'un certain penchant au sadisme. Par exemple, dur envers les hommes, il montrait aux bêtes la plus grande sollicitude.[50]

He [Bonnet] believed that a man worthy of the name must be as tough as nails. He had moreover proved himself to be such a man during the war in Poland, in France, during the Occupation. But he was much less following principles than the impulsiveness of his extreme youth. . . . He proved to be benevolent or cruel depending on the impression that he got from things or people. . . . He was cruel, but it was the cruelty of adolescence . . . one doesn't take pity on the suffering of others: one doesn't see it, one only sees oneself. There entered into this cruelty a bit of affectation that came from his age as much as from a certain penchant for sadism. For example, even though he was hard on men, he displayed the greatest concern for animals.

These indications make Bonnet appear closer to Louis Malle's alternately callous and affectionate young collaborator Lucien in *Lacombe Lucien* than some ruthless member of the SS. Although Némirovsky's characterization of Bonnet doubtless owes something to the French stereotype of Germans as both cruel and sentimental, it is her dissociation of his behavior from ideology that carries the greatest significance for our present analysis. As elsewhere, we see the specific situation not as a result of political decisions taken in reference to a

50  Némirovsky, *Suite française*, 337–38.

coherent ideology, but as a sort of happenstance produced by an un-
scrutable history, just as storms inevitably arise as part of the Earth's
meteorological process. The title *Tempête en juin* is in that respect revealing, as are Maurice Michaud's musings on the great movements
of history.

This explicit neutralization or distancing of ideology in the characterization of Madeleine and Bonnet becomes all the more striking when we see that certain characters are presented in highly ideological terms, beginning with the Viscountess of Montmort and to
a somewhat lesser extent Benoît Labarie, both of whom not coincidentally appear in tandem. The tense confrontation between Mme de
Montmort and her most restive tenant farmer over the latter's raids
on plants and animals jealously hoarded by the former easily constitutes the episode the most highly charged with class politics and the
most momentous in the development of the plot: M. de Montmort's
denunciation of Benoît's hidden gun precipitates the killing of Bonnet, which then compels Madeleine to seek Lucile's assistance in
hiding the fugitive farmer, thus forcing the previously detached and
disaffected Lucile to take sides in a way that puts her life in danger.
The most psychologically and politically dramatic actions in *Dolce* are
driven by a bitter socioeconomic enmity: the politics of class puts the
aristocratic Montmorts in diametrical opposition to the peasant Labarie family. This highly visible socioeconomic polarization moreover
coincides with sharply contrasting attitudes and behaviors toward
the Germans. Neither Benoît's unabashed defiance of the Montmorts' imperious assertion of economic privilege and political authority nor the infuriated aristocrats' appeal to the German occupation
forces come as a surprise, for Némirovsky foreshadows these developments with narrative commentary revealing the deep roots of their
long-standing and bitter hatred of each other.

By placing Bonnet's impudent query about the French reaction
to their own defeat immediately after Mme de Montmort's emphatic expression of disgust ("Pouah!")[51] at having to embrace the children of commoners, Némirovsky invites the reader to compare the

51  Némirovsky, *Suite française*, 357.

peasants' discourse with that of the Viscountess. It is in this same chapter 8 of *Dolce* that we find Benoît bragging to his apprehensive wife about poaching and snitching food from their haughty landlords. Even though he risks a German firing squad, he takes pride in having retained his gun instead of having surrendered it with obsequious courtesy as the Viscount allegedly has. Némirovsky's narrative commentary implicitly attributes his bravado to class resentments that have been simmering for many long years: "De père en fils, les Labarie étaient métayers sur les terres des Montmort. De père en fils, on se haïssait. Les Labarie disaient que les Montmort étaient durs aux pauvres, fiers, pas francs, et les Montmort accusaient leurs métayers d'avoir le 'mauvais esprit'"[52] (Generation after generation, the Labaries had been sharecroppers on the Montmorts' land. Generation after generation, they had hated each other. The Labaries would say that the Montmorts were hard on the poor, proud, and devious, while the Montmorts would accuse their sharecroppers of having a "bad attitude").

On the one hand, Benoît's defiance of the Germans' ban on firearms seems to stem much less from abstract ideological stances than the age-old rancors arising from the aristocrats' haughty social and material domination over their tenant farmers. On the other hand, however, Némirovsky describes their strongly conflicting analyses of the defeat in terms that tend to discredit Amaury de Montmort while aligning Benoît with those whom she depicts courageously confronting an unjust plight in *Tempête en juin:*

Aux yeux du vicomte, Benoît était un soldat de 40, et c'était l'indiscipline des soldats, leur manque de patriotisme, leur "mauvais esprit" enfin qui avaient causé la défaite, songeait-il, tandis que Benoît voyait en Montmort un de ces beaux officiers aux guêtres jaunes qui filaient vers la frontière espagnole, bien à l'aise dans leurs voitures, avec leurs femmes et leurs valises, pendant les journées de juin. Puis il y avait la "collaboration." . . .
—Il lèche les bottes aux Allemands, fit sombrement Benoît.[53]

52  Némirovsky, *Suite française,* 363.
53  Némirovsky, *Suite française,* 364.

In the eyes of the Viscount, Benoît was a soldier from the 1940 campaign, and it was the soldiers' lack of discipline, lack of patriotism, and finally their "bad attitude" that had caused the defeat, he thought, while Benoît saw in Montmort one of these handsome officers in yellow gaiters hightailing it for the Spanish border, taking it easy in their cars with their women and their suitcases during the days of June. Then there was "collaboration.". . .
"He's licking the Germans' boots," Benoît remarked somberly.

Némirovsky confirms Benoît's blunt assessment by depicting the Viscount as turning to the Germans at the behest of Mme de Montmort, who is intent on punishing her tenant farmer's provocative refusal to respect her claims of property and social authority. Ultimately, we see that these relentless socioeconomic conflicts not only produce different perspectives on the May–June debacle, but also result in crucial differences in attitudes toward the Germans. Having penned an article titled "Tout pour le Maréchal!"[54] (Everything for the Marshal!), which railed against the illicit use of grain to fatten livestock, the Viscountess unmistakably appears as a quintessential Pétainist, as we have amply demonstrated.

Némirovsky's depiction of Mme de Montmort's attitude toward the enemy occupier is once again devastating. *Dolce* first exposes the Viscountess's fundamental hypocrisy by juxtaposing her melodramatic lamentations over the tragedies that have stricken France and sorely afflicted her tenants with her coy indulgence in the black market, as she arranges to exchange a bit of her coal for some of Mme Angellier's wheat in order to feed her hens.[55] Némirovsky's prose later reveals that the Viscountess views the defeat as a merited punishment of France's, or perhaps more accurately the common people's, errant thoughts and deeds. The Viscountess is accordingly grateful for the occupation by the Germans, whom she in reality admires:

Ah! le nouvel esprit, le déplorable esprit qui soufflait sur la France! Elle seule savait le reconnaître et lui donner un nom. Le peuple devenait

54  Némirovsky, *Suite française*, 382.
55  Némirovsky, *Suite française*, 382–83.

bolchevik. Elle avait cru que la défaite lui serait salutaire, le détournerait de ses dangereuses erreurs, le forcerait de nouveau à respecter ses chefs, mais non! Il était pire que jamais.

Parfois elle en arrivait, elle, ardente patriote, à se féliciter de la présence de l'ennemi. . . .

On avait beau dire, les Allemands avaient bien du mérite. Voilà un peuple discipliné, docile pensa Mme de Montmort en écoutant presque avec plaisir le pas cadencé qui s'éloignait, et la voix rauque qui criait *Achtung* dans le lointain.[56]

Ah! This new attitude, the deplorable attitude that was catching on all over France! She alone knew how to recognize it and give it a name. The common people were becoming Bolsheviks. She had thought that the defeat would be salutary, that it would turn them away from their dangerous errors and force them to respect once again their leaders, but no, they were worse than ever.

Sometimes even she, the ardent patriot that she was, found herself to be glad that the enemy was there. . . .

Whatever one might say, the Germans did indeed have their merits. Now there were people who were disciplined and docile, thought Madame de Montmort while listening almost with pleasure to the slowly fading sound of the soldiers marching in step and the harsh voice shouting *Achtung* in the distance.

Even before the Viscountess decides to have her husband inform the local *Kommandantur* about Benoît's hidden gun, Némirovsky thus has us view the Viscountess as clearly aligned not only with Pétain but also with the German occupying forces. Here again, we observe that *Suite française* portrays characters primarily in terms of social class and that the image of the Germans emerges as coextensive with varying sets of collective attitudes and individual situations among the French personages. As an aristocrat eager to bolster her own privileged position of socioeconomic power, Mme de Montmort is attracted to the elements of order and discipline that she perceives as characteristic of Hitler's soldiers.

56  Némirovsky, *Suite française*, 445–46.

### From Resentment to Resistance

Benoît's bold trespass and theft of the Montmorts' property appears first and foremost as an act of resistance to an oppressive social order that forces the Viscountess's hand and leads her to consummate, as it were, her alliance with the Germans. Yet at the same time he openly provokes Mme de Montmort, as if to strip away the veneer of patriotic piety to reveal the underlying collaborationism. When all is said and done, the seething class hatreds in this little provincial corner erupt into naked socioeconomic conflicts that ineluctably place individual characters before stark choices with weighty political implications. We can observe this progression from local rivalries to ideological confrontations in Benoît's highly charged encounter with Mme de Montmort. Caught in the act of stealing, Benoît protests that he was taking the corn for a neighbor woman whose husband is a prisoner of war and that the Viscountess's haughty refusal to sell anything has left him no choice but to steal. "Tout ce que vous refusez, sans raison, par méchanceté pure, on le prend. Et ce n'est pas fini. Attendez l'automne! Monsieur le Maire chassera avec les Allemands"[57] ("Everything that you refuse for no reason, out of pure meanness, we will take. And that's not all. Just wait for the fall! The honorable mayor will go hunting with the Germans").

Not content with defying his landlord, he taunts Mme de Montmort by alluding to the Germans and by flouting the traditionally exclusive aristocratic privilege of hunting. When the Viscountess tries to intimidate the upstart peasant by threatening to go get the Germans, Benoît counters that, unlike her husband the Viscount, he has already seen the Germans close up on the battlefield. Her ensuing outrage and renewed threats only prompt greater defiance, as Benoît brandishes the menace of a punitive uprising against aristocratic oppression: "C'est ça, appelez les Boches! Vous êtes bien contente qu'ils soient là, hein? Ça fait la police, ça garde vos propriétés. Priez le Bon Dieu qu'ils restent longtemps parce que le jour où ils

57  Némirovsky, *Suite française*, 448.

seront partis . . ."⁵⁸ ("That's right, call the krauts! You're quite happy they're there, aren't you? Those guys act as a police force and guard your property. Pray to the good Lord that they might stay a long time, because the day they're gone . . .").

Benoît's unblinking defiance of the Montmorts acts as a catalyst, precipitating the denunciation that not only reveals their inclination to collaborate with the occupying enemy forces but also calls attention to the sinister reality of the German presence on French soil. His refusal to remain humble and silent sets him apart from other French personnages, whose quiescence to the Wehrmacht in their midst leads them to regard the Germans as benign and to indulge in friendly interaction. As we have seen, Némirovsky's portrayal of Bussy features shopkeepers happy to see these courteous, well-paying new customers, numerous onlookers eager to take in this new spectacle, and carefree children happy to play virtually unrestrained in the Perrin residence requisitioned by Germans. In each case, the townspeople's casual mode of habitual interaction with these soldiers considerably modifies their perception of the Germans: what initially appears as an intrusive contingent of hostile forces is gradually transformed into a number of familiar, friendly faces worn by largely amusing outsiders.

Benoît's response to the German officer forcibly lodged in his modest rural home differs sharply. He shatters what had been a more or less peaceful coexistence between the residents of Bussy and their German occupiers, and therefore dissipates the illusion of neutrality. Though motivated to a significant degree by bitter class resentment and intense sexual jealousy, Benoît's killing of Bonnet, who was about to arrest him for possessing a gun, nevertheless represents an act of radical defiance of German power, and therefore constitutes an act of resistance. Just as his defiance of the Viscountess exposes her affinity with and reliance on the Germans, so his slaying of Bonnet forces Lucile to determine where her true allegiance lies: ultimately, she must choose between protecting a compatriot or aban-

58  Némirovsky, *Suite française*, 449.

doning him to a German firing squad or worse. The fundamental hypocrisy of la Vicomtesse de Montmort is precisely that of Pétain, only transposed onto the local scene: pompously claiming to be France incarnate, the soul of the nation, they both carry out highly partisan actions harmful to the common people, whom they nevertheless, as Ousby so aptly points out, "invited to confuse prejudice, grievance and envy with patriotism, even patriotic duty."[59] Némirovsky's text thoroughly dispells such confusions.

On another level, Benoît's cunning attack on Bonnet parallels the assassinations of German officers carried out by the communist Resistance at the outset of their militancy in 1941, when they knowingly sought to drive a wedge between the German army and the French populace. As anticipated, such assassinations led to fierce reprisals: for every one of their own who had been assassinated, the Germans shot large groups of French hostages. Such bloodletting increased fear and anxiety among the occupation forces, while at the same time making it much more difficult for the French populace to cozy up to their uninvited guests. It is hardly surprising to observe that in her plans for *Captivité*, which was to follow *Dolce* in the subsequent development of her *Suite française*, Némirovsky planned to depict Benoît as having espoused the communist Resistance and joined forces with Jean-Marie Michaud. Even more significant are the terms in which she outlines Jean-Marie's gradual progression from highly personal preoccupations to political commitment:

il [Jean-Marie] essaie de vivre comme si le grand et urgent problème commun ne se posait pas, comme s'il n'avait qu'à résoudre que ses propres problèmes. Mais voici qu'il apprend que Lucile a aimé et aime peut-être encore un Allemand. Du coup il prend parti car l'abstraction a pris tout à coup figure de haine. Il hait un Allemand et, en lui, à travers lui, il hait ou croit haïr, ce qui est la même chose, une forme d'esprit. En réalité, ce qui se passe, c'est qu'il oublie son propre destin et le confond avec celui d'autrui.[60]

59    Ousby, *Occupation: The Ordeal of France, 1940–1944*, 137.
60    Némirovsky, *Suite française*, 536.

he [Jean-Marie] tries to live as if the great, urgent collective issue were not there, as if he only had to resolve his personal issues. But then he learns that Lucile has been and perhaps still is in love with a German. At that point, he takes sides, now that the abstract issue has suddenly taken on the face of hatred. He hates a German and, in him, through him, he hates or believes he hates, which is the same thing, a certain mind-set. What actually happens is that he forgets his own destiny and confuses it with that of someone else.

As we shall amply see in the following chapter, the question of private lives and public destinies lies at the heart of Némirovsky's artistic enterprise in *Suite française*. The various reactions to the presence of German soldiers in Bussy that we have explored in the previous pages expose the unsettling conflicts and ambiguous connections between personal prerogatives and collective mandates. Benoît's violent clash with Bonnet offers a highly revealing case in point. The French peasant instinctively perceives the intrusion of the bourgeois German officer into his household as a violation of his personal dwelling space, just as he considers Bonnet's provocative flirtation with his wife as an affront to both his masculinity and his humble social status as a tenant farmer. Némirovsky depicts Benoît's immediate motivation as being intensely personal, not as stemming from either patriotism or antifascist political commitment. In the end, however, questions of virility and sexual relations between German soldiers and French women will, far from appearing marginal, prove to be dangerously invested with political implications in the final traumatic phases of the Occupation as well as in the violent settling of scores that marked the Liberation of French territory. And underneath its disarmingly idyllic appearances, the romantic interlude foregrounded by Némirovsky in *Dolce* figures the most vexing and potentially explosive issues of the German occupation of France as well as of her narrative representation of the era.

CHAPTER 7

# PRIVATE LIVES AND PUBLIC STORIES

## A Little Night Music

After the sound and fury of *Tempête en juin*, the second install-
ment of Némirovsky's war narrative portrays a relative return to normal. Suggesting a "soft" or "sweet" musical interlude, the title *Dolce*
functions as a metaphor for the whole series of plot developments.
The term also serves as a metonymy of the part for the whole, since
it points to the thematic and compositional centrality of the relationship between Némirovsky's most prominent feminine protagonist
and the German officer Bruno von Falk, who so uncannily resembles
Vercors's von Ébrennac.[1] The paradigmatic quality of this musical
trope resonates on both the biographical and the textual levels. Lucile initiates her romantic, although unconsummated, idyll with Bruno by inviting him to play the piano: "Mettez-vous au piano et jouez.
Nous oublierons le mauvais temps, l'absence, tous nos malheurs"[2]
("Sit down at the piano and play. We'll forget the bad weather, the absence of our loved ones, all of our misery and misfortunes"). Lyrical-

1  I am not suggesting that Némirovsky was in any way "influenced" by Vercors's *Le
Silence de la mer*. The latter was only distributed in late 1942 to a select few. She would
therefore not have had access to it before her arrest in July 1942.

2  Némirovsky, *Suite française*, 406.

ly interpreting one of his own compositions, Bruno fulfills his lady's wish to find momentary respite from the surrounding anxieties. In explaining his music's symbolism, the German officer describes the all-encompassing conflict between the individual and the community, and then characterizes the privileged moment shared with Lucile as the calm at the eye of a cyclone.

Némirovsky's indirect free style then reveals that Lucile indeed experiences such a fleeting haven from the dismal circumstances of the war and her own virtual emprisonment in her bourgeois marriage:

Ce qui était plus délicieux que tout, c'était cet isolement au sein de la maison hostile, et cette étrange sécurité: personne ne viendrait; il n'y aurait ni lettres, ni visites, ni téléphone. . . . Bienheureux oubli. . . . Jusqu'au soir, rien, des heures lentes, une présence humaine, un vin léger et parfumé, de la musique, de longs silences, le bonheur.[3]

Most delightful of all was this isolation within this hostile home, and this strange security: no one would come; there would be neither letters, nor visits, nor phone calls. . . . Blissful oblivion . . . Until the evening, nothing, the slow passing of the hours, a human presence, a light, fruity wine, music, long moments of silence, happiness.

Némirovsky herself poignantly expressed a similar yearning for an escape from the stranglehold of history in notes dating during the early months of 1942.[4] Increasingly isolated in the provincial town of Issy-l'Évêque, highly restricted in her movements, cut off from friends and associates, and prohibited from publishing, Némirovsky understandably seems to share Lucile's desire to flee far from the madding crowd of all those who "s'entendent tous sur un point: il faut vivre, penser, aimer avec les autres, en fonction d'un État, d'un pays, d'un parti"[5] (all agree on one point: you have to live, think, and love with all the rest, based on a certain regime, a certain country,

---

3  Némirovsky, *Suite française*, 412–13.

4  Philipponnat and Lienhardt, *La vie d'Irène Némirovsky*, 408–12.

5  Némirovsky, *Suite française*, 457.

or a certain party). Alienated from the nation and society whose language and culture she had ardently espoused, she paints the main protagonists of *Dolce* as private individuals longing for companionship and happiness made impossible by the war, and not, as is the case in *Le Silence de la mer*, as humble citizens seeking to escape the monotony of provincial life through courageous adhesion to a national cause that transcends personal inclination.

Here again, in order to best appreciate her historical narrative, we must first of all analyze the work in relation to its historical and political context. While Némirovsky's apparent—but misleading—reluctance to become engaged on the ideological theater of the momentous confrontation with Nazi Germany that would ultimately claim her life seems incongruous from our present perspective, her historical despondency is in many ways only a posture that she shared with the vast majority of people in France during the first part of the German occupation. Like Vercors, who penned *Le Silence de la mer* in the last few months of 1941,[6] she wrote *Dolce* during the darkest, most uncertain moments of the Occupation, well before November 8, 1942: that is, long before the Allied invasion of North Africa and the Red Army's decisive victory at Stalingrad in February 1943 had put victory over Nazi Germany and thus the liberation of French territory on the horizon. While Vercors's clandestinely published narrative is now celebrated for its defiance of the German stranglehold on French publishing as well as for its lucid, if variously received, summons to resist the insidious propaganda of cultural seduction, Némirovsky's representation of women struggling under the psychological and material rigors of the Occupation provides a much richer and more realistic account of the attitudes and behaviors that were in fact displayed during these highly uncertain times.

That Némirovsky's text conveys a woman's perspective can hardly be incidental to the particularly intense and highly nuanced portraits of women so prominently featured in *Dolce*. The contrast with Ver-

6    Lawrence D. Stokes, "Historical Introduction," *The Silence of the Sea / Le Silence de la mer*, edited by James W. Brown and Lawrence D. Stokes (New York and Oxford: Berg Publishers, 1993), 10.

cors's text is dramatic, for the niece's narrator in *Le Silence de la mer* is little more than a caricature of the quietude, subordination, and domestic devotion so often expected of women of that era. Seen only through the eyes of the first-person male narrator, the sole female of Vercors's text is depicted as a stern embodiment of patriotic constancy and virtue who does nothing but knit, serve coffee, and utter a watery-eyed "Adieu!" to von Ébrennac as he leaves for the Russian front. Némirovsky's indirect free style, however, takes us far inside the hearts and minds of several strong female personages, including not only Lucile, but also Madeleine Labarie, Mme de Montmort, and Mme Angellier. Although discrete and mild-mannered, Lucile is portrayed as keenly intelligent and exquisitely sensitive, both emotionally and aesthetically. At the end of the day, she proves to be both courageous and resolute, since she defies cultural and familial strictures by opening her heart to Bruno and finally decides to shelter Benoît from the Germans at the risk of her own life. While in each case highly emblematic of their social class, Madeleine Labarie, Mme de Montmort, and Mme Angellier are equally portrayed as strong-willed, articulate women who pursue their own priorities independent of masculine directives.

### Dangerous Liaisons

Beyond its incontestably superior complexity, however, Némirovsky's characterization of provincial women living through the Occuaption proves to have serious historical implications for both her time and ours. The fact of the matter is that *Dolce* provides a rare and doubtless one of the earliest unblinkered views of a widespread occurrence that we now know was prominent in the everyday lives and preoccupations of the French populace during the Dark Years: the direct association and frequent sexual encounters between French women and German soldiers. Némirovsky shows the young women of Bussy attracted to the virile presence of the Wehrmacht troops and consorting with them in a whole range of behaviors, from furtive glances and casual conversation to stolen kisses, heart-to-heart discussions, and prolonged sexual adventures. Young girls tarry at the public square the very day of the German contingent's arrival;[7] the flushed tavern waitress excitedly rebuffs the raucous advances of soldiers ordering champagne;[8] even Madeleine, who as we have seen will have nothing of Bonnet's flirtation, finds herself unsettlingly attracted by the sharp profile of the German officer who surprises her with her dress unbuttoned from breastfeeding: "Malgré elle, elle était fascinée par ses bottes et la boucle de son ceinturon; le cuir et l'acier lançaient des éclairs"[9] (She was in spite of herself fascinated by his boots and his belt buckle; the leather and the steel reflected flashes of light). The sound of French girls laughing, kissing, and embracing German soldiers moreover forms a conspicuous backdrop for several scenes, including the regiment's departure from Bussy, when "Ça et là, dans l'ombre d'une porte, on entendait un murmure, un bruit de baisers . . . quelques adieux plus tendres que d'autres"[10] (Here and there, in the shadow of a doorway, you could hear a murmur, a sound of kissing . . . some farewells were more tender than others"), and even more ironically, the Viscountess's highly contrived lamentation of France's suffering.

Némirovsky's juxtaposition of Mme de Montmort's righteous indignation with the licentious frivolity of local girls at the end of chapter 9 offers some of her most ferociously satirical pages of the disarmingly named *Dolce*. The text first reveals the true motive for Mme de Montmort's visit, for which her overwrought signs of pity for war suffering had only served as a moral fig leaf: she has in fact come to strike a deal with Mme Angellier, hoping to illegally barter some of her coal in order to procure some wheat to fatten her poultry. Némirovsky then gives us this aristocratic practitioner of the black market's reaction to the sounds of smooches and giggles that drift in off the town square outside the window. The passage bears citing at length:

7  Némirovsky, *Suite française*, 324.

9  Némirovsky, *Suite française*, 335–36.

8  Némirovsky, *Suite française*, 318.

10  Némirovsky, *Suite française*, 515.

Des ténèbres montaient un rire, un frôlement de jupes. Puis une voix d'homme, une voix étrangère demanda:

—Comment, en français, ça? Baiser? Oui? Oh, ça bon . . .

Plus loin, des ombres erraient; on voyait vaguement la blancheur d'un corsage, un noeud dans des cheveux dénoués, le miroitement d'une botte et d'un ceinturon. . . . Deux soldats, dans un groupe de jeunes filles, chantaient:

> Trink'mal noch ein Troepfchen!
> Ach! Suzanna . . .

et les jeunes filles fredonnaient ensuite en sourdine.[11]

The rustling of skirts and laughter rose up out of the darkness. Then a man's voice, the voice of a foreigner, asked:

"What, that, in French? Kiss? Yes? Oh, that nice . . .

A bit farther off, shadows were wondering about; you could barely make out a bust, a thick strand of hair that had been let down, the glimmer of a boot and a belt buckle. . . . Two soldiers were singing amid a group of young girls:

> Trink'mal noch ein Troepfchen!
> Ach! Suzanna . . .

and the young girls were humming softly.

Even more important than Némirovsky's description is the manner in which she frames it thematically by showing how the same scene is differently filtered through the eyes of the Viscountess and those of Lucile. On the one hand, the text indicates the genuinely scandalous nature of such carefree fraternization with invading troops who have visited considerable human and material destruction on towns and villages such as Bussy. Looking out over the little town square, Lucile thinks of those who live there, including the blacksmith who has lost three sons and an impoverished woman who has lost her husband to the war. Expecting words of sorrow to echo faintly from these residences, Lucile instead overhears not just one but an entire group of local girls frolicking with the Germans and humming their

11  Némirovsky, *Suite française*, 384.

drinking songs. As one could expect, the Viscountess bristles with moral outrage and announces her intention of informing the town priest of these flagrant transgressions. As Némirovsky's narrative voice points out, however, Mme de Montmort's indignation stems as much from the resultant doubts about her moral authority as a purveyor of chastity and her own sexual frustration as from her wounded patriotism.[12]

Most noteworthy is the passage that leads us to compare the Viscountess's ostentatious displeasure with Lucile's much more discrete and nuanced reaction:

—C'est un scandale! s'exclama-t-elle [la vicomtesse Mme de Montmort].

—C'est triste, dit Lucile, songeant à toutes ces filles dont la jeunesse s'écoulait en vain: les hommes étaient absents, prisonniers ou morts. L'ennemi prenait la place. C'était déplorable, mais personne ne le saurait demain. Ce serait une de ces choses que la postérité ignorerait, ou dont elle se détournerait par pudeur.[13]

"That's an outrage!" she [the Viscountess Madame de Montmort] exclaimed.

"It's sad," said Lucile, thinking of all these girls whose youth was flowing away in vain: the men were absent, prisoners, or dead. The enemy was taking their place. It was deplorable, but no one would know about it tomorrow. It would be one of these things of which posterity would not be aware, or from which posterity would turn away out of embarassment and modesty.

Placing the Viscountess's histrionics so closely after her black market transaction, Némirovsky only accentuates the satire on moral pretension that we have already noted in many other passages. Conversely, nothing in the text contradicts or even calls into question the lucid, humane assessment of the situation that Némirovsky's indirect free style places in her subtle mind.

---

12  Némirovsky, *Suite française*, 384–85.
13  Némirovsky, *Suite française*, 385.

### The Gender Gap and the Crisis of Virility in Occupied France

When we weigh Lucile's (and arguably Némirovsky's) gentle musings in light of the historical record as well as in relation to current perspectives on the war and the Occupation, we can confirm both their accuracy and their pertinence. As she observes, occupied France had indeed suffered an acute shortage of men as a result of the humiliating defeat that had killed ninety thousand men, wounded two hundred thousand more, and left some two million others to waste away in German prisoner of war camps. The World War II debacle thus aggravated the demographic problem created by the death of some 1.6 million men and the crippling of several hundred thousand more during the butchery of World War I. The obvious sexual, economic, and ethical crises that ensued were devastating to the hundreds of thousands of French citizens who experienced them firsthand.[14] Seeking to galvanize French resolve in the face of what in late 1941 could often appear as the virtually invincible master of Europe for the forseeable future, Vercors understandably had little interest in a realistic representation of the grim socioeconomic picture and murky mores of the early Occupation. As we noted at the outset, Némirovsky firmly resolved to shun partisan portrayals and focused on leaving an enduring narrative of the period. Paradoxically, however, she provides a much more interesting representation of occupied France precisely because of her frank approach to the sensitive topic of French women taking on German lovers.

Given the widely accepted imperative of preserving a minimum of national dignity by maintaining a clear distance between oneself and the sometimes ostentatious, often beguiling demeanor of the German conquerors, on the one hand, and the deep-seated misgivings about French virility severely stressed by the traumatic effects of both World War I and World War II, on the other, it is hardly surprising that the subject of French women who took German lovers has proved to be

---

14  See Burrin, *La France à l'heure allemande*, 210–11, and Vinen, *The Unfree French*, 157–58.

204 PRIVATE LIVES AND PUBLIC STORIES

highly sensitive from the earliest stages of the Occupation to the dramatic turnabout of the Liberation period and even today. In the same "Conseils à l'occupé" (Advice to the occupied people") enjoining his compatriots to refrain from any familiarity with the Germans, Jean Texcier ominously observes that women who chat and flirt with enemy soldiers would be publicly whipped in Germany and even encourages his readers to look forward to such a day in France: "Devant le marivaudage d'une de ces femmes que l'on dit honnêtes, avec un de tes occupants, rappelle-toi qu'au delà du Rhin cette jolie personne serait publiquement fouettée. Alors, en la détaillant, repère soigneusement la tendre place, et savour d'avance ton plaisir"[15] (When you see one of these supposedly respectable women bantering with one of the soldiers occupying your country, remember that on the other side of the Rhine this pretty person would be publicly flogged. Then, noting the details, carefully situate the tender location, and savor your pleasure ahead of time). Within this series of thirty-three such "Conseils" that otherwise offer a remarkable model of an uncompromising lucidity and wry wit coupled with a serenity all too uncommon amid the hysteria and confusion of the debacle and its immediate aftermath, this invitation to prepare for savage revenge to be publicly inflicted on women is a striking anomaly. Since so many French women ultimately did indeed suffer horrendous treatment, we can only conclude that Texcier here again expressed a widely held sentiment that was moreover particularly strong in the rural provinces.[16] Fabrice Virgili confirms that from 1943 to 1946, some twenty thousand women of all ages and professions all over France were victims of head shavings. Far from representing an anomaly at the margins of national liberation, these head shavings, notes Virgili, were most often jubilantly witnessed by the entire local population and functioned "tout à la fois spectacle et manifestation du châtiment des traîtres"[17] (both as a spectacle and as a demonstration of the punishment of traitors).

15  Texcier, *Écrit dans la nuit*, 11–12.

16  Cf. Burrin, *La France à l'heure allemande*, 213.

17  Fabrice Virgili, *La France "virile." Des femmes tondues à la Libération* (Paris: Petite Bibliothèque Payot, 2004), 7.

Dating from the outset of the Occupation and continuing up until the present, this tendency to judge sexual relations between French women and German soldiers as acts of collaboration and treason has a long, but problematic history. A quick survey of discourses contemporaneous with Némirovsky's *Suite française* attests to the paradigmatic reprobation of sexual relations with German soldiers as a shameful betrayal. In this light, we should recall that von Ébrennac's perversely idealistic invitation for France to collaborate with Germany to build a new Europe comes as a proposal of marriage and erotic satisfaction in *Le Silence de la mer*. In his famous postwar essay "Qu'est-ce qu'un collaborateur?" (What is the definition of a collaborator?") Sartre first noted that the most vociferous literary zealots for collaboration, including Alphonse de Chateaubriant, Drieu la Rochelle, and Robert Brasillach, had all depicted France as the willing sexual partner of Nazi Germany. Sartre then concluded that such sexual submission was emblematic of the collaborationist attitude in general: "Pour autant qu'on puisse concevoir l'état d'esprit de la collaboration, on y devine comme un climat de féminité"[18] (To the extent that one can conceive of the mind-set of collaboration, one senses something like a climate of femininity within it). On one level, Sartre reiterates what is perhaps the most well-known of misogynist clichés, "Frailty, thy name is woman," for he assumes that all forms of French weakness in facing the Germans must be inherently feminine. There is an equally stubborn and widely held corollary to this prejudice: namely, that any and all sexual relations between French women and soldiers of the Wehrmacht constituted acts of political treason.

Although Virgili admits that during the war years, the French viewed head shavings as punishment for having had sexual relations with the enemy, he never tires of insisting that these head shavings should actually not be understood as retribution for sleeping with German soldiers, but rather as a gendered punishment for collaboration of several sorts: "Il est pourtant essentiel de dire que la coupe

18  Jean-Paul Sartre, "Qu'est-ce qu'un collaborateur?," *Situations III* (Paris: Gallimard, 1945), 58.

des cheveux n'est pas le châtiment d'une collaboration sexuelle, mais le châtiment sexué de la collaboration"[19] (It is nevertheless crucial to state that the cutting of hair is not punishment for sexual collaboration, but the gendered punishment for collaboration). While providing a highly detailed view of the phenomenon and a coherent exposition of the gendered ideological underpinnings of those who carried out the head shavings, Virgili's largely sympathetic reading of the practice is not without problems. First, his claim that the case of the young girl shorn for having slept with a German was only one instance among many others is a bit misleading. For even though Virgili tries to minimize the accusations of collaboration based on sexual relations, his own statistics and charts are clear: on page 23, we see that 42.1 percent of the *tondues* (shorn women) were accused of having relations with the enemy, while 26.7 percent were shorn for "collaboration indéterminée." This salient fact tends to get buried in all sorts of subtle statistical comparisons, but the dominant tendency remains clear. Second, in repeatedly invoking the "patriotism" that supposedly inspired the head shavings, Virgili never considers all that was (and remains) problematical about the specific origins, nature, and composition of such national sentiment, except for the obviously gendered notion of "virility." After all, Pétain and Vichy had presented themselves as the models of patriotism, and enabled their countless followers to consider themselves as "patriotic" in everything from singing "Maréchal, nous voilà" to denouncing Jews and resisters. Finally, Virgili's insistence that head shaving always sanctioned treason simply postulates the guilt of those shorn and conveniently ignores the problem of scapegoating and score settling, or perhaps simply relegates the issue to the domain of collectively held notions of sexual identity. While admitting that the supposed offenses attributed to the shorn women are ambiguous and problematical, Virgili nevertheless assumes that sexual relations with a German soldier constituted collaboration, even if it had no effect on the war itself. Indeed, Virgili presents sexual relations with Germans

19   Virgili, *La France "virile." Des femmes tondues à la Libération*, 56.

as unmitigated treason: "Perçue à travers le prisme de l'Occupation, la relation sexuelle avec l'ennemi est plus qu'une transgression des règles communautaires, elle est—faut-il le rappeler?—une trahison et revêt une gravité supérieure."[20] (Perceived through the prism of the Occupation, sexual relations with the enemy are more than a transgression of community rules. Must we recall that it is an act of treason and takes on a higher level of gravity?) Virgili's argument is ultimately circular: the women were guilty because the community considered them to be traitors.

Such was the pretext for the outpouring of collective hatred and resentment that marked the pathologically degrading scenes of women subjected to having their heads shaved (and sometimes much worse) in public that occurred on such a large scale. While there is of course at present an equally widespread condemnation of such violence, one can still detect evidence of the persistent notion that amorous contacts between French women and German soldiers represented acts of political treason. Writing for the widely read newsmagazine *L'Express* on 16 April 2008, historian Jean-Pierre Azéma, one of France's leading scholars of the Occupation era, implicitly considers relations between French women and German soldiers as shameful "collaboration" that we should sweep under the rug:

*Restons pudiques* en évoquant *la collaboration des cœurs*. Les historiens parlent de 50 000, voire 80 000 enfants nés des amours franco-allemandes. Des chiffres éloquents, car la naissance de ces "enfants de boche" valait au père le transfert disciplinaire sur le front de l'Est, et à la mère l'opprobre ("Je devins sa femme dans le crépuscule, le bonheur et la honte", dit dans Hiroshima mon amour l'héroïne de Marguerite Duras).[21]

*Let us remain respectful of modesty* when talking about *the collaboration of hearts*. Historians speak of 50,000, perhaps even 80,000 children, born from Franco-German love affairs. Such figures speak volumes, for the

---

20   Virgili, *La France "virile." Des femmes tondues à la Libération*, 293.

21   Jean-Pierre Azéma, "Cette France 'allemande,'" *L'Express*, 16 April 2008; emphasis mine.

birth of these "Krauts' children" meant that the father would be sent to the Russian front and that the mother would be subjected to opprobrium. ("I became his mistress in the midst of twilight, happiness and shame," says Marguerite Duras's heroine in *Hiroshima mon amour*.)

Azéma confirms Lucile's prediction that future generations would likely turn their attention away from this embarrassing chapter of history, for in his introduction to a set of feature articles in *L'Express* symptomatically titled "Les derniers secrets de l'Occupation" (The last secrets of the Occupation) he passes hastily over the thorny issue of the French women who slept with German soldiers, devoting to this matter only one short paragraph consisting of these three terse sentences. It is hardly a coincidence that another article in the same 16 April 2008 feature story takes the opposite approach, zooming in on Franco-German sexual encounters in lurid detail. The summary paragraph placed at the beginning of this article in order to entice us to read the full text is little more than an invitation to historical voyeurism:

Dans un livre dérangeant, *1940–1945, années érotiques*, Patrick Buisson, directeur de la chaîne Histoire, revisite l'Occupation sous l'angle de la libido. Ou comment une France dévirilisée par la défaite—qu'il s'agisse des citoyens de base, des intellectuels ou des ministres collabos—eut les yeux de Chimène pour les "grands barbares blonds." Extraits.[22]

In a disturbing book, *1940–1945, Erotic Years*, Patrick Buisson, the director of the [French] History channel, revisits the Occupation from the perspective of the libido. Or how a France—including ordinary citizens, intellectuals, and collaborationist government ministers—stripped of its virility by the defeat, made coyly seductive eyes at the "great blond barbarians." Here are a few excerpts.

Instead of advising us to turn our eyes discreetly away, as does Azéma, this unsigned article thus encourages us to examine the subject with punctilious titillation. The assumption is once again that sexual

22    "Les Derniers Secrets de l'Occupation," *L'Express*, 16 April 2008, available online at www.lexpress.fr/actualite/politique/les-derniers-secrets-de-l-occupation-472644.html.

promiscuity between French women and German men unfailingly corresponds to ideological attraction or treason.

Némirovsky's depiction of the subject in *Dolce* constitutes a clear departure from both the dominant discourses of her own time and the common perspectives of our present era. Instead of representing one such relationship as paradigmatic of all women who consorted with enemy troops, her text offers an entire range of encounters between French women and soldiers of the Wehrmacht. We have already observed that her narrative depicts such encounters as frequent and widespread among the young women of the Bussy area, and that, although rebuffed, Bonnet's advances to Madeleine not only highlight the tensions within her marriage to Benoît but also precipitate the most dramatic plot development in *Dolce,* since the killing of Bonnet ultimately forces a detached and somewhat confused Lucile to make a decisive commitment. Némirovsky's portrayal of another woman who on the contrary gladly indulges in an extended love affair with a German soldier provides not only a contrapuntal echo of Lucile's own intense attraction to Bruno von Falk, but also a highly suggestive representation of a discomfiting and most often greatly distorted historical reality.

### Forbidden Fruit

In narrating Lucile's dialogue with a seamstress struggling amid the economic rigors of the Occupation, Némirovsky juxtaposes two women from highly disparate socioeconomic milieus that condition their contrasting attitudes toward the Germans. The text underscores Lucile's social status by calling attention to the subtext of the seamstress's compliment on the fine silk fabric that Lucile has brought to be fashioned into a dressing gown:

—Vous avez de la chance d'avoir encore de la soie comme ça. Nous, on n'a plus rien.
Elle le disait sans jalousie apparente, mais avec considération, comme si elle eût reconnu à la bourgeoisie non un droit de priorité, mais une

espèce d'astuce naturelle qui lui permettait d'être servie avant les autres.[23]

"You are lucky to still get silk like that. On our end, we don't have any more."

She said it without any apparent jealousy, but with consideration, as if she acknowledged that the bourgeoisie had not a right to priority, but a sort of natural clever knack for getting what they wanted before everybody else.

The seamstress is significantly never named, but simply designated by her social station. She vigorously reiterates her class-conscious comparison of Lucile's bourgeois privilege with her own material and social discomfort in defending her sexual relationship with the German soldier whose belt lies revealingly on her bed.

Though measured, Lucile's reaction is nevertheless highly judgmental: "Comment pouvez-vous?"[24] ("How can you do such a thing?") Writing as we have seen for posterity, Némirovsky uncannily echoes the very question that we contemporary readers automatically ask when approaching the issue of French women who took German lovers during the Occupation. How could the seamstress give herself over to an enemy soldier of the army that had so humiliatingly defeated France and now arrogantly occupied French territory? The seamstress's forthright answer echoes the conflict between private lives and public stories that is so poignantly developed throughout the entire text of Némirovsky's Suite française. Flatly refusing to view her love affair in terms of history and national loyalty, the seamstress adamantly asserts her personal desire for considerate and courteous masculine affection regardless of nationality or, what was even more scandalous at the time, race: "Entre un homme et une femme, ça ne joue pas, tout ça [les guerres]. S'il était anglais ou nègre et que je le trouvais à mon goût, je me l'offrirais, si je pouvais"[25] ("Between a man and a woman, that stuff [wars] doesn't come into play. If he were

23  Némirovsky, Suite française, 398.        24  Némirovsky, Suite française, 398.
25  Némirovsky, Suite française, 399.

English or black and I found him to my liking, I'd have a fling with him if I could"). The seamstress moreover points out to Lucile that her German lover is a well-mannered, polite man who shows consideration by bringing gifts and flowers. Unlike the locals who reek of alcohol and are only interested in one thing, this German, affirms the experienced seamstress with no little confidence, offers love. In response to Lucile's chiding expression of surprise, the seamstress once again stresses the matter of class difference, explaining that she is only naturally more appreciative than would be Lucile of the German's little demonstrations of attention because she has neither the material comforts, cultural education, nor leisure time that characterize Lucile's bourgeois existence.[26]

For all these reasons, the seamstress stubbornly brushes aside the matter of nationality and persists in viewing her lover as a man: "Alors, vous comprenez, qu'on me dise: 'Allemand, Allemand, c'est un Allemand,' ça ne me fait ni chaud ni froid. C'est des gens comme nous"[27] ("Well, then, you know, if people tell me: 'German, German, he's a German,' I could care less. They're people like us"). Lucile replies with condescension, addressing her as "ma pauvre fille" (my poor girl), and serves up a brief moral lesson, pointing out the people refer to "un Allemand" (a German) not to denounce any innate difference but to recall that the Germans have killed French soldiers, taken loved ones prisoner, and begun to create food shortages.[28] These edifying words only spur the seamstress's most forceful expression of defiance and class resentment. Recalling that her father had been killed in the previous war, she protests that she has indeed taken all these facts into consideration but has finally decided to take care of herself, since no one else will. Her refusal to act in accordance with the expectations of others is all the more adamant in that she is an outcast: "Dans le pays on dit que je suis une chienne. Non! Les chiens, c'est ceux qui vont en bande et mordent si on leur ordonne de mordre. Moi et Willy . . ."[29] ("People around here say that I am a dog.

---

26  Némirovsky, *Suite française*, 398–99.    27  Némirovsky, *Suite française*, 399.

28  Némirovsky, *Suite française*, 399.    29  Némirovsky, *Suite française*, 400.

No! The dogs are those that go around in bands and bite if people order them to bite. Me and Willy . . ."). In her own truculent words, the seamstress affirms her prerogative of pursuing happiness and fulfillment on her own terms, and not those of who claim authority all while despising her. Finally letting her defenses down, she protests that she simply loves him and believes his promise to come marry her after the war. Lucile nevertheless renews her reproaches, warning her that she may face dangerous consequences once her brothers, momentarily held as prisoners of war, return to Bussy.

### Truth and Consequences

Having analyzed the seamstress's impassioned defense of her highly contested relationship with her German lover, we are now poised to appreciate its significance as a literary representation of an aspect of the Occupation that, as evidenced by the recent publications mentioned above, continue to attract a great deal of attention on the part of scholars and public alike. For her own time as well as ours, Némirovsky's text implacably confronts its readers with unsettling truths ill-suited for either moral edification or political appropriation. The socioeconomic origins of the dissonance between Lucile's gentle, yet patronizing admonitions and the seamstress's undaunted articulation of personal desire point to a long-standing inability or refusal to consider Franco-German love affairs during the Dark Years for what they really were. The most recent historical research suggests that the better set of lenses through which to view such relationships in general can be taken from the seamstress's frank, plaintive defense of her personal desires and her private life, and not from Lucile's somewhat sympathetic, yet ultimately patronizing reminders of France's story. The fact of the matter is that, like Némirovsky's seamstress, the majority of French women who consorted with German soldiers during the Dark Years were from the lower classes.[30] Similarly, they found themselves facing loneliness and economic

30   Vinen, The Unfree French, 162–63.

hardship in a society beset with a whole host of economic woes exacerbated by the absence of so many men. Even though the question of sexual relations between a local population and enemy troops is invariably—and understandably—a highly sensitive matter, it is not surprising under such circumstances to find that a disproportionate number of women from the most vulnerable and least respected segments of French society sought consolations of various sorts with members of the Wehrmacht.[31] Most pertinent to our analysis of Némirovsky's historical narrative is the seamstress's refusal to view her relationship with her German lover as a political matter. If during the Liberation period such women often suffered dreadful treatment, including not only the long-lasting trauma of public shaving but also socioeconomic ostracism that extended to their children, it was almost always on the pretext of their alleged "collaboration" with the occupying army.

Virgili stubbornly ignores the fact pointed out by Vinen: namely, that the vast majority of those who had relations with the Germans were poor, lonely women who were uninterested in politics. In adamantly presenting head shavings as a highly understandable manifestation of a supposedly unanimous and supposedly pure collective will and as a virtually necessary phase of national liberation, Virgili tends to minimize the violence and injustice visited on many lower-class women who, as Vinen points out, had no interest in public affairs. Indeed, Virgili himself points out that the sanction only began with head shaving: the real punishment was a radical exclusion followed by internment, banishment, and even execution.[32] Instead taking this notion of "punishing traitors" at face value, we need to subject it to thoroughgoing scrutiny. Virgili merely ignores the obvious issues of scapegoating and historical exorcism: focusing implacably on a few individuals whose association with the Germans was known unfortunately also made it possible to avoid the vexing issues of a more general, widespread complicity of the local and national com-

31  Cf. Burrin, *La France à l'heure allemande*, 210–11.

32  Virgili, *La France "virile." Des femmes tondues à la Libération*, 294.

munity in collaborating with the Germans. And as Richard Vinen points out, the overwhelming majority of French women who slept with German soldiers were uninterested in politics and in an equally disproportionate number of cases, there was little evidence that such women actually assisted the German war effort in any way.[33]

Némirovsky's totally uncompromising depiction of such relationships through her portrayal of the seamstress would obviously not be anything but disastrous in a narrative such as *Le Silence de la mer*, which Vercors penned in order to galvanize psychological resistance to Nazi Germany's insidious enterprise of cultural seduction. But neither does it constitute the slightest basis for suspicions of Pétainist sympathies of any sort. The seamstress's unabashed rejection of bourgeois propriety as well as of the National Revolution's insistence on feminine fidelity and devotion to family and country would have mortified any and every Vichyite who ever read the text. We can instead once more confirm the historical accuracy of Némirovsky's *Suite française,* which here again proves to be much closer than Vercors's *Le Silence de la mer* or even Sartre's "Qu'est-ce qu'un collaborateur?" to the way in which the common people actually experienced the ordeal of the war and the Occupation in France. At the same time, we see traces of a political sensitivity that makes Némirovsky's own resolutely apolitical aesthetic and her highly sympathetic portrayal of Lucile all the more complex and intriguing. Like the seamstress, Lucile proves to be fiercely attached to her own desire for personal fulfillment independent of sociohistorical strictures.

### Intimacy, History, and National Identity

The revealing exchange between the seamstress and Lucile in fact announces a thematic conflict between private lives and public stories, individual persons and collective or national destinies, and ultimately between the human subject and history. Némirovsky lyrically develops this same theme in narrating the long, intimate con-

33  Vinen, *The Unfree French,* 176–77.

versations between Lucile and Bruno that take on crucial imporance at a critical juncture in the plot. Immediately after Lucile soberly assesses the local girls' frolicking with the Germans as a sad but understandable fact of life, she allows herself to be drawn into an even closer confidence with the German officer who had already pleasantly intrigued her. She eventually lets Bruno enter into the "inner sanctum" of her personal life, just as Marthe lets Bruno into the "inner sanctum" of the house by inviting him into the kitchen.[34] Lucile takes the habit of quietly slipping into Bruno's room and opening up her heart to him, thus indulging in a sort of moral and political adultery by entering into close moral intimacy with a soldier of the Third Reich: "Pas un aveu, pas un baiser, le silence . . . puis des conversations fiévreuses et passionnées où ils parlaient de leurs pays respectifs, de leurs familles, de musique, de livres"[35] (No confession, not one kiss, silence . . . then feverish and impassioned conversations during which they would talk about their respective countries, their families, music, books). While this relationship is never sexually consummated, it clearly constitutes intercourse in the wider, traditional sense of the term. Némirovsky moreover leads us to ask whether Lucile's spiritual communion with Bruno does not go just as far as the seamstress's sexual relations in befriending, comforting, supporting, and thus entering into complicity with the enemy, since the text later describes Lucile's haste to pour out her heart to Bruno as "une hâte d'amant qui est déjà un don, le don de l'esprit avant celui du corps"[36] (a lover's haste which is already a gift, the gift of the mind before that of the body).

This highly detailed and extensively developed relationship between Lucile and Bruno von Falk clearly constitutes the narrative, thematic, and aesthetic capstone of *Dolce*. It moreover exemplifies both the singularity and limits of Némirovsky's historical narrative. As we have found to be the case in the rest of the novel, the image of the Germans that emerges is coextensive with the attitude, social

---

34  Némirovsky, *Suite française*, 388; cf. 390.
35  Némirovsky, *Suite française*, 460.      36  Némirovsky, *Suite française*, 460.

identity, and personal situation of the French character interacting with them. Lucile provides a particularly striking case precisely because her contacts with the German officer lodged in the same house are so close and frequent and because she strives so forcefully to ignore the dramatic historical circumstances that have brought her into contact with Bruno in the first place. Her deep disaffection from her bourgeois family and her desperate desire to forget the war and escape the imperative of silent dignity in the presence of the enemy, however proper and refined he may appear to be, make her the virtual antithesis of the quiescent and rigorously patriotic niece of Vercors's narrator in *Le Silence de la mer*.

Yet Némirovsky ultimately aligns Lucile's most momentous decision with the demands of social solidarity and national loyalty. Bruno von Falk, on the other hand, uncannily seems to parallel Vercors's Werner von Ébrennac. Both are young German officers who conduct themselves with discipline and courtesy in their requisitioned lodgings. They speak an elegant, if imperfect, French, and display their cultural refinement with literary discourse and musical performance. As aspiring and talented composers called into the service of Hitler's army, both Bruno and von Ébrennac present readers with a highly nuanced and problematical image of the German occupying forces. Bruno, however, presents a crucial difference. Whereas Vercors depicts von Ébrennac consciously (and naïvely) dreaming of an individual and collective Franco-German marriage providing personal fulfillment while at the same time serving national grandeur, Némirovsky portrays Bruno much in the same vein as Lucile: caught in an unhappy marriage, he appears first and foremost as an individual longing for companionship, lyrical beauty, and personal contentment.

Like Bruno, Lucile pretends to flee or forget history in order to live only in the blissful world of the amorous couple contemplating nature, music, art, and literature. She does not relate the war and the Occupation to ideology or politics, nor does France's destiny seem to motivate her thought and action. History appears as something totally exterior, similar to a storm or an earthquake that ravages people's lives. Socioeconomic structures, traditions, and "le sang"[37] ("blood") seem to trump virtually everything. Similarly, Lucile views her attraction to Bruno as socially dangerous, but adamantly rejects the idea that it could in any way be harmful. While frequently and energetically mocking Vichy discourse, and alluding to the brutally repressive policies carried out by the German occupying forces, Némirovsky lets virtually nothing of Nazi ideology filter through, except for a brief mention of propaganda posters against the English and the Jews.[38] The text nevertheless indicates that the matter of Bruno's national identity and his role as an officer in Hitler's army remain ominously present in the peripheral shadows of Lucile's consciousness.

We indeed find a number of passages of *Dolce* that call attention to Bruno's German cultural identity and his role and function as an officer of the Wehrmacht. When Bruno first comes to take up lodging at the Angellier residence, Lucile must make a willful effort to put his participation in the German war machine out of her mind in order to consider him only as a private person. Impressed "malgré elle"[39] (in spite of herself) by the handsome young officer's imposing profile, she nevertheless wonders how many French troops he has killed and whether he could have taken her own husband prisoner. At this point, Némirovsky shows her perception of Bruno to be highly ambivalent. Lucile observes that an enemy soldier could never appear as a simple human being but inevitably conjured up to the mind rival armies of cohorts and adversaries, including the missing and the dead: "On ne s'adressait pas à un homme mais à une multitude invisible"[40] (One wasn't talking to one man, but to an invisible multitude). Ultimately, however, Lucile concludes that the resulting impossibility for one person to speak to another on a purely individual basis constituted another of the war's perverse effects. Aided in her determination to ignore the overriding historical circumstances

---

37   Philipponnat and Lienhardt stress the importance of "sang," a key thematic motif in several of Némirovsky's novels, including *Suite française*. See *La vie d'Irène Némirovsky*, 383–84.

38   Némirovsky, *Suite française*, 314.          39   Némirovsky, *Suite française*, 320.

40   Némirovsky, *Suite française*, 320.

by her aversion to her despotic mother-in-law Mme Angellier's icy demeanor and her own desire to break out of her gloomy solitude, Lucile manages to keep her misgivings at bay while baring her soul to the German officer who offers both a sensitive ear and lyrical confessions of his own.

When examined closely, however, Némirovsky's text presents Bruno's charm as containing a number of distinctly Germanic elements that seem seductively exotic to Lucile. Performing a piece of his own composition, Bruno presents the successive movements as a Germanic saga featuring a lone soldier, dramatic battles, "Un peuple en marche" (A people marching forward), and a chorus of "milices divines"[41] (divine militias). While the enchanted Lucile swoons over this display of musical and linguistic virtuosity and joins him in bemoaning the sacrifice of the individual to the community, Bruno's artful program notes are reminiscent of the aesthetics of fascism, since they adumbrate a celebration of war and death viewed as the *summum* of human experience. In Némirovsky's narration of Lucile's sensual attraction to the German officer, Bruno's warriorlike virility takes on a disturbingly sexual charge:

Elle ressentait un plaisir bien féminin, une sorte de sensuelle douceur à voir cet air enfantin sur un visage qui était, après tout, celui d'un ennemi implacable, d'un dur guerrier. "Car il ne faut pas nous dissimuler, songea-t-elle, que nous sommes tous entre ses mains. Nous sommes sans défense. Si notre vie et nos biens sont saufs, ce n'est que parce qu'il le veut bien." *Elle eut presque peur des sentiments qui s'éveillaient en elle et qui ressemblaient à ce qu'elle eût éprouvé en caressant une bête sauvage, quelque chose d'âpre et de délicieux, un mélange d'attendrissement et de terreur. . . .*

Il l'écoutait en fouettant légèrement d'une badine le revers de ses bottes. Il se tourna vers les soldats et les apostropha rudement. Lucile compris qu'il leur enjoignait de mettre de l'ordre dans la maison, de raccommoder ce qui était brisé, de nettoyer les planchers et les meubles. *Lorsqu'il parlait allemand, surtout avec ce ton de chef, sa voix prenait une*

*sonorité vibrante et métallique qui procurait à l'ouïe de Lucile un plaisir du*
*même ordre qu'un baiser un peu brutal qui s'achève en morsure.* Elle porta
doucement ses mains à ses joues brûlantes et se dit à elle-même:
"Arrête-toi! détourne de lui tes pensées, tu es sur un chemin red-
outable."[42]

She felt a very feminine pleasure, a sort of sensual gentleness, in seeing
this childlike aspect on a face that was, after all, that of an implacable
enemy, a tough warrior. "For we must not hide from ourselves," she
thought, "the fact that we are all in his hands. We are defenseless. If our
lives and our possessions are safe, it is only because he wants it that way."
*She was almost afraid of the feelings that were being aroused in her and that*
*resembled what she would have experienced when petting a wild beast,*
*something rough and delightful, a blend of tenderness and terror.* . . .
    He was listening to her all while lightly slapping the back of his
boots with a switch. He turned toward his soldiers and lashed out against
them. Lucile understood that he was instructing them to put the house
in order, to mend what had been broken, and to clean the floor and the
furniture. *When he spoke German, especially with the tone of a leader, his*
*voice took on a vibrant, metallic quality and gave Lucile's sense of hearing a*
*pleasure similar to that produced by a slightly brutal kiss ending in a bite.* She
quietly brought her hands up to her burning cheeks and said to herself:
"Stop! Turn your thoughts away from him, you are on dangerous path."

    The narrative context is highly significant, for this last passage de-
picts Bruno outside the private realm of the Angellier household:
here in the Perrin residence degraded by his soldiers, he has fully assumed the persona of a German officer carrying out his official military duties, ordering the troops under his command to clean up and
restore the damaged home. Yet it is precisely the foreign elements of
brute force that exercise a power of erotic attraction on a simultaneously fascinated and intimidated Lucile.
    The association of Germany with untamed force and implaca-
ble discipline was of course hardly invented by Némirovsky. While
more stylized, similar thematics figure prominently in the discourse

---

42  Némirovsky, *Suite française*, 423; emphasis mine.

articulated by von Ébrennac in hopes of attracting the narrator and his niece to the idea of a bold new Franco-German union. In contrast with the lacy winter covering seen in delicate French forests, the dense snow on German forests, declares von Ébrennac, has a rather bestial quality to it: "Chez moi on pense à un taureau, trapu et puissant, qui a besoin de sa force pour vivre"[43] ("Where I come from, you think of a bull, stocky and powerful, who needs his strength to live"). The virile potency of the bull image is entirely consonant with von Ébrennac's systematic portrayal of France as the quintessentially feminine bride offering graceful, tender refinement to the quintessentially masculine Germany. Von Ébrennac accordingly uses the tale of "Beauty and the Beast" as an extended metaphor for the gradual alliance of civilized elegance and rough-hewn force. Both Vercors and Némirovsky incorporated well-known tropes of German power and order into the narratives that they wrote during the first half of the Occupation. As is once again evident, however, they wrote from very different perspectives. Whereas in courting the niece's nephew von Ébrennac presents himself as an emissary of Germany, Lucile persists in trying to view Bruno as a kindred spirit whose German identity is merely cultural, unrelated to defeat and Occupation, and circumstantial, a geographical accident due to the inscrutable whims of destiny.

Equally persistent in Némirovsky's text, however, are indications of undeniable and deep-seated cultural differences associated with the German officer's national origins. In the same passage depicting Lucile as being alone with Bruno and experiencing a rare moment of unadulterated happiness merely from sharing Bruno's company ("Pas un aveu, pas un baiser, le silence ... puis des conversations fiévreuses et passionnées où ils parlaient de leurs pays respectifs, de leurs familles, de musique, de livres "[44] [Not one confession, not one kiss, silence ... then feverish and impassioned conversations in which they would talk about their respective countries, their families,

43    Vercors, *Le Silence de la mer*, 27.

44    Némirovsky, *Suite française*, 460.

music, books]), the prose mentions the accoutrements of his military role, including the belt buckle inscribed with the words *Gott mit uns,* his revolver, and his helmet. Némirovsky's indirect free style moreover shows Lucile captivated by the Germanic quality of Bruno's respectful, courteous patience:

Allemands, allemands. . . . Un Français ne m'aurait pas laissée partir sans autre geste d'amour que celui de baiser mes mains et ma robe. . . .
    Elle sourit, haussa légèrement les épaules; elle savait que ce n'était ni de la timidité ni de la froideur, mais cette profonde et âpre patience allemande qui ressemble à celle du fauve, qui attend son heure, qui attend que la proie fascinée se laisse prendre d'elle-même. "A la guerre, disait Bruno, il nous arrivait de passer des nuits en embuscade, dans la forêt de la Moeuvre. L'attente, alors, est érotique. . . ." Elle avait ri de ce mot. Il lui semblait moins drôle maintenant.[45]

Germans, Germans. . . . A Frenchman would have never let me leave without any gesture of love other than kissing my hands and my dress. . . .
    She smiled and gently shrugged her shoulders; she knew that this was neither shyness nor coldness, but that deep, rough German patience that resembles that of a wild animal waiting for his time, waiting for his dazzled prey to let herself get caught. "At war," Bruno was saying, "we sometimes spent entire nights waiting in ambush in the forest of La Moeuvre. Waiting in those circumstances is erotic . . ." She had laughed at these words. They seemed less funny at present.

Although Lucile repeatedly insists that her love for Bruno concerns only their two private lives, these other notations in the text indicate that her interest in him is dangerously connected to the very public stories of the war and the Occupation, since it is precisely his warriorlike virility that exercises a power of sexual attraction.

---

45  Némirovsky, *Suite française,* 460–61.

## Love's Labors Lost

Paradoxically, these very same elements of German military masculinity suddenly appear utterly alien and repulsive when Lucile ends up vigorously rebuffing the sexual advances that in many respects had seemed to be the logical culmination of her idyllic interludes of soul-sharing conversation with Bruno. Analyzed closely, Némirovsky's text indicates both Lucile's own surprise at her sudden turnabout and the sensory perceptions that act as a catalyst, precipitating the enemy identity out of the mental suspension in which she has for so long kept it dissolved. No longer can she now put the war and the Occupation out of her mind:

Elle avait peur de lui. . . . L'amour, qu'elle avait accueilli si complaisam-ment qu'elle avait refusé de le croire coupable, lui apparaissait tout à coup comme un honteux délire. Elle mentait; elle le trahissait. Pouvait-on appeler cela l'amour? Alors? une heure de plaisir seulement? . . . Mais le plaisir lui-même, elle était incapable de le ressentir. Ce qui les faisait ennemis, ce n'était ni la raison ni le coeur mais ces mouvements obscurs du sang sur lesquels ils avaient compté pour les unir, sur lesquels ils n'avaient pas de pouvoir. Il la touchait avec de belles mains fines mais ces mains dont elle avait souhaité la caresse, elle ne les sentait pas, tandis que le froid de cette boucle de ceinturon pressée contre sa poitrine la glaçait jusqu'au coeur. Il lui murmurait des mots allemands. Étranger! Étranger! ennemi, malgré tout et pour toujours ennemi avec son uniforme vert, avec ses beaux cheveux d'un blond qui n'était pas d'ici et sa bouche confiante.[46]

She was afraid of him. . . . She had previously welcomed love with such complacency that she refused to believe it could be a transgression: now it suddenly appeared to her like a shameful delirium. She was lying, she was betraying him. Could you call that love? Well then, only an hour of pleasure? . . . But she was incapable of experiencing pleasure in itself. What made them enemies was neither reason nor sentiment of the heart, but these obscure movements of blood which they had counted on to

46  Némirovsky, *Suite française*, 491–92.

unite them and over which they had no power. He was touching her with his distinguished hands. She had wanted them to caress her, but now she wasn't feeling them, while his belt buckle pressing against her breasts sent chills right through to her heart. He was softly murmuring words in German. Stranger! Foreigner! He was an enemy in spite of everything, forever an enemy with his green uniform, his pretty blond hair like no other around her and his confident mouth.

Even though, as conveyed by Némirovsky's indirect free style, Lucile's feverish thoughts attribute this brusque repulsion to "ces mouvements obscurs du sang" (these obscure movements of blood), the text underscores the concrete details that irrepressibly call attention to his status as a soldier of the occupying enemy army: his belt buckle, his uniform, his hair and facial features, and of course his use of German. Nor is it incidental that just before her firm rejection, Bruno had seized her roughly in exactly the manner that Lucile had previously fantasized as being erotic: that of a beast finally pouncing on the prey that it had so patiently stalked.[47]

We shall have much to say about the ethical implications of Lucile's pivotal decision to hide Benoît from the very troops that Bruno was leading in searching for the fugitive assassin of his comrade Bonnet. Consideration must first be given, however, to the image of the Germans that Némirovsky composes with her complex characterization of Bruno. Bruno's embodiment of the Wehrmacht indeed proves all the more interesting in that, like Lucile, he tries to push overriding historical events into the background and refuse any and all political implications of his actions. Entertaining fantasies of proudly escorting Lucile to the festivities being prepared on the château grounds, Bruno ostensibly lays claim to a totally private sphere, autonomous from the surrounding matters of assassination and repression: "Mais ça n'a aucun rapport. Ce sont vos histoires à vous. Est-ce que ça me regarde? . . . En mon âme je suis libre"[48] ("But that doesn't have anything to do with it. Those are *your* problems. Does

---

47    See above, the citations from pages 423, 460–61.

48    Némirovsky, *Suite française*, 486.

that concern me? . . . In my soul, I am free"). This passage comes not coincidentally just a few pages before Lucile's dramatic refusal of his advances in the most edenic of settings, that of a fragrant, blooming garden on a beautiful evening in late spring. Here again, as was the case for Lucile, Némirovsky's text belies the conscious claims of her protagonist and depicts Bruno's supposedly private and personal thoughts and deeds to be in reality heavily invested with national identity and commitment to the German military.

We have already seen that his most lyrical expression, in other words, his own musical composition, in fact celebrates the military adventures of an individual and his hometown.[49] Némirovsky's text shows that Bruno's irrevocable commitment to the Wehrmacht extends well beyond historical circumstances, directing his actions and in fact shaping his aspirations. His devotion to the German army proves in fact to be total and unquestioning. Informing a surprised Lucile that, contrary to expectations, his regiment will not be leaving Bussy just yet, he conveys a rather fatalistic attitude with the words "C'est la vie militaire"[50] ("That's military life"). The poetic autobiography that he then composes to give Lucile an idea of his personal itinerary is even more revealing, since he casts himself in the role of a generic, timeless soldier: "le soldat reste puéril par certains côtés, et par d'autres il est si vieux, si vieux. . . . Il n'a plus d'âge. Il est contemporain des choses les plus anciennes de la terre, du meurtre d'Abel par Caïn, des festins de cannibales, de l'âge de pierre"[51] ("the soldier remains puerile in some ways, and in others, he is so old, so old. . . . He's ultimately ageless. He is contemporaneous with the most ancient things on earth: Cain's murder of Abel, the feasts of cannibals, the Stone Age").

Whatever he may try to tell himself and Lucile about the ineffable moments of romantic escape, Bruno in fact adheres to the collective identity that he presents only a few pages later as the underlying German cultural belief: "Nous autres Allemands, nous croyons en l'esprit de la communauté dans le sens où l'on dit qu'il y a chez

49   See above, our citation of 408.        50   Némirovsky, Suite française, 405.
51   Némirovsky, Suite française, 406.

les abeilles l'esprit de la ruche. Nous lui devons tout: sucs, éclats, par-fums, amours"[52] ("We Germans believe in the spirit of the communi-ty, in the sense that one speaks of bees having a spirit of the hive. We owe everything to it: lifeblood, appearances, scents, passions"). Any il-lusions that we might have as to the supposed autonomy of Bruno's affectivity are shattered by his own expression of his most passionate feelings as conveyed by Némirovsky's indirect free style. Once again, Bruno fantasizes about sharing his regiment's festivities with Lucile:

Cette femme auprès de lui, par une nuit comme celle-ci, dans le parc de Montmort, avec les fanfares et les feux d'artifice au loin . . . une femme, surtout, qui comprendrait, qui partagerait ce frisson presque religieux de l'âme, né de la solitude, des ténèbres et de la conscience de cette obscure et terrible multitude—le régiment, les soldats au loin—et plus loin encore l'armée souffrante et militante et l'armée victorieuse campant dans les villes.[53]

To have this woman at his side on a night like this on the grounds of the château de Montmort, with bands and fireworks in the distance . . . especially a woman who would understand, who would share this quasi-religious shivering of the soul that is born out of solitude, dark-ness, and the awareness of that dark, terrible multitude—the regiment, the soldiers in the distance—and even farther off, the suffering, cam-paigning army, and the victorious army camping in cities.

Bruno's most ardent aspiration is thus to see his desire for Lucile to be at once consummated and subsumed into a sort of Hegelian ab-solute spirit incarnated by the conquering German army. This com-plete identification with the military also expresses itself in a much more prosaic way in the following pages when Bruno unblinkingly tells Lucile first that he cannot allow himself to feel pity for his fallen comrade Bonnet, and second, that he would like to personally kill the assassin: "Si jamais je le découvre, cet homme, ce sera pour moi un plaisir de l'abattre de mes propres mains"[54] ("That man: if ever I find him, it will be a pleasure for me to slay him with my own hands").

52  Némirovsky, *Suite française*, 409.    53  Némirovsky, *Suite française*, 487.
54  Némirovsky, *Suite française*, 490.

It is therefore not surprising to find only a few paragraphs later in the text that Lucile, having heard Bruno state his intentions so coldly, perceives his uniform, language, and physiognomy as a repulsive enemy presence.

### Literature, Culture, and Politics

Having thus traced the contours of Némirovsky's coextensive portrayal of Lucile and Bruno, we can more clearly define its significance by referring back to the historical and ideological contexts of the early Occupation. If, as we have already noted, the Bruno von Falk of *Dolce* so strikingly recalls the Werner von Ébrennac of *Le Silence de la mer*, it is because both Némirovsky and Vercors did not simply develop their characters out of some mystical artistic inspiration, but instead drew heavily on the stock of images and clichés widely circulating within their common cultural network, that is, the discourses familiar to both as highly learned writers keenly attuned to the latest developments in French arts and letters. Both Bruno and von Ébrennac are molded in the image of genteel cultural refinement, respectful courtesy, and disciplined military service that Nazi propaganda had been skillfully displaying in these most prestigious Parisian cultural milieus by means of the Comité France-Allemagne ever since the mid-1930s.[55] What better means of defusing French hostility and lulling them into complacency, first with the lure of pacifism and cooperation displayed before the war, then with mirage of cultural renaissance with the "new Europe" constructed by the Third Reich featured during the Occupation?[56] Though subverted more explicitly by Vercors, the figure of the well-spoken, chivalrous, and aesthetically sensitive young German used by both Vercors and Némirovsky as a metonymy of German occupying forces corresponds to the image skillfully disseminated by Nazi propaganda and variously decoded from a number of different French perspectives.

It was precisely because this façade of high-brow culture flourish-

---

55  Jackson, *France: The Dark Years, 1940–1944*, 88.

56  Burrin, *La France à l'heure allemande*, 93–94.

ing under the Nazis was so dangerously alluring that Vercors set out to undermine it with his clandestinely published narrative. *Le Silence de la mer* nevertheless drew sharp criticism from some of the most perspicacious and ideologically savvy readers of the early 1940s: Jean Paulhan, Arthur Koestler, and Ilya Ehrenburg found Vercors's highly stylized figuration of Franco-German relations under the Occupation inadequate to the task of denouncing the Nazis and inciting resistance.[57] *Suite française* has similarly been criticized for ignoring the reality of Nazism: René de Ceccatty complains that Némirovsky makes no mention of "l'abomination nazie et antisémite"[58] (the abomination of Nazism and anti-Semitism). It is certainly fair to say that neither *Le Silence de la mer* nor *Suite française* provides a satisfactory primer on what we know today to be the monstrous nature of Nazi ideology and its highly unsettling and far-reaching cultural implications. While Vercors does expose the Nazi intention to conquer, exploit, and reduce France to total servility, the text of *Le Silence de la mer* (contrary to Melville's film adaptation) makes no allusion to the many severe persecutions of the Jews that were being carried out even in 1941 when the book was written.

Neither the Nazi strategy of total economic and political domination nor the pervasive racism of the German occupying forces is explicitly designated by the text of *Dolce*. Not versed in either history or politics, Némirovsky most likely did not perceive the ideological implications of Nazi Germany's campaign to extend its stranglehold from Europe to the rest of the planet, and thus did not depict either Bonnet or Bruno in those terms. Instead of totally discounting her metonymical portrayal of the Germans, however, we can here again most fruitfully understand her text in reference to its context. To a great extent, Némirovsky's characterization of the Germans corresponds to the incoherent and fragmentary perceptions that Philippe Burrin indicates were common to the majority of the French populace, whose high-

---

57   Brown and Stokes, "Historical Introduction," *The Silence of the Sea / Le Silence de la mer.*

58   René de Cecatty, "Le *Guerre et paix* d'Irène Némirovsky," *Le Monde des Livres*, 30 September 2004.

ly imperfect knowledge tended to be dominated by stereotypes accumulated over the years from previous German occupations. Unable to grasp the radical implications of the agenda of conquest and racial extermination laid out in *Mein Kampf,* which was nevertheless available in translation in France prior to the war, the popular imagination defined the Germans according to clichés that had for the most part been in circulation ever since 1870: namely, notions of Germanic discipline, force, cruelty, sentimentality, and organization.[59] When one adds to that the distinct strains of pacifism (evident in Lucile's reference to two million men lost to World War I on page 409) that mitigated French enthusiasm for another war with Germany, the yearning to take a vacation from history, which was shared by a large segment of the French populace, becomes even more understandable.

Némirovsky clearly strove to make politics secondary—though not absent—in the narrative composed primarily to convey the experience of individual private lives amid the upheaval of historical events. At the same time, however, her rich and complex portrayal of Bruno is in several important ways more sinister and more ambivalent that the image projected by Vercors's von Ébrennac. While the latter finally resigns himself to a bitter fate of destruction, Bruno presents a much more flesh-and-blood human figuration of fears and desires that curiously includes a romantic image of love, Wagnerian musical exaltation, and then the unsettling amalgam of hatred, revenge, and pleasure all mixed together in his hope of killing Benoît. And as we have already observed, Némirovsky's narrative confronts the embarrassing reality of the many French women who, without political motivation, found Germans sexually attractive. Most significant in this light is Lucile's sudden and vigorous rejection of Bruno's advances: this plot development constitutes a symbolic rejection of the New Order enticingly held out by German propaganda that is even more dramatic than the resolute silence immortalized by Vercors's *Le Silence de la mer.* Lucile's largely unexpected anti-German stance provides the central focus of our next chapter.

59  Burrin, *La France à l'heure allemande,* 46–47.

# CHAPTER 8

# REACHING THE RENDEZVOUS WITH DESTINY

## Women in Love

In order to fully discern the implications of Lucile's intimate but never-consummated conversations with Bruno that lead up to her decisive refusal to make love with this culturally refined and emotionally sensitive member of the Wehrmacht, we cannot take her at face value. Although the highly articulate expressions that Némirovsky attributes to her in both direct and indirect discourse often do echo the pronouncements found in the author's personal notes, we have to go beyond what Lucile explicitly states. We must once again take into account the particular historical context while at the same time analyzing the highly suggestive configurations of plot and character that Némirovsky has also woven into the text of *Dolce*. Contrary to what Lucile so adamantly claims, both the text and the context show that her ambivalent attraction to this German officer is neither just a matter of her private life nor totally isolated from the drama of history. Nor are Lucile's affection for and rejection of Bruno, as Philipponnat and Lienhardt have suggested,[1] reducible to the inscrutable inclinations of "sang" (blood),even though, as we have seen, concrete im-

---

1  Philipponnat and Liendhardt, *La vie d'Irène Némirovsky*, 383–84.

ages of Bruno's German identity are what appear as the immediate source of her feelings.

Whether interpreted in terms of Némirovsky's own text, which prominently features Mme Angellier's disgust at having to house a member of the enemy detaining her son, or in reference to Pétain's rhetoric, which incessantly recalled the hardships occasioned by the absence of some two million men in uniform, Lucile's extended and close fraternization with a German officer is all the more scandalous since she is the wife of a prisoner of war and thus expected to embody familial loyalty, domestic devotion, and patriotic fidelity. Lucile determines instead to pursue her own individual happiness and desire for personal fulfillment, outrageously flouting her mother-in-law's bourgeois strictures as well as Vichy's narrow definitions of women's roles. We contemporary readers can peremptorily dismiss the highly restrictive, self-serving directives emanating from both the National Revolution and from the largely antipathetic mother-in-law figure. However, Némirovsky's text contains a number of other elements that cannot be so easily discounted and that call into question Lucile's attempted flight from history. Largely ignored by most critics of *Suite française,* these components of the narrative prove crucial in avoiding several common misinterpretations.

Within Némirovsky's text as well as its historical context, Lucile's highly dangerous sessions of soul sharing with Bruno can be called into question by the widely recognized code of conduct that called on French people to keep their distance from the Germans. The text suggests that Lucile is quite aware of this code, to which she deftly claims exception when Mme Angellier tartly recalls it to her attention.[2] Némirovsky nevertheless suggests that Lucile herself knows that her blissful moments of companionship with Bruno violate the requirement to keep the occupying army at a distance by remaining discreet in word and deed. Why else would she repeatedly issue such plaintive protests of her innocence, if not because she knew full well that she was transgressing the norm?

2  Némirovsky, *Suite française,* 434.

Némirovsky's plot structure invites us to compare Lucile's relationship with Bruno to the seamstress's sexual liaison with another German soldier, since their previously analyzed dialogue occurs almost immediately after Lucile had first indulged in her illicit friendship by inviting Bruno to have coffee in Marthe's jealously guarded kitchen. Némirovsky highlights the transgression by showing the otherwise complicit Marthe to be outraged: "cela lui semblait scandaleux et presque sacrilège: il violait le coeur de la maison"[3] (to her, it seemed an outrage and almost a sacrilege: he was violating the most intimate area of the home). The encounter with the seamstress that occurs only a few pages later thus juxtaposes two women in love with German soldiers. When studied closely, the seamstress's situation proves to be closely analogous to Lucile's in several important ways. Although the prominently featured difference of class grants to Lucile material comforts and leisure that the seamstress can only dream of, both are in fact lonely women who find themselves neither respected nor appreciated: they thus yearn for a masculine presence offering both love and friendship beyond the crude desire for possession from which both have suffered in the company of their male compatriots. Just as the seamstress appreciates her German soldier's cleanliness, manners, and gifts, so Lucile finds that Bruno's disciplined restraint compares favorably with her compatriots' more straightforward advances: "Allemands, allemands. . . . Un Français ne m'aurait pas laissée partir sans autre geste d'amour que celui de baiser mes mains et ma robe"[4] ("Germans, Germans. . . . A Frenchman would have never let me leave without any gesture of love other than kissing my hands and my dress"). Consciously or unconsciously echoing the seamstress's ironic "Allemand, Allemand,"[5] Lucile thus finds herself charmed by previously unknown attentions now given by a German companion who, like the seamstress's lover, vows to reunite with his French mistress after the war.[6]

3   Némirovsky, *Suite française*, 390.      4   Némirovsky, *Suite française*, 460.

5   Némirovsky, *Suite française*, 399.

6   Cf. Némirovsky, *Suite française*, 400, 410.

More telling, if less obvious, than these circumstantial similarities are Lucile's reasoned justifications of her love for the German officer: here again, her spirited protests in fact echo the seamstress's
feisty arguments against those who would judge her. While the seamstress expresses herself with no little truculence, and without the linguistic elegance or nuance of sensibility visible in Lucile's lyrical affir-
mations, the seamstress shows herself no less mindful than Lucile of
the moral dimensions of her love for a German soldier. When Lucile
admonishes her to remember that these Germans have killed and imprisoned French soldiers and are now starving the country, the seamstress proceeds to set her straight in no uncertain terms about her
own ability to confront moral issues. The text bears citing at length.

Vous croyez que je n'y pense jamais? Des fois, je suis couchée contre lui
et je me dis: "C'est peut-être tout de même son père qui a tué le tien";
papa, vous savez, est mort pendant l'autre guerre. . . . J'y pense bien, et
puis, au fond, je m'en fous. D'un côté il y a lui et moi; de l'autre, il y a les
gens. Les gens ne se soucient pas de nous; ils nous bombardent et nous
font souffrir, et nous tuent pis que des lapins. Eh bien, nous, on ne se
soucie pas d'eux. Vous comprenez, s'il fallait vraiment marcher pour les
autres, on serait pires que des bêtes. Dans le pays on dit que je suis une
chienne. Non! Les chiens, c'est ceux qui vont en bande et mordent si on
leur ordonne de mordre. Moi et Willy . . .
    Elle s'interrompit, soupira.
    —Je l'aime, dit-elle enfin.[7]

"You think that I never think it about that? Sometimes I'm lying there up
against him and I say to myself: 'After all, it may be his father that killed
yours'; my Dad, you know, was killed during the other war. . . . I do think
about it, and then, in the end, I don't give a damn. On the one hand, you
have him and me; on the other, there are the people around here. People
don't care about us; they bomb us and make us suffer, and kill us worse
than rabbits. Well, we don't care about them. You know, if we really had
to do what others want us to do, we would be worse than animals. In
these parts, people say that I am a dog. No! The dogs are those who go

7  Némirovsky, Suite française, 400.

around in bands and bite when people order them to bite. Me and Willy
. . ."

>She cut herself off, and sighed.
>"I love him," she finally said.

Having lost her own father during World War I and finding herself ignored by the very people who would now judge her, the seamstress is visibly irked by Lucile's rather smug bourgeois condescension. Clearly having no need for lessons in patriotism nor any desire for a director of conscience, the lower-class woman vehemently underscores her own vigorous ethical reflections. Her integrity consists precisely of her refusal to submit to the moral injunctions of the very people who despise her. In sum, the seamstress simply asserts the primacy of her love for this particular German over the supposed moral authority of society, or in her terms, "les gens" (people). Pithily refusing to conform to the collective dictates of "ceux qui vont en bande" (those who go around in bands) she deftly turns her detractors' insult, "on dit que je suis une chienne" (people say that I am a dog), on its head by laying claim to a self-consciously autonomous moral agency that is superior to theirs. On another level, the seamstress's vehement rejection of the local community's judgment shows that the passion for equality in French society so clearly identified by Tocqueville is driven by a demand for recognition of human dignity defined in terms of social identity. As Philippe d'Iribarne points out, the place and status of individuals within society in turn concerns their degree of "nobility," which is the extent to which their honor and dignity as human beings are recognized, or, on the contrary, the degree to which they are considered "base," "common," or "vulgar."[8] By refusing to stoop and bow to the dictates of society and by defending the principles that she herself has freely and autonomously espoused, the seamstress lays claim to her own sense of honor and nobility.

Lucile invokes the exact same principle, but expresses it in more abstract, general terms. Exasperated by expectations that she should fall in line with some nationally defined community, she declares her

8    See Philippe d'Iribarne, *L'Étrangeté française*, 75–76, 85.

intimate conversations with Bruno to be exempted from moral judgments.

"Eh bien, oui, la guerre, se disait-elle, eh bien, oui, les prisonniers, les veuves, la misère, la faim, l'occupation. Et après? Je ne fais rien de mal. C'est l'ami [Bruno] le plus respectueux, les livres, la musique, nos longues conversations, nos promenades dans les bois de la Maie. . . . Ce qui les rend coupables, c'est l'idée de la guerre, de ce malheur universel. Mais il n'en est pas plus responsable que moi! Ce n'est pas notre faute. Qu'on nous laisse tranquilles. . . . Qu'on nous laisse!" Elle s'effrayait parfois et s'étonnait même de sentir en son coeur une telle rébellion—contre son mari, sa belle-mère, l'opinion publique, cet "esprit de la ruche" dont parlait Bruno.[9]

"Well, yes, the war," she kept saying to herself, "Well, yes, the prisoners, the widows, the utter destitution, hunger, the occupation. So what? I'm not doing anything wrong. He [Bruno] is the most respectful of friends: books, music, our long conversations, our walks in the woods of la Maie. . . . It's that universal tragedy, the idea of war, that makes all those things transgressions. But he is no more responsible for all that than I am! It's not our fault. People should let us alone. . . . They should let us be!" She sometimes frightened herself and was even surprised to feel in her heart such rebellion against her husband, her mother-in-law, public opinion, and that "hive mentality" that Bruno had spoken of.

Like the seamstress, Lucile insists that the historical circumstances of which she is well aware are nevertheless completely exterior to her life. And in precisely the same manner as the seamstress, only using slightly different terms, she congratulates herself for her independence in choosing to pursue her pleasure with Bruno, claiming that she would be more submissive than a slave if she renounced her own happiness for the sake of some idea of war. Brushing aside her own father's and her husband's combat against German troops, she like the seamstress finds herself more enlightened than those who simply allow themselves to be guided by collectively imposed directives: "Ils ne sont même pas conscients de leur esclavage, se dit-

9  Némirovsky, *Suite française*, 456–57.

elle"[10] (They are not even aware of their own enslavement, she said to herself).

## Class Privilege and Ethical Responsibility

At this point, Lucile sets out in a direction opposite to that followed by the narrator's niece in *Le Silence de la mer:* instead of aligning her personal stance with the collective posture imposed by the overriding historical circumstances of defeat and occupation, Lucile seeks to isolate her private life from France's public story. She has knowingly violated the widely recognized code of conduct by befriending a German officer and laying bare her soul to him. In depicting her protagonists' thought and actions as socially contingent, sexually anchored, and psychologically conflicted, Némirovsky elaborates a narrative that proves more plausible, and therefore more engaging, than Vercors's *Le Silence de la mer.* Némirovsky first has Lucile explore the extreme limits of the acceptable and then puts her to concrete tests of ethical action by having her respond first to Madeleine's urgent appeal for help and then to Bruno's passionate embraces. In each case, Lucile's actual conduct belies her previously expressed refusals of ethical responsibility and national loyalty. When forced to choose between protecting Benoît from a certain death and pursuing her captivating romantic idyll with Bruno, she firmly refuses to collaborate and hides Benoît under her own roof at the risk of her life. Since the ambivalence of Lucile's feelings has made her decision infinitely more problematic than that of the narrator's niece's in *Le Silence de la mer, Dolce* foregrounds a rejection of collaboration that is arguably more dramatic and more compelling than that featured in *Le Silence de la mer.*

Analyzed closely, Némirovsky's uncompromising representation of French women finding themselves strongly attracted to some of the German soldiers who had overrun French territory, taken almost two million of their compatriots prisoner, and proceeded to occupy

---

10  Némirovsky, *Suite française,* 457.

the country in ways that imposed severe economic hardships and limitations on basic freedoms explores a widespread ethical dilemma with both honesty and sensitivity. All while holding up Vichy's moralism to ridicule by relentlessly satirizing the discourse of the ultra-Pétainist Viscountess Mme de Montmort and by foregrounding highly sympathetic portraits of two women, the seamstress and Lucile, who thoroughly flouted the National Revolution's exhortations for women to offer models of personal self-sacrifice and patriotic devotion, Némirovsky's *Suite française* conveys a keen awareness of the urgent beckoning of ethics in the face of history. This adumbration of a responsibility grounded in the primacy of historical events can be found on the levels of plot structure, characterization, and narrative technique.

The plot induces us to compare the behavior and attitudes of Lucile with those of her less privileged counterparts, including not only the seamstress, but also Madeleine Labarie, who likewise comes into close contact with a German soldier seeking a romantic relationship with a French woman. Overworked and largely unappreciated by her husband, Benoît, whose coarse manner seems to bruise her sensibility, Madeleine would have just as much reason as does Lucile for seeking amorous consolation from the handsome, sophisticated Bonnet. Madeleine's encounter with Bonnet occurs in chapter 5, after the exposition of Lucile's unhappy marriage and suffocating existence within Mme Angellier's household provided by chapters 3 and 4. Némirovsky juxtaposes Lucile's love for Bruno with the seamstress's passion for her German lover by placing the two women's long dialogue in chapter 11, only a few pages after the text depicts Lucile, having shared coffee and delightful conversation with Bruno, as being in love with the young German: "Elle se sentait légère et joyeuse; elle rentra en courant"[11] (She felt lighthearted and joyful; she ran back into the house). The most telling juxtaposition occurs, however, in chapter 18, when Madeleine dramatically asks Lucile to hide Benoît from the Germans. Némirovsky's sequencing of the plot is unmis-

11  Némirovsky, *Suite française*, 395.

takable, since Madeleine's urgent plea for help intervenes immediately after Lucile's most intimate interlude with Bruno has produced her most intense feelings of happiness and freedom, and has furthermore prompted her previously cited outcry against "l'esprit communautaire" (community mind-set).

As sublimely lyrical and close to her own sentiments as Lucile's protest against the tyrannies of history and national loyalty may be, Némirovsky's narrative ultimately shows Lucile's renegade stance to be untenable. That Lucile's privileged moments with Bruno have brought her into an enemy community whose interests and values are incompatible with those of her French counterparts is suggested by the fact that she takes care to hide her meeting with Madeleine from the German officer. Némirovsky calls attention to the involuntary ethical repercussions of Lucile's idyll with Bruno by means of Madeleine's observation: "pardon, madame Lucile, on m'a dit qu'il était amoureux de vous et que vous en faisiez ce que vous vouliez"[12] ("excuse me, Mrs. Lucile, they told me that he was in love with you and that you did what you wanted with him"). This pointed reminder of the considerable sway that Lucile holds over Bruno moreover echoes a similar remark by Benoît in his earlier request for Lucile to have Bonnet removed from his household.[13] Since Némirovsky has shown Madeleine to be much more psychologically stressed and materially burdened than Lucile, there is no little irony in the peasant woman's forthright appeal to one of the most wealthy bourgeois wives in the area. Here also, the text clearly encourages us to compare Lucile's ethical dilemma with the predicament faced by French women in much less privileged milieus. Conceding that Lucile risks prison or possibly even death for hiding Benoît, Madeleine points out that a neighboring farmwife, Louise, was not afraid to shelter Benoît even though she had to provide for her four children in the absence of her prisoner of war husband. Just as Lucile is about to let herself be entirely swept away by her German soul mate, history, or

---

12   Némirovsky, *Suite française*, 465.

13   See Némirovsky, *Suite française*, 389.

at least the most dramatic local circumstances directly caused by the presence of the Wehrmacht in Bussy, makes a brusk intrusion into her private world, irremediably tying Lucile to her compatriots and people in the community, as she fully realizes after having firmly rebuffed Bruno's most ardent advances in chapter 20: "Elle se sentait—ligotée—captive—solidaire de ce pays prisonnier qui soupirait tout bas d'impatience et rêvait; elle laissa s'écouler la nuit vaine"[14] (She felt . . . bound . . . captive . . . in solidarity with this imprisoned country that was softly sighing with impatience and dreaming; she let the empty night go by).

Ostensibly manifesting itself in the form of physical repulsion, Lucile's refusal to make love with Bruno is in fact only the most dramatically visible attestation of ethical responsibility that Némirovsky's narrative implicitly indicates by means of plot sequencing and characterization. When analyzed in the context of the changing perspectives of narrative voice that we have already identified as one of the linchpins of Némirovsky's technique, and in relation to broader thematic patterns, Lucile's dilemma of having to choose between her romantic yearnings and the urgency of saving a compatriot from a certain death can be best understood not simply as some melodramatic and anecdotal resolution of the plot's main conflict, but as emblematic of the inescapably ethical dimensions of life under the Occupation, and arguably of human existence in general.

We have seen that in *Tempête en juin* the repeated ironic reversals of perspective underscore the radical discrepancy between the various characters' discourses about the debacle and the reality of the historic event, on the one hand, and between the hubris of aesthetic and moralistic pronouncements and human frailty, on the other. In the first part of *Suite française*, Némirovsky thus uses dramatic shifts of narrative voice primarily to satirize the hypocrisy and injustice of upper-class pretensions by focusing on the socioeconomic and psychological divisions between the highly privileged members of the bourgeoisie and the common people. While the satirical vein contin-

14  Némirovsky, *Suite française*, 494.

ues in the second part of *Suite française,* it is largely concentrated in the ironic portrayal of the Viscountess Mme de Montmort and in the explicit challenges to her moral posturing. Némirovsky continues to make liberal use of the indirect free style in *Dolce:* while poignantly foregrounding the unbridgeable chasm separating the self from others, Némirovsky uses this direct textual access, as it were, to the innermost thoughts of her protagonists to reveal that, for all the tensions and conflicts that set them against each other, Lucile, Bruno, and Mme Angellier nevertheless all seek, at least within the isolation of their subjective existence, to assert the primacy of their relations with lovers or loved ones over the collective imperatives stemming from historical events. In other words, they assert the primacy of their private lives over the demands of public stories.

### Far from the Madding Crowd

Neither the compelling desire to escape the burdensome moral and material rigors of the Occupation, nor the attempt to transcend the limitations of history are distinctively Lucile's. Similar aspirations are pursued by the seamstress, who as we have seen vehemently refuses to let "les gens" (people) dictate her conduct and limit her happiness. Bruno likewise vaunts the eternity of aesthetic pleasure[15] and, comparing the present moment to the eye of a hurricane, affirms the inviolability of his lyrical intimacy with Lucile.[16] Némirovsky's characters thus develop their own variation on the well-known romantic aspiration to absolute love within the supposedly transcendent confines of the amorous couple. We find the most striking rendition of this theme, however, not in her narration of Lucile's fleeting rapture nor in Bruno's lyrical flights, but where we would least expect it: namely, in Némirovsky's depiction of Mme Angellier. On the one hand, Mme Angellier seems to offer a textbook example of two often excoriated bourgeois vices, pervasive materialism and the obsession with order. *Dolce* foregrounds an obsession with family heirlooms

15  Némirovsky, *Suite française,* 409.    16  Némirovsky, *Suite française,* 412.

and treasures that seems to border on fetishism in her case, since we see her repeatedly inventorying prized possessions that serve no purpose but to embody wealth and status. The veritable tyranny that she exerts over her daughter-in-law Lucile moreover makes the latter's friendship with Bruno easily understandable.

Yet Némirovsky avoids reducing Mme Angellier to a mere caricature of everything odious within the provincial bourgeoisie by showing that she too suffers and, in her own way, also yearns to escape her condition to a realm of transcendent beauty and human intimacy. Even before surprising Lucile reading aloud to the German officer who had requisitioned lodging in her home, Mme Angellier largely confines herself to her room, accentuating her seclusion by closing the shutters and drawing the curtains.[17] It is in this state of resolute solitude that Némirovsky's indirect free style shows her desperately attempting to relive the most precious moments of her life, and in particular, the memory of her son's childhood. We cite at length to highlight the rich, nuanced texture of these inner musings:

jamais elle n'avait été plus consciente d'elle-même, mais [c'était] une sorte de comédie volontaire, qui seule lui procurait quelque soulagement comme en peuvent donner le vin ou la morphine. Dans l'obscurité, dans le silence, elle recréait le passé; elle exhumait des instants qu'elle avait crus elle-même oubliés à jamais; elle mettait au jour des trésors; elle retrouvait tel mot de son fils, telle intonation de sa voix, tel geste de ses petites mains potelées de bébé qui, vraiment, pour une seconde, abolissaient le temps. Ce n'était plus de l'imagination mais la réalité elle-même lui était rendue dans ce qu'elle avait d'impérissable, car rien ne pouvait faire que tout cela n'eût pas lieu. L'absence, la mort même n'étaient pas capables d'effacer le passé; un tablier rose que son fils avait porté, le mouvement par lequel il lui avait tendu en pleurant sa main piquée par une ortie, tout cela avait existé et il était en son pouvoir, tant qu'elle était vivante encore, que cela existât de nouveau. Il ne fallait que la solitude, l'ombre, et autour d'elle ces meubles, ces objets qu'avait connus son fils. . . . Pour de brefs instants, elle était heureuse. Il n'y avait plus à son bonheur ces limites imposées par le réel.[18]

17  Némirovsky, *Suite française*, 436.     18  Némirovsky, *Suite française*, 437.

never had she been more conscious of herself, but it was sort of a deliberate exercise in make-believe, the only thing that brought her a bit of relief such as that provided by wine or morphine. In the darkness, in the silence, she would re-create the past; she would bring treasures into the light; she would retrieve something her son had said, a certain inflexion of his voice, a certain gesture made by his chubby baby hands. For an instant, these memories would abolish the passing of time. It was no longer simply her imagination. It was rather that the very reality of these moments had been restored to her in all that made it imperishable, for nothing could change the fact that all that had taken place. Neither absence nor even death could obliterate the past: a pink apron that her son had worn, the movement with which he had cried and held out his hand stung by nettles . . . all that had existed and it was within her power to make it come to life again as long as she herself was still living. All she needed was solitude, darkness, and the presence of this furniture and these objects that her son had been familiar with. . . . For a few fleeting moments, she was happy. Reality no longer imposed its limits on her happiness.

Even though Mme Angellier's indulgence in these reminiscences is totally personal, Némirovsky stresses the fact that she is fantasizing about what would be possible only if the war were over: "Tout était possible, tout était à sa portée. D'abord la guerre était finie. C'était cela le point de départ du rêve, le tremplin d'où l'on s'élançait vers une félicité sans bornes. La guerre était finie "[19] (All was possible, everything was within her reach. First of all, the war was over. That was the starting point for her dreams, the springboard from which one could leap into unbounded bliss. The war was over). And although her pursuit of personal happiness in no way brings her into contact, much less compromises her, with the occupying forces, the text indicates that Mme Angellier seeks to escape from history no less than does Lucile, since the elderly woman wants only to be reunited with her son and could not care less about the victory or defeat of Hitler's armies: "Victoire des Anglais ou des Allemands, que lui importait! Elle ne se souciait que de son fils"[20] (It mattered little to her whether victory was for the English or for the Germans! She only cared about her son).

19  Némirovsky, *Suite française*, 437–38.    20  Némirovsky, *Suite française*, 438.

**The Pursuit of Happiness**

When we analyze the impassioned demands for happiness that Némirovsky articulates through the voices of the seamstress and Mme Angellier as well as in the words of Lucile and Bruno, we observe that although somewhat different in their specific content, they all conform to a common paradigm: all vigorously disregard the grim reality of the war and the Occupation and cling desperately to what they consider a radically personal relationship exempted from all strictures imposed by social or national imperatives. Far from being incidental or accessory, their perceived total isolation from collectivity and autonomy from history constitute an integral (and perhaps the most important) part of the intense pleasure that they experience in these private relationships. Thus the seamstress takes pride in keeping society at bay ("D'un côté il y a lui et moi; de l'autre, il y a les gens"[21] [On the one hand, you have him and me; on the other, there are the people around here]) and defiantly asserts her dignity by refusing to run with the pack ("Non! Les chiens, c'est ceux qui vont en bande et mordent si on leur ordonne de mordre. Moi et Willy . . ."[22] [No! The dogs are those who go around in bands and bite when people order them to bite. Me and Willy . . .]). We have already seen that Bruno tries to deny his intimate, firsthand involvement in the war and the Occupation ("Mais ça n'a aucun rapport. Ce sont vos histoires à vous"[23] [But that doesn't have anything to do with it. Those are your problems]), even though he is actively looking for Benoît and hoping to kill him with his own hands. Enjoying his first moment of confidence with Lucile, he first eulogizes the eternal beauty of music that will remain when the war has passed, and then composes a veritable fairy-tale scenario of postwar bliss in the company of his beloved:

Je sonnerai un soir à la porte. Vous m'ouvrirez et vous ne me reconnaîtrez pas, car je serai en vêtements civils. Alors, je dirai: mais je suis . . . l'officier allemand . . . vous rappelez-vous? C'est la paix maintenant, le

---

21  Némirovsky, *Suite française*, 400.    22  Némirovsky, *Suite française*, 400.

23  Némirovsky, *Suite française*, 486.

bonheur, la liberté. Je vous enlève. Tenez, nous partons ensemble. Je
vous ferai visiter beaucoup de pays. Moi, je serai un compositeur célèbre,
naturellement, vous serez aussi jolie que maintenant.[24]

"One evening, I will come and ring your doorbell. You'll open the door
and you won't recognize me, for I will be in civilian clothes. Then I will
say:'But I am . . . the German officer . . . remember? It's peacetime now:
happiness, freedom. I'll take you away. Come, we are leaving together. I
will have you visit many countries. As for me, I will be a famous
composer, of course, you will be as pretty as you are now."

Sharing her first moment of rapture with Bruno and his music, Lucile first shuts the war out of her mind ("J'aime mieux ne pas y penser"[25] [I prefer not to think about it]) and then savors the feeling of being sheltered from all outside intrusions:

Ce qui était plus délicieux que tout, c'était cet isolement au sein de la
maison hostile, et cette étrange sécurité: personne ne viendrait; il n'y
aurait ni lettres, ni visites, ni téléphone. . . . On n'entendrait plus ces voix
maudites, invisibles, funèbres, parler de navires coulés, d'avions brûlés,
de villes détruites, dénombrer les morts, annoncer les futurs massacres. . . . Bienheureux oubli. . . . Jusqu'au soir, rien, des heures lentes,
une présence humaine, un vin léger et parfumé, de la musique, de longs
silences, le bonheur.[26]

Most delightful of all was this isolation within this hostile home, and
this strange security: no one would come; there would be neither letters,
nor visits, nor phone calls. . . . No longer would one hear those accursed,
invisible, gloomy voices talking about sunken ships, burned planes,
destroyed cities, giving the number of those killed, announcing future
massacres. . . . Blissful oblivion. . . . Until the evening, nothing, the slow
passing of the hours, a human presence, a light, fruity wine, music, long
moments of silence, happiness.

Némirovsky's variation on the paradigm of the couple seeking the absolute, or at least unmitigated bliss, within their own intimate relationship emphasizes their alienation from history more than from family

24  Némirovsky, Suite française, 410.      25  Némirovsky, Suite française, 412.

26  Némirovsky, Suite française, 412–13.

and society. Lucile's flight to this haven sheltered from the sound and fury of the world at war clearly generates the privileged moments of beauty and pleasure she enjoys with Bruno. In addition to its close parallels with the other attempts to escape history found in *Dolce*, the idyllic moment articulated so lyrically here through Némirovsky's indirect free style moreover offers a paradigmatic example of the inherent injustice of the amorous couple that objectively seeks to negate socioeconomic relations and historical circumstances in order to remained totally consumed with its own rapture.

### Ethical Summons

It is precisely this attempt to dwell solely within a realm of personal intimacy that raises the issue of ethics, not in terms of the justice or injustice of such and such specific act, but in terms of what constitutes the ethical as an essential dimension of human existence. While on the most immediate textual level, Némirovsky narrates the poignant dilemma of a sensitive woman trapped in the stultifying monotony of a provincial bourgeois mariage during the ordeal of the war, the thematic and narrative components of her text also lead us to explore what Lévinas considers to be the very foundation of the ethical, that is, the attention to and respect of otherness that permeates our own existence. Lévinas indeed views the presence of the other not only as constituting our very humanity, but also as irrevocably defining the self as responsible for fellow human beings. Human thought accordingly consists neither in the ego's detached, methodical cogitation nor in the utilitarian problem solving of the naked ape. Human thought rather exercises itself in the fundamental and inescapable ethical dimensions of responding to the gaze of the other that summons the self to care for and protect the other's well-being. Hence the lapidary affirmation of one of the most pivotal tenets of Lévinas's analysis of intersubjectivity: "La pensée commence avec la possibilité de concevoir une liberté extérieure à la mienne"[27] (Thought be-

---

27   Emmanuel Lévinas, "Le Moi et la totalité," in *Entre nous. Essais sur le penser-à-l'autre* (Paris: Éditions Grasset et Fasquelle, 1991), 27.

gins with the possibility of conceiving of a freedom outside of my own). Lévinas thus holds that, whether thinking in the most theoretical terms or in the most utilitarian mode, humans are in relationship with each other and that these relations have inescapably ethical implications. Simply stated, then, Lévinas defines the human not in a capacity for abstract thinking nor in an ability to make and use tools, but in our responsibility for others. This responsibility is not the product of our thought nor does it result from our choice. It instead issues from what remains outside the grasp of our conceptual analysis and affective empathy: the gaze of the other irrevocably summons us to care for the well-being not just of one person but of all humans.[28]

To return to Lévinas's previously cited philosophical maxim, human "thought" (or "individual consciousness," "subjectivity," "the self") is inescapably intersubjective, in relation with the other. The ethical thus begins with the realization that "thought" neither constitutes itself as an autonomous totality nor generates its own spontaneous ethical principles. The existential root of violence and injustice lies precisely in such ontological solipsism, in the self's claim to constitute a world apart, sufficient to itself, even if it be in communion with another human being. Hence the inherent injustice of the amorous couple totally absorbed in a private world of shared thought and sentiment. Be it between lovers, family, or friends, the rapturous intimacy of the romantic couple objectively perpetuates the illusion of the autonomous, self-sufficient human subject by turning its back on socioeconomic structures and historical events. The romantic couple thus negates the imperative of justice.[29]

It is crucial to recall that for Lévinas the ethical is not a code of prescriptions and interdictions, but a summons to justice. Since sentiment and intention, whatever be their origins or tenor, invariably find themselves outstripped by the web of economic relations, the ethical cannot be based on subjective will and affect: it must be encoded into law and embodied in society. The private relations of

28   See Lévinas, "L'ontologie est-elle fondamentale?" in *Entre nous*, 12–22.
29   See Lévinas, "Le Moi et la totalité," 27–30.

lovers and family therefore cannot constitute the realm of the ethical. While friends and lovers can right their offenses or simply pardon each other on the basis of their own mutual will and sentiment, social injustices and historical violence must be addressed through laws, institutions, and collective efforts not accessible from the realm of intimacy.[30]

Like Lévinas, Némirovsky is uninterested in configuring her narrative in view of inculcating specific moral or political watchwords. By explicitly portraying the dramatic conflicts between private lives and public stories, individual and collective destinies, however, she uses her own artistic means and narrative terms to explore the same compelling drama of the self in history that can be seen as the concrete backdrop of Lévinas's entire philosophical project. On that textual level, we can point to several series of elements which in the long run undermine Bruno's and Lucile's otherwise exquisitely articulated flights from the ethical repercussions of personal actions in the dramatic contexts of the war and the Occupation. We have already seen that Némirovsky's sequencing of the plot forces Lucile's hand, making it impossible for her to escape choosing between her desire for Bruno and the imperative of protecting Benoît from the Germans. Némirovsky's indirect free style moreover shows that Lucile herself recognizes that she has been placed before this ethical dilemma and has unavoidably committed herself and taken sides: "Et moi? Je dois prendre parti. J'ai déjà pris parti, déjà . . . malgré moi. Et je me croyais libre"[31] ("And how about me? I must take sides. I have taken sides already . . . in spite of myself. And I thought I was free"). Although unlike her mother-in-law, Mme Angellier, who, to her credit, unhesitatingly proposes to hide Benoît in her own room, Lucile has had to struggle, it was not possible for her not to choose. In so doing, she has come to the conscious conclusion that moral obligations occasioned by exterior events have trumped her individu-

---

30  Cf. Bracher, "Samuel Moyn," in *Origins of the Other: Emmanuel Lévinas between Revelation and Ethics* (Ithaca, N.Y.: Cornell University Press, 2005), available online at www .h-france.net/vol16reviews/bracher.html (August 2006).

31  Némirovsky, *Suite française*, 479.

al inclinations. On that score, it is crucial to note that this admission that she must willy-nilly "prendre parti" (take sides) precedes the scene in which she rebuffs Bruno's sexual advances. Though her immediate sensations of disgust crystallize at the sight of Bruno's helmet and belt buckle, her action cannot simply be attributed to the inscrutable whims of "blood": the sequencing of the text shows on the contrary that her refusal to engage in "horizontal collaboration" has clearly been prefigured by her previous commitment to hide Benoît at the risk of her life.

While Némirovsky's narrative sequencing provides the most visible refutation of her protagonists' claims to complete autonomy within their own private world of intimate relationships, there are also more subtle thematic motifs that contest such ethical solipsism. Without passing judgment one way or another on Lucile's intimate friendship with Bruno, the text nevertheless indicates that her willful construction of a purely personal realm concerning only the amorous couple is an untenable fiction. Here again, it is important to observe that perhaps even more than she admires Bruno, Lucile treasures the very notion of a world apart, outside the suffocating monotony of her marriage and free from the imperatives of the Occupation.

Cette amitié entre elle et l'Allemand, ce secret dérobé, un monde caché au sein de la maison hostile, que c'était doux, mon Dieu! Elle se sentait alors un être humain, fier et libre. Elle ne permettrait pas à autrui d'empiéter sur ce qui était son domaine propre. "Personne! Ça ne regarde personne! Qu'ils se battent, qu'ils se haïssent! Que son père et le mien se soient battus autrefois! Qu'il ait fait de sa main mon mari prisonnier (idée qui obsède ma malheureuse belle-mère)! Qu'est-ce que ça fait? Lui et moi, nous sommes amis."[32]

My God, how sweet it was, this friendship between her and the German, this unseen secret, a world hidden deep within a hostile home! At that moment, she felt herself to be a human being, proud and free. She would not allow another person to encroach on what was her own domain. "Nobody! That's nobody's business! Even if he might have taken my

32  Némirovsky, *Suite française*, 457–58.

husband prisoner with his own hands (the idea that my miserable mother-in-law is obsessed with). What does it matter? As far as he and I are concerned, we are friends."

Némirovsky's indirect free style thus presents this notion of "son domaine propre" (her own domain) as one of Lucile's most tenaciously held convictions while at the same time leaving open the possibility that hers is not the last word on the subject. Far from incidental, Lucile's explicit exclusion of all that might connect her and Bruno to both World War I and World War II represents one of the barriers necessary to construct such a domain. Lucile's adamant disclaimer moreover illustrates by counterexample Lévinas's critique of the inherent fallacy of the amorous couple's claim to ethical self-sufficiency. Whatever the intensity of her soul-sharing affection for Bruno, the violence and injustices of war remain outside the purview of her own personal will and sentiment: they are not hers to pardon or forget.

### Self and Other

Némirovsky's text moreover indicates that just as Lucile cannot invoke subjective autonomy to supplant the reality of the other in history, so she cannot escape the other's gaze. The first challenge to Lucile's supposedly secret world is posed by Benoît, who comes to seek her assistance in having Bonnet transferred out of his household. When Lucile protests her incapacity to influence Bruno, Benoît bluntly announces that she has been seen talking, laughing, and eating strawberries with the German officer. Lucile's displeasure in discovering herself thus subjected to the Bussy community's stern gaze is palpable: "Quel pays! pensait cependant Lucile. Les gens ont des yeux qui percent des murs"[33] ("What a region!" thought Lucile in the meantime. "People have eyes that pierce the walls"). Let us recall that, in Lévinas's analysis, it is precisely the gaze of the other that dissipates the fantasy of subjective self-sufficiency, disrupts the comfortable pursuit of self-interest, and summons the self to responsibil-

33  Némirovsky, *Suite française*, 389.

ity. Instead of dominating the other under the scrutiny of my eyes and thought, and thus subjecting the other to a conceptualization of which I remain the master, I find myself under the eyes of the other, whose perception and judgment outstrip my control. The gaze of the other thus compels me to respond and account for my action or inaction.

Némirovsky's text suggests that such is precisely Lucile's experience, not only in this initial encounter with Benoît, but also in a more subtle way throughout the various passages of *Dolce* that depict her tense coexistence with her mother-in-law Mme Angellier. It is after all from Mme Angellier's relentlessly scrutiny of anything and everything within her household that Lucile strives unsuccessfully to hide first her intimate conversations with Bruno and then her protection of Benoît. When Mme Angellier stumbles across Lucile returning with an empty plate, the discovery appears to the latter as the realization of the inevitable: "Elle n'aurait pu lui cacher plus longtemps une présence étrangère: cette vieille femme semblait, du regard, sonder les murailles"[34] (She would not have been able to hide the presence of an outsider from her any longer: the elderly woman seemed to probe the thick walls with her gaze). Even when, having indignantly retreated to the confines of her own room for the duration of the German officer's stay, Mme Angellier was not physically there, Lucile felt her implacable presence throughout her mother-in-law's entire house, as we learn once again from Némirovsky's indirect free style: "Quelle immense maison vide, mon Dieu! Sa belle-mère, comme elle l'avait promis, ne quittait plus sa chambre; on lui montait ses repas là-haut, mais même absente on croyait la voir. Cette maison était le reflet d'elle-même, la part la plus vraie de son être"[35] (My God, what a huge empty house! As she had promised, her mother-in-law confined herself to her room; they brought her meals up to her, but they thought they saw her even when she wasn't there. This home was her very reflection, the truest part of her being). Rath-

34  Némirovsky, *Suite française*, 478.
35  Némirovsky, *Suite française*, 458–59.

er than suggesting that Mme Angellier exerted a sort of metonymical presence through objects that recalled such and such a trait or anecdote, the text merely underscores that everything inescapably fell under her ceaseless surveillance, which appears as her principal mode of maintaining her invisible influence at a time when a German officer had commandeered a room in her house and her daughter-in-law defiantly fraternized with the enemy:

Et que pouvait-elle faire? Les hommes ont les armes, savent se battre. Elle ne pouvait qu'épier, que regarder, qu'écouter, que guetter dans le silence de la nuit un bruit de pas, un soupir, pour que ça au moins ne soit ni pardonné ni oublié. . . . Lorsque tout dormait enfin dans la maison, la vieille femme faisait ce qu'elle appelait sa ronde. Rien alors ne lui échappait.[36]

And what could she do? Men have weapons and know how to fight. She could only spy, look, listen, and in the silence of the night lie in wait for the sound of a step or a sigh, so that there would at least be something that would be neither forgiven nor forgotten. . . . When at last the entire house was asleep, the elderly woman made what she called her rounds. Then nothing escaped her attention.

Just as Mme Angellier makes her rounds to monitor her possessions, so Lucile senses her surveillance in contact with the various objects in the home. Neither Proustian reminiscence nor Balzacian metaphor, the Angellier household and the objects within it appear in Némirovsky's text as embodiments of social and intersubjective relationships. The first pages of *Dolce* thus show Mme Angellier reacting to the Germans' entry into Bussy by inventorying her prized possessions and hiding heirlooms "pour dérober aux regards sacrilèges de l'ennemi la vue de la grand-tante Adélaïde en communiante et celle de l'oncle Jules à six mois, tout nu sur un coussin"[37] (in order to prevent the pictures of great-aunt Adélaïde at her first communion and that of the six-month-old Uncle Jules, totally naked on a pillow, from

36  Némirovsky, *Suite française*, 473.
37  Némirovsky, *Suite française*, 310.

falling under the enemy's desecrating gaze), while the last few chapters focus on Mme Angellier's pervasive presence.

In undercutting Lucile's claims to a haven sheltered from the demands of history and society, these elements of Némirovsky's text illustrate an often misunderstood aspect of the inescapably ethical dimensions of intersubjectivity. In Lévinas's analysis, such material objects might be considered the nuts and bolts of the intersubjective ties that ineluctably implacate the self in ethical questions. Far from some mystical intimation, the presence of the other manifests itself not only through the gaze that summons the self to care and accountability but also through material objects that spontaneously appear as belonging to other persons, thus outside the domain of the self's individual desires and prerogatives:

Les choses comme choses tiennent leur indépendance première du fait qu'elles ne m'appartiennent pas—et elles ne m'appartiennent pas parce que je suis en rapport avec des hommes de qui elles viennent. Dès lors, le rapport du moi avec la totalité est un rapport avec les êtres dont je reconnais le visage. Envers eux je suis coupable ou innocent. La condition de la pensée est une conscience morale.[38]

The fundamental independence of objects as such stems from the fact that they do not belong to me, and they do not belong to me because I exist in relation to the human beings from whom they come. The relation of the self with totality is therefore a relation with beings whose face I recognize. I am guilty or innocent with respect to them. Moral awareness is the condition of thought.

Our contact with material objects leads us straight back to human relations and therefore to the problem of ethics.

It is no accident that several passages in the last few chapters of *Dolce* show Mme Angellier and Lucile focusing intensely on intersubjective relations vividly called to mind by their contact with the material world. Checking on her precious wine cellar, Mme Angellier shudders at the prospect of German intrusion: "Elle pense à des

---

38   Lévinas, "Le Moi et la totalité," 27.

mains sacrilèges fouillant le grenier, la resserre à provisions, et la cave! à y bien réfléchir, c'est pour la cave que Mme Angellier tremble surtout"[39] (She was thinking of desecrating hands rummaging around searching the attic, the food supplies, and the cellar! When one thinks about it, it was first and foremost for her cellar that Madame Angellier was trembling). The text specifies it is not the potential loss of the wine in and of itself that troubles her, since she never indulges in the pleasure of drinking. The elderly widow rather fears losing what she regards as a sort of sacred trust handed down over generations in her family: "Mais le vin fait en quelque sorte partie de l'héritage et, à ce titre, est sacré, comme tout ce qui est destiné à durer après notre mort"[40] (But wine is in a way part of the patrimony, and as such is sacred, as is everything destined to last after our death). That the quintessentially bourgeois Mme Angellier thus reifies family relationships and transforms her wine collection into a veritable fetish is beside the point here. She immediately perceives material phenomena in terms of intersubjective relations, as is also the case for both her and Lucile when, without seeing who is there, they immediately recognize the thud of boots as coming from the German officer, "parce que cette démarche ne pouvait être que celle d'un vainqueur, fier de lui-même, foulant le pavé ennemi, piétinant avec joie la terre conquise"[41] (because this step could only be that of a victor striding down the enemy's street, and who was proud of himself as he strutted over the conquered land).

In this light, Lucile's repulsion at seeing the accoutrements of German military service becomes all the more understandable as an ethically motivated response, especially since Némirovsky's indirect free style shows her pondering the sinister presence of the Nazi flag in terms of the human destruction wrought by Hitler's armies. In this case, the Germans had hoisted the banner above the chateau grounds in preparation for their festivities: " l'étendard à croix gammée, teint, dirait Lucile à voix basse, de tout le sang de l'Europe. Hé-

39  Némirovsky, Suite française, 476.          40  Némirovsky, Suite française, 476.
41  Némirovsky, Suite française, 477.

las, oui, de l'Europe entière, Allemagne comprise, le plus noble sang, le plus jeune, les plus ardent, celui qui coule le premier dans les combats"[42] ("the flag with the swastika, stained," Lucile would mutter softly, "with all the blood of Europe. Alas, yes, from all of Europe, including Germany: the noblest, youngest, most ardent blood, that which was the first to flow in combat"). Without attempting to moralize by indicating that such and such choices are reprehensible while others are laudable, Némirovsky's narrative nevertheless depicts as illusory her protagonists' attempts to escape all that ties them to the social context and historical events of their time. The text accordingly presents their thought, speech, and actions not as arising from the putatively unfathomable depths of "blood," but as inescapably fraught with ethical implications. However, these ethical dimensions do not eliminate a certain number of shortcomings, particularly in terms of Némirovsky's portrayal (or lack thereof) of the war and the Occupation in terms of history and politics.

## Epilogue

Those seeking a thorough assessment of the German occupation of France or a probing analysis of Nazism would come away empty-handed from reading Némirovsky's *Suite française*. For two interrelated reasons, however, we may ask if it is reasonable to criticize her text for not representing what we now know to have been the full range of historical crimes committed by Vichy and the Nazis. In the first place, we must always keep in mind that she was able to complete only two of the projected five volumes that were to compose the full *Suite française*. Second, having been deported to her death in the summer of 1942, she had no possibility of coming to grips with the most unsettling implications of Vichy's collaboration with Nazi Germany and the war in general, namely, the massive round-ups and deportations, the death camps, the "univers concentrationnaire," and even the atomic bomb. As we have repeatedly stressed, we

42  Némirovsky, *Suite française*, 484.

can best assess *Suite française*'s narrative of the fall of France and the Occupation by comparing it with other texts written at approximately the same time under comparable conditions. To gauge the intellectual limitations of her representation of the Dark Years in *Suite française*, we can therefore compare it with Jean Guéhenno's *Journal des années noires*.

As one of the rare authors having resolved to publish nothing as long as both Vichy and the Germans maintained their censorship over all public venues while they were trying to give the appearance of a return to cultural "normalcy," Guéhenno like Némirovsky destined his writing to a postwar readership. His determination to keep on writing without being able to publish in the foreseeable future is remarkably similar to that we have already observed in Némirovsky's notes to herself: "Voici le temps venu d'écrire pour rien, pour le plaisir. Nous voici réduits au silence, à la solitude, mais aussi peut-être à la gravité"[43] (Now is the time to write for no reason, for the pleasure of writing. Now we have been reduced to silence, to solitude, but perhaps also to thinking gravely). Guéhenno's most salient similarity with Némirovsky resides in the fact that for the first two years, he had to pursue his writing amid the unsettling anxiety and uncertainty that marked the first phase of the German occupation before the Allied invasion of North Africa in November 1942 and the Soviet victory over von Paulus at Stalingrad in February 1943 raised hopes for a victory over Nazi Germany. On April 9, 1941, seeing the Nazis' seemingly inexorable advances in Greece and Yugoslavia, he feels on the verge of despair: "Nous vivons les jours les plus sombres. Je ne peux rien écrire sur ce cahier"[44] (We are living the darkest days. I cannot write anything in this notebook). Although not subject to the many persecutory measures aimed at the Jews (and thus at Némirovsky and her family), Guéhenno repeatedly speaks of being virtually imprisoned and struggles to maintain his lucidity and morale in the face of German oppression, Vichy's collaboration, and a

43   Jean Guéhenno, *Journal des années noires* (Paris: Gallimard, 1947), 82.

44   Guéhenno, *Journal des années noires*, 142.

severe lack of dependable information. The following reflection from November 28, 1941, testifies to a widely shared frustration that is often overlooked by present-day observers benefitting from some sixty-five years of historiography and impeccable hindsight:

C'est l'une de nos misères de vivre ainsi sans rien savoir, rien sur quoi nous puissions prendre appui, construire le moindre raisonnement, la moindre espérance, dans une sorte de nuage mental fait de vagues bruits, de fausses nouvelles, de mensonges intéressés, d'illusions imbéciles. Dans ce monde cotonneux, le courage est aussi vain que la peur.[45]

One aspect of our misery is to live like this without knowing anything, in a sort of mental cloud made of a few rumors, misinformation, self-serving lies, and idiotic illusions. There is nothing that we could use as a basis to build the slightest analysis or hope. In this fuzzy world, courage is as pointless as fear.

With the Nazis maintaining their stranglehold over the greater part of Europe and with Vichy propaganda incessantly denouncing the intellectual values of the Enlightenment and the political heritage of 1789 as prime causes of France's disastrous defeat, the temptation to flee the reality of current events and take a vacation from history was widespread among the French populace.

Némirovsky responded on the literary level by steeling herself against adversity in order to produce a Tolstoy-like novel about various protagonists pursuing personal happiness in the throes of historical upheavals that called their very lives into question. She wrote a narrative unparalleled in its representation of the pathos occasioned by the civilian exodus, its disturbing satire of social class, and its unblinkered portrayal of isolated women encountering German soldiers in complex and often disturbing ways. While Némirovsky unsparingly ridicules the sententious moralism emanating from Pétain and even exposes the ethical dimensions of the private lives that clearly remain her prime focus, nothing in *Suite française* indicates that she

45  Guéhenno, *Journal des années noires*, 249.

really grasps the most crucial issues at stake in the dramatic events confusedly unfolding in the early 1940s. There is nothing in her narrative that suggests that the war and the Occupation represent much more than simply the most recent of the countless vicissitudes of power and national dominance that had always characterized European history. Nothing indicates that in facing Hitler's armies, Europe and the world find themselves at a pivotal moment in history which critically poses the most crucial questions of humanity and which call into question the very possibility of intellectual freedom, individual autonomy, and private life.

For Guéhenno, on the other hand, the invasion, defeat, and occupation of France by Nazi Germany are not merely exterior circumstances that upset the pursuits of private life. They represent on the contrary mortal perils to the ongoing struggle for intellectual, social, and political emancipation that, in his view, constitute the essential narrative visible in European history and common to all mankind. For Guéhenno, the struggle against the Third Reich is not just the latest political squabble: it is a resistance to a systematically degrading oppression that threatens to engulf all of culture and society. He is thus keenly aware of the radical contingency of all the events that he chronicles in his *Journal:* at stake is nothing less than the future of all he holds dear in France, Europe, and even universal human history. We accordingly find him striving to decipher the Serbian radio's account of anti-Nazi demonstrations in Belgrade and explaining why he clings to every word: "Mais j'entendais l'histoire se faire"[46] (But I could hear history being made). Guéhenno listens so intently because, as a prominent intellectual figure and teacher intent on promoting the ideal of progress and social justice through education, he feels directly implicated in the drama that is unfolding and thus accountable for what is transpiring in occupied France.

Guéhenno can indeed be considered as one of the finest emissaries of "La République des Lettres" that saw the unfettered pursuit of knowledge not only as the noblest expression of humanity but

---

46  Guéhenno, *Journal des années noires,* 139.

also as the prime instrument of social and political justice. The ultimate achievement thus consists of living according to the values and ideas that, after engaging in a scrupulous study of history, literature, and philosophy, one has identified and espoused on one's own. Amid the barrage of defeatism, Nazi propaganda, and Pétainist scoldings, Guéhenno thus harks back to the smile of reason to reaffirm what he considers to be the most sacred vocation within this République des Lettres:

Voltaire forma cette expression: homme de lettres, pour désigner une nouvelle charge et un nouvel honneur. Comme il y avait eu en d'autres siècles des hommes d'armes, des hommes de robe pour mener la cérémoniale sociale, il y aurait désormais des hommes de lettres, libres, faiseurs d'hommes libres, et la liberté serait leur arme et leur honneur.[47]

Voltaire formulated the expression "man of letters" in order to designate a new mandate and a new honor. Just as in previous centuries there had been men at arms and men in robes to lead social formalities, from now on there would be men of letters, free men who would make others free, and freedom would be their arm and their honor.

It is crucial to notice that Guéhenno defines these "hommes de lettres" not as aesthetic virtuosi or literary gurus, but as active citizens whose task can only be carried out within the nation, the people constituted as body politic. On the one hand, Guéhenno affirms that "On est libre ou esclave à la mesure de son âme"[48] (We are free or enslaved according to the measure of our soul). On the other hand, he hastens to add that such liberty cannot exist in isolation, simply in the mind of the intellectual or in the writer's text. Liberty must be made a reality for all the citizens of the Republic: "Pour tout homme de coeur, la liberté, c'est davantage encore que sa propre liberté, la liberté des autres"[49] (For all who take themselves seriously, freedom is, much more that one's own, the freedom of others). It is therefore im-

47  Guéhenno, *Journal des années noires,* 84.
48  Guéhenno, *Journal des années noires,* 84.
49  Guéhenno, *Journal des années noires,* 85.

possible, points out Guéhenno, to feel free when two million compatriots are being held prisoner while some forty million fellow citizens remain virtually shackled under the Occupation.

The prime difference between Némirovsky and Guéhenno can be defined in their sharply contrasting perspectives on history. Némirovsky sees herself and her protagonists as battered by the inexplicable storms of a history "full of sound and fury, signifying nothing" and largely exterior to individual lives. Guéhenno on the contrary understands his existence as configured by and contingent upon the historical events that have been structured by countless influences of the past that are unfolding before his very eyes, and in which he participates through his work as a teacher and writer. Well versed in philosophy and history, Guéhenno clearly delineates the critical stakes of the Dark Years in terms of politics, society, and culture, while Némirovsky focuses on the concrete experience of those who confront the ordeal in their personal lives without really grasping what is taking place in institutional or intellectual terms. While Némirovsky implacably satirizes socioeconomic hubris and Pétainist propaganda, Guéhenno subjects Vichy's authoritarian obfuscations to a withering analysis. Although Némirovsky exposes the hypocrisy and self-interest that drive the discourse of the National Revolution, she does not seem capable of understanding the war and the Occupation in terms of intellectual or political history as does Guéhenno.

Both writers observe, however, that the war tends to expose people for what they really are. "Ces jours que nous vivons révèlent les êtres" (These days that we are living reveal people for what they are), writes Guéhenno at the outset of the Occupation in July 1940.[50] From her own perspective as a novelist, Némirovsky offers a highly similar observation when her indirect discourse develops Lucile's reflections on the discrepancy between the Bruno von Falk with whom she has shared privileged moments of beauty and friendship and the officer of the Wehrmacht who will vigorously pursue Hitler's military objectives on the Russian front:

50  Guéhenno, *Journal des années noires*, 28.

Enfin, il y a un abîme entre le jeune homme que je vois ici et le guerrier de demain, se dit-elle. On sait bien que l'être humain est complexe, multiple, divisé, à surprises, mais il faut un temps de guerre ou de grands bouleversements pour le voir. C'est le plus passionnant et le plus terrible spectacle, songea-t-elle encore; le plus terrible parce qu'il est plus vrai; on ne peut se flatter de connaître la mer sans l'avoir vue dans la tempête comme dans le calme. Celui-là connaît les hommes et les femmes qui les a observés en un temps comme celui-ci, pensa-t-elle. Celui-là seul se connaît lui-même.[51]

In the end, there is an abyss between the young man that I see here and the warrior that he will be tomorrow, she said to herself. It is well known that human beings are complex, multifaceted, contradictory, and full of surprises, but it takes a time of war or great upheaval in order to see it. That is the most fascinating and the most terrible spectacle, she thought. The most terrible because it is the most real: you cannot take it for granted that you know the sea without having seen it during a storm as well as during calm weather. The person who knows men and women is somebody who has observed them during an era such as this one, she thought. Only such people know themselves.

These words aptly describe one of the strongest virtues of Némirovsky's narrative of the war and the Occupation, while at the same time revealing a weakness. The strength of *Suite française* resides precisely in the rich, complex ambivalence of its characters in face of traumatic events that bring their private lives into intense conflict with public stories. The novel's principal weakness stems from the absence of elements that could allow us to see these historical events not as the more or less arbitrary occurrence, or "le plus passionnant et le plus terrible spectacle" (the most fascinating and the most terrible spectacle) of natural tragedies such as earthquakes or hurricanes, but rather as the products of culture and ideology. Yet the passage contains a metaphor uncannily reminiscent of Vercor's central image of the sea: a deceptively calm outward appearance can belie the complex and powerful elements seething beneath the surface and capable of

---

51 Némirovsky, *Suite française*, 511.

overwhelming those who underestimate its fury. While keenly aware of such powerful ambivalence on the level of individuals and social groups, Némirovsky seems not to have perceived lurking in the sea of history the Leviathan of Nazism whose sinister emergence would, as for millions of others, make her own rendezvous with destiny tragically fatal.

# BIBLIOGRAPHY

"Les Alcoves de la collaboration." *L'Express*, 16 April 2008. Available online at www.lexpress.fr/info/france/dossier/occupation/dossier.asp?ida=470000.

Amouroux, Henri. *Quarante millions de Pétainistes*. Paris: Robert Laffont, 1978.

Azéma, Jean-Pierre. "Cette France 'allemande.'" *L'Express*, 16 April 2008. Available online at www.lexpress.fr/info/france/dossier/occupation/dossier. asp?ida=469998.

———. *De Munich à la libération, 1938–1944*. Paris: Seuil, 1979.

Benjamin, René. *Le Printemps tragique*. Paris: Plon, 1940.

Bloch, Marc. *L'Étrange défaite*. Paris: Gallimard, 1990.

Boulouque, Clémence. "Irène Némirovsky: Échec à l'oubli." *Le Figaro Littéraire*, 11 September 2004.

Bracher, Nathan. "The Burden of History and the Politics of Memory." Published as "Die Last der Geschichte und die Erinnerungspolitik," in Michael Meimeth, John Robertson, and Susanne Talmon, eds., *Integration und Identität in inwanderungsgesellschaften Herausforderungen und transatlantische Antworten 2008*. Denkart Europa. Schriften zur europäischen Politik, Wirtschaft und Kultur, Bd. 4, 117–33. Baden-Baden, Germany: Nomos Verlaggesellschaft.

———. "Commémorations du Jour-J 2004: Les Jeux de la mémoire et de l'histoire." *Contemporary French Civilization* 29, no. 1 (Winter–Spring 2005): 105–36.

———. "Samuel Moyn, *Origins of the Other: Emmanuel Lévinas between Revelation and Ethics*. Ithaca and London: Cornell University Press, 2005. Available online at www.h-france.net/vol6reviews/bracher.html (August 2006).

———. "Soixante ans après: Pour un état des lieux de mémoire." *French Politics, Culture, and Society* 25, no. 1 (Spring 2007): 49–69.

Bruckner, Pascal. "Elle s'appelait Irène." *Le Nouvel Observateur*, 21 October 2004.

Burrin, Philippe. *La France à l'heure allemande*. Paris: Éditions du Seuil, 1995.

Cecatty, René de. "Le *Guerre et paix* d'Irène Némirovsky." *Le Monde des Livres*, 30 September 2004.

Cremieux-Brilhac, Jean-Louis. *Les Français de l'An 40.* 2 vols. Paris: Gallimard, 1990.

Diamond, Hanna. *Fleeing Hitler.* New York: Oxford University Press, 2007.

Douzou, Laurent. *La Résistance française: Une histoire périlleuse.* Paris: Éditions du Seuil, 2005.

Fink, Carole. *Marc Bloch: A Life in History.* New York: Cambridge University Press, 1989.

Finkielkraut, Alain. *Nous autres, modernes.* Paris: Ellipses, 2005.

———. "Qu'est-ce qu'une nation?" In *La défaite de la pensée,* 43–52. Paris: Gallimard, 1987.

Fishman, Sarah. *We Will Wait: Wives of French Prisoners of War, 1940–1945.* New Haven, Conn.: Yale University Press, 1991.

Franklin, Ruth. "Scandale Française: The Nasty Truth about a New Literary Heroine." *The New Republic,* January 30, 2008, 38–43.

Guéhenno, Jean. *Journal des années noires.* Paris: Gallimard, 1947.

Hoffman, Stanley. "Le Désastre de 1940." In *Études sur la France de 1939 à nos jours,* 22–37. Paris: Éditions du Seuil, 1985.

Iribarne, Philippe d'. *L'Étrangeté française.* Paris: Éditions du Seuil, 2006.

Jackson, Julian. *France: The Dark Years, 1940–1944.* New York: Oxford University Press, 2003.

Kershaw, Angela. "Finding Irène Némirovsky." *French Cultural Studies* 18, no. 1 (February, 2007): 59–81.

Le Naire, Olivier. "La Passion d'Irène." *L'Express,* 27 September 2004.

Lévinas, Emmanuel. "L'Ontologie est-elle fondamentale?" In *Entre nous: Essais sur le penser-à-l'autre,* 12–22. Paris: Grasset et Fasquelle, 1991.

———. "Le Moi et la totalité." In *Entre nous: Essais sur le penser-à-l'autre,* 23–48. Paris: Grasset et Fasquelle, 1991.

Lloyd, Christopher. "Irène Némirovsky's *Suite française* and the Crisis of Rights and Identity." *Contemporary French Civilization* 31, no. 2 (2007): 161–82.

Mauriac, François. "Ce Reste de fierté." In *Journal. Mémoires politiques,* 763–64. Paris: Robert Laffont, 2008.

———. "Le Métier d'écrivain." *L'Express,* 5 April 1957, pp. 17–20.

———. "Mussolini envahit l'Abyssinie—Un Dessin de Sennep." In *Journal. Mémoires politiques,* 704. Paris: Robert Laffont, 2008.

Michelet, Jules. *Histoire de France: Choix de textes présentés par Paule Petitier.* Paris: Flammarion, 2008.

Montherlant, Henry de. *Essais.* Paris: Gallimard, 1963.

Némirovsky, Irène. *Destinées et autres nouvelles.* Pin-Balma: Sables, 2004.

———. *Suite française.* Paris: Denoël, 2004.

Nettlebeck, C. E. "Saint-Exupéry, Antoine de." In *Historical Dictionary of World War II France,* 323–24. Westport, Conn.: Greenwood Press, 1998.

Nora, Pierre. "Le Nationalisme nous a caché la nation." *Le Monde,* 17 March 2007.

Ousby, Ian. *Occupation: The Ordeal of France, 1940–1944.* New York: St. Martin's Press, 1998.

Petitier, Paule. "Introduction." In Jules Michelet, *Histoire de France: Choix de textes présentés par Paule Petitier,* 7–31. Paris: Flammarion, 2008.

Philipponnat, Olivier, and Patrick Lienhardt. *La vie d'Irène Némirovsky.* Paris: Grasset-Denoël, 2007.

Poznanski, Renée. "Vichy et les Juifs: Des Marges de l'histoire au coeur de son écriture." In *Le Régime de Vichy et les Français,* edited by Jean-Pierre Azéma et François Bédarida (Paris: Fayard, 1992), 59–67.

Rousso, Henry. *Les Années noires: Vivre sous l'occupation.* Paris: Gallimard, 1992.

———. *La Hantise du passé.* Paris: Les Éditions Textuelles, 1998.

———. *Le Régime de Vichy.* Paris: Presses Universitaires de France ("Que sais-je?"), 2007.

Saint-Exupéry, Antoine de. *Pilote de guerre.* Paris: Gallimard, 1942.

Saint-Just, "Sur le mode d'exécution du décret contre les ennemis de la Révolution." Available online at www.royet.org/neal17891794/archives/discours/ stjust_decret_ennemies_revolution_03_03_94.htm.

Sartre, Jean-Paul. "M. François Mauriac et la liberté." In *Situations I,* 36–57. Paris: Gallimard, 1947.

———. "Qu'est-ce qu'un collaborateur?" In *Situations III,* 43–61. Paris: Gallimard, 1945.

Sobanet, Andrew. *Jail Sentences: Representing Prison in Twentieth-Century French Fiction.* Lincoln: University of Nebraska Press, 2008.

Stokes, Lawrence D. "Historical Introduction." In James W. Brown and Lawrence D. Stokes, eds., *The Silence of the Sea / Le Silence de la mer,* 1–23. New York: Berg Publishers, 1993.

Texcier, Jean. *Écrit dans la nuit.* Paris: La Nouvelle Édition, 1945.

Todorov, Tzvetan. *Devoirs et délices d'une vie de passeur: Entretiens avec Catherine Portevin.* Paris: Éditions du Seuil, 2002.

———. *Mémoire du mal, tentation du bien.* Paris: Robert Laffont, 2000.

Vercors. *Le Silence de la mer et autres récits.* Paris: Albin Michel, 1951.

Vinen, Richard. *The Unfree French.* New Haven, Conn.: Yale University Press, 2006.

Virgili, Fabrice. *La France "virile." Des femmes tondues à la Libération.* Paris: Petite Bibliothèque Payot, 2004.

Welch, Edward. *François Mauriac: The Making of an Intellectual.* New York: Rodopi, 2006.

Weiss, Jonathan. *Irène Némirovsky.* Paris: Éditions du Félin, 2005.

Werth, Léon. *33 jours.* Paris: Magnard, 2002.

Wieviorka, Annette. "On ne disait pas qu'on était juif." Interview. *Les Drames de l'été 1945. Les collections de l'Histoire* 28 (July–September 2005): 36–39

Wylie, Laurence, and Brière, Jean-François. *Les Français.* 3rd ed. Upper Saddle River, N.J.: Prentice-Hall, 2001.

# INDEX

Daladier, Édouard, 120
Dark Years, x, xvi, 133, 138, 146, 157, 162,
    165, 212, 254, 258
De Gaulle, Charles, 3, 92, 103, 138, 146
Diamond, Hanna, 31n6, 50, 63, 66, 69,
    90–91, 93–96, 113–14
Diderot, Denis, 130
Dunkirk, 139

1870 (year), 123, 125, 179, 228
England, 75, 241
Ehrenburg, Ilya, 227
Epic, xvii, 34, 66–69, 85, 141
Esménard, Robert, 8
Étrange défaite, L', xviii, 107–12, 125–27

Fèvre, Lucien, 33
Finkielkraut, Alain, 59
Fragonard, Jean-Honoré, 130n1
French Revolution, 32, 37, 107, 111
Franklin, Ruth, xii

Germans, ix, xviii–xix, 6, 13, 23–24, 29,
    80, 86, 92, 103, 114–24, 130–34, 138,
    144–46, 158, 162–63, 164–95, 199–201,
    205–9, 214–32
Germany, 135–36, 156, 205, 219–20, 241,
    252–60
Gide, André, 2, 3, 44
Giraudoux, Jean, 44
Goering, Hermann, 120
Golsan, Richard J., x
Great Britain, 170
Guéhenno, Jean, xi, xx, 177–79, 184, 254–58

Hegel, Georg Wilhelm Friedrich, 1, 3–4,
    12, 17, 225
Heidegger, Martin, 58, 61–62
History, 1, 10–20, 23–27, 30, 32–38, 41,
    43, 56–57, 60–61, 67, 70, 82–83, 101,
    113, 132, 143, 165, 197, 207–10, 214–15,
    223–24, 229–60
Hitler, 115, 119–20, 122–23, 130, 164, 167,
    170, 174, 180, 191, 216–17, 241, 252, 256
Hoffman, Stanley, 62n61
Holocaust, xii, 94, 99, 127, 160, 165

Hôtel du Parc, 75
Husserl, Edmund, 58

Indirect free style, 15–16, 46, 69, 89, 97,
    142, 197, 202, 221, 223, 225, 238, 240,
    244, 246, 248–49, 252
Intersubjectivity, 38, 65, 73, 81–84, 93, 111,
    235–60
Iribarne, Philippe d', 139–40, 233

Jackson, Julian, 31n6
Jeux interdits, 99
Jews, ix, xii, xvi, 2–3, 13, 24, 27, 29, 91, 93,
    96, 113, 124–27, 146, 157, 162, 206, 254
Journal des années noires, xi, 178–79, 254–58

Kershaw, Angela, 160–61
Koestler, Arthur, 227

La Bruyère, 44
Lacombe Lucien, 157, 187
Lamirand, Georges, 155
La Rochefoucauld, 44
La Rochelle, Drieu, 205
Le Naire, Olivier, xin3
Lévinas, Emmanuel, 58–61, 64, 244–46,
    248–49
Lloyd, Christopher, xii, xiv, 143, 148, 161

Maginot Line, 3, 62, 88–89
Malle, Louis, 157, 187
Marx, Karl, 1, 17
Mauriac, François, xx, 40–41, 60, 176–79,
    184
Mein Kampf, 122, 228
Mendès France, Pierre, 95
Mers-El-Kebir, 182–83
Michelet, Jules, 36–39, 41, 63–64, 82,
    89, 92
Montaigne, Michel de, 57
Montesquieu, 111
Montherlant, Henry de, 4, 14, 77, 98
Mussolini, 115

Nanking, 108
National Assembly, 77

*After the Fall: War and Occupation in Irène Némirovsky's* Suite française was designed in Scala by Kachergis Book Design of Pittsboro, North Carolina. It was printed on 60-pound House Natural Smooth and bound by Sheridan Books of Ann Arbor, Michigan.